Square Peg

To my wife, Elaine,
my children, Brent, Marcia, Scott,
Kimberly, Alysa, and Jess, and
our twenty grandchildren—
all of whom have sacrificed and supported me
throughout a driven and hectic life.

Square Peg

*Confessions of a
Citizen Senator*

Orrin Hatch

 BASIC
BOOKS

A MEMBER OF THE PERSEUS BOOKS GROUP
NEW YORK

A cataloging-in-publication record for this book is available
from the Library of Congress.
ISBN 0-465-02867-5 (hc); ISBN 0-465-02868-3 (pbk)
03 04 05 / 10 9 8 7 6 5 4 3 2 1

Contents

Preface

M ORE than fiery speeches, more than dramatic cross-examina-
tions in a hearing room, more than acclamation and hand-
shaking and applause, a political career is built on moments like this:

My first campaign was for a Utah Senate seat in 1976, and by late
June, we were struggling. We were operating on a shoestring, my
political inexperience was showing, and the predictions that I would
lose badly looked depressingly accurate. Late one night, I was at our
campaign headquarters, a small white house we had rented in Salt
Lake City, going through the day's mail, when I found a letter from an
elderly woman. She wrote that she liked what I had to say and wanted to help—so she was enclosing $5, which was all she could afford
on her fixed income of $98 a month.

I groaned. How could I possibly keep her money? She needed it to
live, not to waste on a silly political campaign, especially one that
looked as if it was going nowhere. I showed the letter to Carol Nixon,

a friend who was helping with the campaign. "We can't accept this," I said. "We have to send it back to her."

Carol took the letter and the five-dollar bill and looked thoughtfully from one to the other. "No, you won't," she said finally. "You don't get off that easy. She made a decision to send this and you have to respect it. You're going to repay her faith by winning this race and then being the best senator you know how to be. Every single day you're in office, you have to do right by her. That's all she asked for; that's all we can expect."

The first obligation my contributor imposed on me was to pick my head up and stay in the race. The second was to speak my mind honestly and to serve with a sense of purpose—to be the kind of person on whom no contribution, especially from someone with so little to spare, would ever be wasted. It's the hardest five dollars I ever earned.

We went on to win that campaign and (with an exception I'll get to) every one since.

UNDOUBTEDLY, that woman was not at the Utah Republican Convention twenty-four years later to see what had become of her candidate. I was being booed, and not lightly. These were not mutterings or grumblings or isolated jeers. They were lusty, full-throated, enthusiastic boos, and there was no way I could get them to stop.

It was May 8, 2000, and we were at the new E Center, a 15,000-seat arena just outside Salt Lake City and one of the few facilities in the area that could easily hold a convention of 7,000. On this day, the Republicans would pick the party's nominees for governor and other state positions, for the House of Representatives, and for the Senate seat I now hold. For each position, any candidate who received more than 60 percent of the delegates' votes automatically became the nominee. If no one reached this level, there would be a primary between the top two to determine the winner.

No incumbent wants to be trapped in a primary. At the time I was one of the most popular politicians in the state, with an approval rating around 75 percent, and yet there were three challengers for my seat. The last thing I wanted to do was campaign against members of my own party. At best, it would waste time and money that could be spent on the general election in November. At worst . . . any race you run, you can lose.

For the convention, the party had built a raised platform at one end of the arena and decked it out with red, white and blue bunting, balloons, and colored drapery. Sitting on folding chairs in front of the stage were the delegates, 5,000 men and women who had been selected in hundreds of small meetings held around the state. Many sat quietly, looking more like members of a church congregation than attendees at a political convention. I knew that if these people decided the nomination, I would win easily.

But they were not the only ones in the audience. A small group of delegates were convinced that the longer they could delay the proceedings, the better their chances of manipulating the outcome. The nominations were scheduled to end at noon, and most of the attendees had neither the time nor the patience to spend the entire day selecting candidates. The further the convention could be pushed into the afternoon, the more the number of delegates would dwindle, and the better the hard core's chances to force a primary or even nominate one of their own candidates.

Their strategy was simple: Contest every aspect of the proceedings, make as much noise as possible, and keep causing disturbances and delay. They were organized and persistent, but by themselves they were too small a group. So they had brought help. On either side of the delegates, clustered in permanent seats close to the stage, were roughly 2,000 nonvoting guests. These were supposedly friends and benefactors invited by state party officials and the various candidates to watch the proceedings. In fact, many were dedicated single-issue activists. Though their causes differed, they shared a deep suspicion of anyone—right, center or left, Democrat or Republican—who runs for elective office or, worse, holds it. Today they had a common objective: Defeat the incumbents.

They went to work the minute the convention began, loudly supporting the interruption of a handful of administrative issues that had to be resolved before nominations could begin. The majority who simply wanted to get on with things became more and more frustrated. Arguments started breaking out among the attendees, who tried to make the "guests" be quiet. By the time the convention got to the nominations, the atmosphere had grown ugly. As my turn came up, I could sense the collective anger waiting to explode.

When I walked onto the stage, the booing started. I looked around the arena, spotting several faces I knew among those making noise. One woman who kept shaking her head had recently visited my office with several others in her organization. They wanted to tell me what I was doing wrong. The list seemed endless, and the meeting ran on for hours. The central accusation was that I was a frequenter of Democrats. I was willing to work on legislation with those on the other side of the aisle—people like Senators Joe Lieberman and Christopher Dodd, and Representative Henry Waxman—and even counted them among my friends. Worst of all, I had cosponsored bills with Ted Kennedy.

In vain did I explain to them that this is how Congress—and the country—works. There are varying points of view. All of my colleagues in both houses of Congress are responsible for representing their different constituencies as best they can, and good legislation emerges when all views are heard and the best ideas, regardless of origin, are put into effect. Working with the other side is not only politically necessary but actually beneficial for everyone.

None of that mattered to this woman and her associates. They couldn't get past the names of my cosponsors.

I looked elsewhere and saw a small, thin man who fervently believed I had betrayed our constitutional right to bear arms. Mind you, my record in Congress as a supporter of the rights of gun owners is well established. Still, for this man and his colleagues, I was the enemy. I had voted for a comprehensive juvenile crime bill even though it contained one provision we both opposed.

When we met, I explained that if I had followed his advice, the entire bill would have been defeated, including many provisions he and I both favored. I had let the bill move through the Senate, I told him, because I knew I could use my position as Judiciary Committee chairman, and chairman of the House-Senate conference committee that would decide on the final form of the bill, to remove the offending language. That way, all that was good in the bill could be enacted.

To this fellow, that answer was just a lot of Washington hooey—further proof, if any was needed, that I was part of a secret cabal to violate his constitutional rights. Even worse, I had refused to endorse a local initiative he supported giving people the right to carry guns in churches and synagogues, public schools, and mental institutions. When I asked why he wanted the state to sanction attending church armed, he grew exasperated. "What if someone comes in and starts shooting up the congregation?" he hissed. "Then you'd want me armed."

Actually, I could think of nothing I'd want less.

Days before the convention, one of the gun groups had distributed a cartoon that portrayed me as a dolphin, jumping through hoops from one barrel to another at the direction of my "trainer," the gun control lobby. The cartoon caused a minor uproar because an animal rights group was incensed that I had allowed myself to be shown as a dolphin.

I had been given a total of five minutes to be nominated, have my nomination seconded, and make an acceptance speech. My two nominators would have one minute each and I would take the rest—three short minutes to make my case for reelection. I knew I needed to make every word count. It was a brief but important opportunity to shape the coming campaign for myself and my party.

It was critical that none of us go over our limit, because the second the arena clock showed that five minutes had elapsed, the sound would be turned off and the last of the three speakers (me) would be caught speaking into a dead microphone—silenced in midsentence. This was no idle threat. The party had done it in the past. It's a humiliating experience; you continue to talk, but the audience can't hear a word, and they stare at you with a mixture of fascination and embarrassment as your speech is suddenly reduced to a pantomime act. Nobody votes for the mime.

Norm Bangerter, a respected and well-liked former governor of Utah, stepped forward to the podium to place my name in nomination. His considerable popularity was no match for the animus that had built up and was now directed toward me. He was welcomed with boos.

I looked out at the crowd. Many of the guests had left off booing in favor of shouting and gesturing. My campaign advisors had warned me not to react. Just stay calm, they said, and above all else don't be the spark that sets things off. This was easier said than done. People tell me I always seem calm, impervious to every complaint, but rest assured, that reputation is highly exaggerated. I felt as if I could hear every word, and I was a mess inside.

And then it happened. As Norm was speaking, the clock counting down my five minutes stopped.

Was it a mechanical glitch? A mistake by a party official? Did someone do it intentionally, for whatever reason? It didn't matter. To the activists, the answer was obvious—a dark conspiracy was at work to give me more than my allotted time. Several people leapt to their feet and began yelling in earnest. If the arena had been noisy before, now the sound was deafening. Norm's speech was completely drowned out, but he kept going, unaware that the clock had stopped. My chance to make a compelling case for myself was evaporating.

Barbara Smith stepped forward to second my nomination. If anyone could quiet the crowd it was she. A remarkable, articulate woman who has dedicated her life to the service of others, she had served as the General President of the Relief Society of the Church of Jesus Christ of Latter-day Saints, the oldest women's organization in the world and one of the highest offices a woman can hold in the Mormon Church. But she fared no better than Norm. Her words almost inaudible over the shouting, she finished in a matter of seconds and stepped away from the podium, visibly shaken.

It was my turn. Despite the good advice, I was angry—angry with the way the crowd had treated Norm and Barbara, and with the way they were now treating me. I had served four terms in the United States Senate. Didn't that at least give me the right to speak in defense of my own nomination?

Twenty-four years earlier, I had spoken at this same convention for the first time. Then the consensus was that I was too inexperienced to run a good race, and too conservative to appeal to a majority of voters. I was sure to ruin any hope the Republicans had of unseating the incumbent, a Democrat thought to hold the safest seat in the country. I was the young outsider, the hopeless underdog, the darling of the so-called ultraconservatives. Now they were calling me a traitor to the issues I had once championed. There were even handbills saying I hated families and was anti-Christian.

And these were the Republicans. I still had a general election to go.

"You've forgotten us, Hatch," one man screamed. "What are you, Hatch?" yelled another. "You're sure not one of us anymore."

I felt awed, overwhelmed for a moment by the force of their belief. Were they right? Had I really changed that much? Had I abandoned what—and whom—I stood for?

I thought back to the woman with the five dollars, whom I sometimes imagine sitting in judgment over everything I do as a senator. It's not like that, I wanted to say—I haven't forgotten you. Sure, I've changed. I've spent a quarter of a century in Washington, and over time you learn things. I'm more open to different ideas than I once was, more interested in the substance of a proposal than its author. I had learned how to pass and stop legislation, how to use the office of senator to accomplish what needs to be done. I have learned that government does matter, that individual Americans who have the courage to stand by their beliefs have literally changed the world.

A lot of things have changed: Congress is different; the presidency, the courts, even our own state, have gone through twenty-five years of history. We all are different from the way we were. It's inevitable. Some of the issues we struggle with today were inconceivable in 1976. Old views and presumptions have to be reexamined.

Still, had I lost my way? Had I overlooked my constituents? I talk to them every single day. I listen to what they have to say and help as many as I can. Had I become part of the problem I was first elected to fix? The principles of governance that I first campaigned on, and was about to invoke yet again, were the same and as critical to the future of our country as they have always been. Had I grown too used to the political machination, corruption and plain wrongheadedness that led me to run for office in the first place? No! These all angered me as much as they did a quarter of a century before, and I continued to battle them daily. I was still earning my five dollars.

None of this was in my prepared speech. There was no way to explain what I had learned about being a senator, about campaigning, legislating and politics in just a few minutes. I would need a book.

I stepped forward to the podium and looked up at the crowd, waiting for a break in the noise so I could begin. For the first time, I could hear some applause, and even some cheering, mixed in with the boos. What I had to say, here and for the rest of the campaign, wouldn't please everyone. It wouldn't conform to a set political perspective with all the standard positions. Like my career, it would be unpredictable. Some would find it illogical. I would say what I felt needed to be said, even if it was not what my listeners wanted.

I don't know how many people even heard me. I don't know whether I spoke eloquently—probably not, given the circumstances—but I said what I stood for, what I have always stood for. The nomination went through, and I ran and was reelected. The speech did what it needed to do.

But the idea of a book to explain the lessons I had learned, the opportunities and limitations of being a legislator, the victories and defeats, the joy and frustration—the idea of a book stayed with me. This is the book.

———————————

I would like to thank Kevin McGuiness for his generous and invaluable help in every aspect of this manuscript's writing and editing; as my former chief of staff, Kevin has been a good friend and trusted advisor, and as my collaborator on this book, his expertise has carefully guided the manuscript to its present state.

I would also like to thank William Frucht, senior editor at Basic Books, who is the most talented editor any author could have. To the highly professional and wonderfully enthusiastic management, editorial, production, marketing, sales and publicity people at Basic Books: you all have my most sincere appreciation and admiration.

I also want to thank my wife of 45 years, Elaine Hansen Hatch, who has been willing to support me during the many hours, weeks, and months it took to complete this book.

In addition, I feel very deeply toward all of those who have worked with me throughout these past 26 years in the United States Senate. I have had one of the most dedicated and loyal staffs in the history of the United States Senate. Without them, many of the good things we have done together would not have come to pass.

Trust in the Lord with all thine heart;
and lean not into thine own understanding.
In all thy ways acknowledge him,
and he shall direct thy paths.

Be not wise in thine own eyes:
fear the Lord, and depart from evil.

PROVERBS 5-7

Do what is right:
Let the consequence follow.

"DO WHAT IS RIGHT"
(MORMON HYMN BY
PARLEY P. PRATT, 1817-1857)

Chapter One

When Is the Right Time to Run?

Service is the rent you pay for room on this earth.

—Shirley Chisholm

WHENEVER people ask me about running for office, I try never to discourage them, no matter how implausible the idea might seem. I have only to look into the mirror to remember that conventional wisdom is not always an accurate predictor of one's political future.

Instead, I suggest they consider the following five questions. If they honestly listen to their own answers, they will have a pretty good idea whether they are personally and professionally ready to take such a life-altering step.

Is running the right thing to do? Is it the right thing for your family, for your state and for your country? Is it the right thing for you and your own future?

The simple fact is that it is hard work trying to reconcile the demands of being a senator or representative with your responsibilities as a parent, let alone deciding where the family should live. Much will depend on the location of your home state or district. If you are from Delaware or Virginia, the travel demands are much different from what they are if you are representing Hawaii or Alaska. Still, I have always felt it important, if possible, to move your family to Washington. Their presence during the week is critical to keeping a sense of balance and perspective.

There will be significant trade-offs no matter where your family is. The constant demands on your time, meeting with constituents, campaigning and fundraising, both in Washington and back home, will force you to choose between your family and job far more often than you could ever imagine. To survive, let alone succeed, you will need an unusually patient and understanding spouse.

Do you have the personal strength, the mental and physical stamina, to run an effective campaign and bear up through the process? Running for office can be physically grueling and emotionally exhausting.

It is no place for the faint of heart or those filled with self-doubt. You can be assured of exposing yourself and your family to public scrutiny; the achievements of which you are most proud will be sullied; and your statements during the campaign will be twisted and distorted until they no longer even remotely resemble their original meanings.

As Barry Goldwater once observed, following his unsuccessful presidential campaign, "If I hadn't known Barry Goldwater in 1964, and I had to depend on the press and the cartoons, I'd have voted against the son of a bitch."[1]

Is it the right time for you to run and are you running against the right opponent? Some consideration has to be given to the political landscape of the moment, and whether you are in tune with the people you hope to be representing. If the voters are uncomfortable with who you really are and what you believe, you may not be the right person to represent that constituency.

Similarly, it helps to be running against the right opponent, against someone who has a different agenda and outlook from yours. As so many have observed, more elections are lost than they are won.

Can you attract the support you will need to put yourself in a position to win? Until a better system comes along or you are independently wealthy, you will have to raise your own funding. Running a campaign is like remodeling a house: It always ends up costing more than twice what the experts predict.

Are you running for the right office? There were some who thought my decision to run for the Senate was a sign of excessive ambition. After all, I had no previous experience in public office. It might have made more sense to run for the House of Representatives first, a more traditional path to the Senate.

Despite the considerable importance of serving in the House of Representatives, I simply was not comfortable risking my law practice for a position that might last only for two years. Moreover, I did not feel I had the economic wherewithal to begin planning the next campaign the minute the first one ended.

The final decision should always the candidate's, and the candidate's alone. No one else can be a more effective judge because ultimately the person running has the most at stake.

My own decision to run had more to do with my opponent than with my own interest in becoming a United States senator. In 1976, the United States was a different place politically than it is today.

The country was headed in the wrong direction. We were struggling with double-digit inflation, high interest rates and growing unemployment. Our military strength was eroding. The nation was still reeling from the war in Vietnam and the scandals that led to the resignation of President Richard Nixon.

Congress was locked tightly in the control of the Democratic Party, and no one thought there was much of a chance that the Republicans would ever be able to regain control of either the House or the Senate. What Congress did best was spend money. The federal budget was expanding rapidly, expenditures were far outpacing revenues, and yet no one seemed concerned or even aware that they were saddling future generations with a massive debt.

Instead, Washington was governed by the belief that government was the answer to every question and the solution to every problem. All that was needed to establish a perfect society was the right number of laws, the right number of rules and regulations, and scores and scores of federal regulators charged with making sure that things worked perfectly.

To many in the western part of the country especially, we were heading toward an American brand of socialism. Naturally, one has to be careful about such generalizations. As Justice Earl Warren noted, "Many people consider the things which government does for them to be social progress, but they consider the things government does for others as socialism."[2] Still, the trend was there, complemented by the growing conviction that Americans could not be trusted to make the right decisions by themselves. It was as if our national motto had become: "Pray for the welfare of the government, for were it not for the fear of the government, a man would swallow up his neighbor alive."[3]

Moreover, the practice of religion was treated with increasing hostility. After 150 years of permissible school prayer, the Supreme Court, in *Engle* v. *Vitale*,[4] banned the practice in public schools. In 1973, the monumental decision in *Roe* v. *Wade*[5] legalized abortion, reading a right to an abortion into the Constitution. For many, these cases epitomized the trend toward the judicial legitimization of a devolution of moral accountability and personal responsibility.

I was convinced that someone needed to stand against these trends. Someone needed to point out the deterioration of our moral fiber, the proliferation and increasing acceptance of drugs and crime, the expansion of the welfare state. There was a need to refocus attention on the diminishment of our military, the federal takeover of our local schools and the bartering of our children's future by politicians who seemed more concerned with their next election than the need for fiscal responsibility. It was time for a different philosophy, a different kind of politician.

I believed that the answer lay in lower taxes, less government, fewer regulations, less centralized power and a wiser use of the power that must be exercised on behalf of the people. As Barry Goldwater once noted, "A government that is big enough to give you all you want is big enough to take it all away."[6]

Unlike many in office at the time, I had a greater faith in the collective wisdom of the public than in the parochial views being espoused in the echo chamber inside the Capital Beltway.

Utah was also a different place then. The governor, Calvin Rampton, a Democrat who had held office for three terms, was extremely popular, although he had decided not to run for reelection. There was only one Republican in the then four-person congressional delegation, Senator Jake Garn, who had been elected in 1974.

The incumbent senator up for reelection, Frank E. "Ted" Moss, an entrenched Democrat who had held his seat for eighteen years, was considered by most political experts to have one of the safest seats in the country. *U.S. News and World Report* claimed he was the only incumbent running who could not be beaten. He was considered a superb campaigner who had not let his leadership position in the Senate interfere with his reputation for constituent service.

Senator Moss was extremely liberal for the state, however. His voting record was far more comparable to representatives from the eastern states than to those from the West. He was clearly part of the Democratic establishment in Washington, a willing advocate and player in the group that was leading the country in the wrong direction. In many ways, he personified the very ideas and attitudes that I found so objectionable.

I had known about Ted Moss for some time. I first saw him in person when he debated Senator Arthur V. Watkins during the 1958 campaign. Senator Watkins was a courageous and respected member of the institution. A Republican, he chaired the Senate Select Committee that recommended censure of Joseph McCarthy over his infamous search for communists in the government. It was a thankless but critical assignment that may have helped the nation weather a dangerous political storm but it probably cost him his seat.

At the time, I was an undergraduate at Brigham Young University, working my way through school. I started out as a janitor and then moved up to selling diamonds and cookware. At BYU, where so many students get married while still in school, someone was always interested in engagement rings or, on a more practical note, pots and pans. Like most people who had been raised in a union household, I was a Democrat. My conversion to the Republican Party would not come until I went to law school.

I came to the debate expecting to support the Democratic candidate but left far more impressed with the thoughtfulness, grace and intelligence of Senator Watkins. Despite my party affiliation, I was surprised and disappointed when Moss defeated Watkins in a three-way race, despite winning only 39 percent of the vote. The third candidate was J. Bracken Lee, a radically conservative former governor of Utah and the mayor of Salt Lake City, who entered the race to protest Watkins's actions against McCarthy. He drew a significant number of Republican votes and threw the election to Moss. For Republicans, the possibility of losing to a Democrat because of the presence of a more conservative third-party challenger has haunted every election since.

By the spring of 1976, Senator Moss had attracted several Republican opponents, all of whom were already campaigning. Sherman Lloyd was a former four-term Republican member of the House of Representatives. Clinton Miller was a conservative Washington lobbyist. Desmond Barker had worked in the Nixon White House and had been in and out of state party politics for years. And the party favorite was Jack Carlson, a former Assistant Secretary at the Department of the Interior.

Jack was certainly qualified. He had two degrees from Harvard University and had served as an economic advisor to three presidents. He also had the benefit of his wife, Renee, who was an excellent politician and in many ways a more natural and instinctive campaigner than her husband. In fact, I thought she would have made a far more effective candidate, and if she had been running I probably would not have entered the race.

All four had more impressive political credentials than I had. All had more experience in Washington and a better working knowledge of Congress. All were better known to Republican Party regulars and, to some degree, to the voters. Yet I knew they also shared one fundamental flaw—none could defeat Ted Moss.

By May 1976, my law practice was just beginning to take off. I was involved in several business transactions that, if they turned out as I expected, would ensure my family a good income for some time. My wife, Elaine, and I had six children, three boys and three girls, ranging from Brent, who was eighteen, to Jess, who was six. We had a wonderful home, a four-bedroom house on the East Bench of the Wasatch Mountains, and a spectacular view of the Salt Lake valley below.

For Elaine and me, the house was especially symbolic of what we had worked so hard to accomplish, a far cry from our first home in Pittsburgh, Pennsylvania. My father, Jesse, a master metal lather and local union leader, had helped me rebuild my parents' chicken coop. Together, we turned it into a tiny two-room bungalow, with a toilet and small stove, that we nicknamed "the cottage," a description that would have made even the most aggressive real estate agent cringe.

One could argue that I should have been content, but I wasn't. I could not escape the powerful and persistent belief that my state and my country were in serious trouble, headed down a dangerous and destructive path, and that if given a chance, I could make a difference. I felt it was my duty, my responsibility, to run and at least give voice to my concerns and my ideas for remedying what was wrong. It was my obligation to give the voters another choice. If they were not interested, I would be more than comfortable returning to the practice of law.

I began to think in earnest about running only a couple of weeks before the filing deadline. Like most potential candidates, I talked to my friends. Andrew Grey Nokes, a fellow attorney and a close family friend, was one of the most supportive. We spent long hours talking politics, discussing what was wrong with the country and what needed to be done. Grey continually counseled me to act on my beliefs and run. His unshakable, irrepressible support at the beginning was critical.

Also critical was the encouragement from Earnest L. Wilkinson, the former president of Brigham Young University. Wilkinson had been a senatorial candidate himself, losing badly to Moss in 1964, the year of President Lyndon Johnson's landslide victory. He introduced me to several individuals who would end up playing a key role in my campaign, particularly W. Cleon Skousen, a former law enforcement official, author, teacher and leading western states conservative.

As I talked to others, I realized that I had two things in my favor. First, an anti-Washington sentiment was sweeping the country and the state. Ironically, my lack of political experience or familiarity with Washington was suddenly a plus instead of a negative.

Second, the key to winning the primary was to survive the Republican state convention. A candidate winning 70 percent of the votes of the 2,500 delegates at the convention would avoid a public primary. If no candidate reached that level, there would be a primary between the top two. So to make it to the primary, I didn't need to convince the entire state. Instead, I needed to contact an identifiable number of delegates, most of whom could be reached in small groups. Talking to them would be very much like addressing a jury or arguing a case in a courtroom. I had spent my entire career learning how to listen and talk on my feet, how to read an audience while speaking to them. Moreover, the number of delegates had been doubled from the previous convention. At least half would be just as new as I was.

Still, more typical of the reactions to my musing was the one I received from Frank Madsen, who was also a close friend, a neighbor and a fellow church member. When I told him I was thinking of running against Senator Moss, he was incredulous.

"You're crazy," he said. "Nobody knows you; you're not known as a Republican; and you don't have any money. It's crazy."

As brutally honest and accurate as this assessment was, it only described my then current political condition. It did not reflect what could be accomplished with the right campaign.

On the other hand, Frank's response did underscore another, more practical problem: money. Unlike some candidates, I had neither amassed nor inherited a small fortune. I simply couldn't afford to take off six or seven months from my law practice to run for office. Before I ran, I needed to make sure that we had enough money to literally put bread on the table through the election in November. I was too naïve at that time to worry very much about financing a campaign, assuming that if I was lucky I might be able to raise just enough funds to operate on a shoestring budget.

Amazingly, the solution to this problem had already come from the most unlikely of sources—Judge Willis Ritter, an irascible curmudgeon who had been appointed to the federal bench by President Roosevelt but who seemed more in sympathy with Judge Roy Bean. He was the chief judge of the United States District Court in Utah, an unlikely location for a man whose hatred of the media was exceeded only by his contempt for members of the Church of Jesus Christ of Latter-Day Saints.

A small, pudgy man rumored to sip Wild Turkey in the courtroom, Judge Ritter was a mystery to many lawyers, often involving himself directly in the cases before him, questioning witnesses and shaping decisions. Yet he also had an unfailing empathy for those who were fighting what he perceived to be the establishment or the vested interest. As a relatively new lawyer in Utah, practicing in a small firm, I had many clients who fit this category, and the judge and I enjoyed a cordial relationship.

In April 1976, Judge Ritter called a scheduling conference to set his trial calendar. Every lawyer with a case currently pending before him had to be there to give a status report and explain whether he or she was ready for trial. I knew from experience that it was a mistake ever to indicate to Judge Ritter that you weren't ready. If he thought it was true, he was apt to schedule the case immediately.

Twenty-seven cases were pending that day, and I was the plaintiff's counsel in twelve. Each time Judge Ritter barked my name, I stood and said I was ready. At one point, he glared down at me, shaking his head slightly, and then a smile crossed his face. He knew there was no way I could be prepared for all twelve. They represented a good two years' worth of work. Still, he scheduled each case, creating an impossible workload if each had actually gone to trial.

Judge Ritter's scheduling put a lot of pressure on my opposing counsel, and I was able to settle every case that month, winning extremely favorable settlements for my clients. In one month, I had generated enough income to cover my own and my law firm's expenses for the rest of the year.

Amazingly, my young law partner, Walt Plumb, never questioned my decision to run, even though we both knew my candidacy would affect the firm no matter what the outcome. He doubted I could win, but never once tried to talk me out of running. Walt has gone on to be a phenomenally successful attorney and is worth literally millions today. He still enjoys teasing me about the money I lost by not staying in the firm.

There remained one final hurdle: Elaine. When I first explained to her that I was thinking of running, she was upset. She had a low regard for politics and for politicians. Moreover, she loved the life we had built for ourselves in Utah, her only complaint being that she wished I could spend more time with the family.

At the time, I normally worked long hours during the weekdays and spent Saturday at the office. Much of Sunday was devoted to church work. Monday night, however, was our "family home evening," and the entire family would spend the evening together. We spent one

Monday night talking about whether I should run. I explained to the children why I thought I needed to run and why I believed it was so important. The older ones, who were able to appreciate what was involved, were excited. Elaine was still worried. Understandably, she was convinced that politics would take up even more time and, if I won, regardless of where we lived, I would be able to spend even less time with her and the children.

I spent the better part of two weeks thinking about running, discussing the possibility with as many people as I could, seeing whether anyone else would jump in at the last second, and talking with Elaine. I also prayed, hoping to be guided to do what was right. It was a painful process. I changed my mind so many times that I began to wonder whether I would ever be able to make a final decision. I ended up filing on the last day, at the last hour.

As Elaine likes to remind me, she was less than thrilled with this and cried for three days. Fortunately, as she has so often done when we've confronted some exigency, she reconciled herself to making the best of the situation and immediately made herself an invaluable and steadying asset to the campaign.

What now might look like an easy, obvious decision was in fact an extremely precarious, illogical and unlikely proposition. In some ways, the seeming impossibility was an incentive, not an impediment. The repeated advice I was given not to run had accomplished the opposite effect. It had made me even more committed to becoming a candidate. The more people cautioned me, the more they told me it would be impossible to defeat someone as entrenched as Senator Moss, the more convinced I became that I would not only run but I would win.

I believed that the real challenge would not be Ted Moss. The attitudes of the state had changed, and I felt he no longer reflected the opinions or positions of most Utahns. He was vulnerable to a Republican opponent who was younger, more articulate, and more conservative. My problem would be the Republican primary, where I would face a group of challengers who all had more experience with campaigning, with the state Republican Party and with real politics. On paper, there was no way I could match the accomplishments of Jack Carlson. My political experience consisted of being elected student body president in college—for the summer school session. Fortunately, races are not won with résumés.

There were moments when I second-guessed my decision. The first occurred right after I filed. I stepped out of the secretary of state's office and found myself in front of the media. For a moment, as I looked at the gaggle of reporters and cameras, I felt as if I were falling into a bottomless pit. My mind swirled. Fortunately, I gathered myself and said something marginally coherent, the words coming more easily once I started. Later, when the doubts reemerged, I would think back to those ten days in May and remember what had led me to run in the first place. Each time, no matter what was going on, I would again become convinced that running was the right thing to do.

My strategy was simple: come in second at the state convention and force a Republican primary. Jack Carlson had been campaigning for almost eighteen months, using his position in the Ford Administration as an effective springboard. My only hope was to meet as many of the delegates to the state convention as possible, and the best way to do that was to attend the local county conventions.

Over the next few months, Elaine, our six kids, and I crisscrossed the state in our green Ford van and attended all twenty-nine Republican county conventions. Everyone got involved, handing out literature, putting up signs and talking with the delegates. To our collective surprise, we ended up spending more time together as a family that year than ever before.

It was a summer vacation unlike any other. Normally, spending July and August driving around in a car with your parents would not be the first choice of most children, but our kids had fun, rarely complaining despite the long hours. We covered the long distances reading stories and singing songs. And naturally I was not above bribery. They well understood that if they behaved, I would spring for milkshakes.

As in most campaigns, we ate an amazing amount of fast food. Kentucky Fried Chicken was the favorite, but the real winners were the milkshakes at Granny's, a tiny hamburger joint in Heber City. Each milkshake is a colossus, a triumph of taste over gravity. The shake is so thick that it can stand inches over the top of the cup, more like an ice cream cone than a beverage. The mapmakers at Rand McNally would be shocked to learn that, according to my children, most cities and towns in Utah can only be reached by passing Granny's.

Despite the predictions of a sure defeat, by the time of the convention in July, the race had tightened. I spoke first, stressing that we needed a candidate who could bring a fresh perspective to Washington. Jack Carlson focused on issues, emphasizing his considerable insider knowledge. When the delegates voted, he won narrowly, with 930 votes to my 778. The others were far back. Our strategy had paid off. We had forced a September primary.

For the next two months, Jack and I traveled around the state, although he spent more time campaigning against Senator Moss than against me. I desperately tried to get him to debate, knowing, as the underdog and lesser-known candidate, that a debate could only raise my profile. He constantly refused, choosing instead to emphasize that I had lived in Utah for only six years.

It seems that almost every opponent I have ever run against has tried to win points by pointing out that I was not born in Utah, even though it never works. On this occasion, my mother stepped into the fray and wrote a letter to the *Deseret News* saying that she was to blame for my not being a Utah native. She pointed out that when I was able to decide on my own where I would live, I chose to move to Salt Lake City.

With only weeks to go before the September primary, I felt I was beginning to pull ahead of Carlson, although not by an overwhelming margin. Something more was needed. Several of my campaign staff suggested I ask Ronald Reagan for his endorsement, even though it was unlikely that a Republican of his stature would get involved in a state primary contest. I resisted. By now the race was personal, and I wanted in the worst way to win the election on my own without having to ride on someone else's endorsement or coattails.

My staff argued back, pointing out that I had welcomed other endorsements, especially from people within the state. The only difference was that Reagan was from California. I swallowed my pride and agreed to make the call, starting with Reagan's pollster, Richard Wirthlin, who was from Utah and was still involved in state politics. His polling indicated I was ahead of Carlson, by as much as nine points in some surveys, and there was a strong possibility that I could win in November. I did not have enough funds to conduct my own polling, but his assessment matched what we were sensing. Wirthlin realized that an endorsement was not as a big a risk as it had seemed only months before. Moreover, for Reagan, an endorsement would give him part of the credit for my victory and a potential ally when he ran for President in 1980.

Four days before the primary, Reagan telegraphed his enthusiastic endorsement, which my campaign quickly got out to the papers. Carlson scrambled to obtain a similar statement from President Ford or his candidate for Vice President, Senator Bob Dole, but they refused to get involved, and the race was suddenly all but over.

In the end, I won the September primary by an almost two-to-one margin. I spent a total of $35,000, $18,000 of which was my own, an amazingly miniscule amount by today's standards.

I could now finally focus on my most formidable opponent, Senator Moss. Once again, I was fortunate. Despite my victory, Moss refused to take me seriously. He had beaten several better-known, more established Republican challengers in the past. Even though I was ahead in the polls, he was confident he could easily win against a political novice, especially one he liked to refer to as a carpetbagger.

We debated for the first time before eight hundred Rotarians at the Hotel Utah. He spoke first, bellowing out the question, "Who is this young—upstart—attorney—from—Pittsburgh?"

He elongated every word, as if each by itself was sufficient to serve as my epitaph. In one question, he had managed to underscore the fact that I was inexperienced, that I was an attorney, an occupation viewed with even more scorn than politics, and that I was not a native Utahn. He seemed confident he was hitting a political trifecta.

He could have added a few more. The debate marked the first time I had ever met a United States senator face-to-face. Moreover, he had been a senator when I was still a janitor. If he had known, I am sure he would have added "scared to death" to his litany.

Knowing there was nothing I could do about my profession or my age, I decided to focus on my place of birth. "Senator," I said, anger overwhelming my nervousness, "my great-grandfather, Jeremiah Hatch, founded Vernal and Ashley Valley in eastern Utah. My great-uncle, Lorenzo Hatch, was one of the founders of Logan and Cache Valley in northern Utah, and my great uncle, Abram Hatch, helped found Heber City and Heber Valley in central Utah. They were all polygamists, and everywhere I go, people come up to me and say, 'You know, I think I'm related to you.'"

People began to laugh, but I was still angry. "If you keep denigrating my Hatch family background," I continued, staring at Moss, "the Hatch vote alone is going to rise up and bite you in the ass."

The Rotarians roared in laughter, and Senator Moss looked shocked and perplexed. The tone for the rest of the campaign was set.

Moss continued to attack my character and place of birth. With only days to go before the election, his campaign made an issue of the fact that I was a named defendant in a lawsuit alleging securities fraud, and the senator repeatedly asked whether someone being sued for fraud should represent the state.

In fact, I was being sued by none other than former heavyweight boxing champion George Foreman, for an alleged error or omission in a security document I had prepared. He had been one of the investors in a proposed real estate deal in Reston, Virginia. My law firm had been asked to prepare a private-placement memorandum, a legal document given to potential and actual investors to warn them of the potential risks associated with investing. As is often done with such documents, we listed every conceivable reason why someone should not participate, but Foreman went ahead. When the deal went bust, he sued me and everyone else involved, including his own lawyers and my law partner, alleging that he had been given insufficient warning of all the potential risks.

The case was settled before trial, and my partner and I were vindicated, my insurance company paying only what would have been defense costs. If I recall correctly, Foreman's own attorneys paid for almost the entire settlement.

Still, at this point, I was the defendant in a lawsuit, and the allegations were hurting me. Fortunately, my campaign staff conducted their own research and found some surprising information about Senator Moss.

The issue came to a head on the Saturday three days before the election. Senator Moss and I were both guests on a local news show hosted by Lucky Severensen, one of the top political shows in Utah at the time.

Moss raised the issue, again asking whether someone being sued for fraud should represent Utah. I patiently waited for him to finish, then explained the nature of the case and my technical involvement. When I had finished, I asked Senator Moss whether he had ever been sued. He sputtered for a minute, then said that, like most attorneys, he had probably been sued at some point during his career. I asked whether he had ever been sued for actual fraud. He emphatically said, "No!"

I paused for a moment while I reached down into my briefcase and pulled out a copy of a lawsuit for fraud that had been filed against Senator Moss. I slowly explained the differences between the lawsuit filed against me and the one against Moss. In my case, the allegations involved a single legal error, or omission, in a lengthy document, and turned on whether the long list of cautions I had included in the document had given the buyer adequate warning. In his case, the allegations involved the senator's own personal conduct and alleged actual fraud.

Senator Moss looked at me in shock, speechless. The host, Lucky Severensen, leapt into the void and began demanding details about the lawsuit, questioning whether it was fair for Senator Moss to make an issue of charges filed against me but not admitting to the lawsuit against him. Moss tried to respond, but it was too late. Nothing he could say or do could remedy the damage.

As often happens in politics, the number of people who actually watched the television show was tiny, probably just a handful of reporters and our respective families and campaigns. But by Monday it was hard to find a person in Utah who didn't know about the show and the blunder Moss had made.

To this day, I have wondered why he would choose to make an issue out of Foreman's lawsuit, knowing he had been sued himself. Whatever the reason, it clearly backfired.

On the day of the election, Utah voted overwhelmingly for President Ford, who won every state west of the Mississippi but still ended up losing to Jimmy Carter, and for Scott Matheson, the Democratic candidate for governor. I defeated Senator Moss, 54 percent to 45 percent, helped by the hard, dedicated work of countless volunteers, campaign staff and my family; by the continued support of Ronald Reagan; and by my opponent's failure to take my candidacy seriously until the last moment.

My decision to run, which had initially seemed so preposterous, suddenly became a far more obvious proposition, as if my election was a virtual certainty the minute I announced. Yet it never would have been possible if so many seemingly unrelated factors had not come together almost simultaneously and so favorably.

When I first decided to run for the Senate, I was perhaps the only person who didn't think I was trying to build castles in the air. Through hard work and perseverance, and the support, advice and encouragement of many different people, I was able to put together a campaign that over only seven months enabled an unknown to survive a crowded Republican convention, best the favorite in the party primary and go on to defeat a supposedly invincible and powerful incumbent. I ran at the right time for me, politically, personally and financially, and for the right office.

None of that would have been possible, however, unless I was convinced, like so many other candidates, not only that I could be of service but that I had an obligation, a duty to run. To quote President Eisenhower, it was my turn in the saddle, my time to "protect the rights and privileges of free people and . . . preserve what is good and fruitful in our national heritage."[7]

Chapter Two

When a Nod Is More than Hello

The better part of one's life consists of his friendships.

—Abraham Lincoln

F OR a freshman senator, no matter how old or politically experienced, the first year in the United States Senate is largely a mystery. It takes time to learn the special vocabulary of the institution, the written and unspoken rules that govern conduct, and the various little bits of information that can spell the difference between success and failure. For someone with no previous political experience—I had never even seen the Senate chamber in person until after I was elected—the learning curve can be staggering.

Most newcomers wear a look of earnest fascination. They appear lost on the Senate floor and are out of sync with the institution's natural rhythm. They tend to show up early for votes and hearings. It takes time to master the real clock of the Senate, to learn how much time you really need to vote or to make a speech on the floor, or when to attend a hearing.

With luck, a newcomer will find a mentor, another member who is willing to serve as a guide to some of the more obvious pitfalls and dangers. If the newcomer is really lucky, the mentor will actually be a good one.

Early in my first year, I was standing on the Senate floor during a late-night session when I noticed Senator James Eastland walking toward me. At the time, he was a titan, one of the last lions of the old Senate where members such as Lyndon Johnson, Everett Dirksen, Scoop Jackson and Eastland himself stood larger than life. The rest were virtually unknown.

In 1977, the Senate was still dominated by its committee chairmen, a small group of men, all Democrats, who were insulated from normal political pressures by the rules of seniority. Their committees were like personal fiefdoms, and they reacted to a challenge to their authority with the same severity once exercised by medieval lords. Their power over the legislative process was nearly absolute; they could destroy a colleague's legislation on a mere whim, so long as it was subject to their committee's jurisdiction. The only bona fide threat to their supremacy was their own mortality.

Senator Eastland was a chairman's chairman, a son of the old South, a master of the rules and a man with an unshakable contempt for the foolish and, worse, the inexperienced. A freshman Republican would have been all but invisible to him. So I was shocked when it became obvious that the Judiciary Committee Chairman wanted to talk.

"Hatch," he barked, "how about going to dinner with me?" It was more an order than a question.

"I'd be delighted," I said quickly. He had forgotten more about the Senate than I would ever know, and I was the newest member of his committee, and belonged to the minority party. I had the least seniority and the most to lose from his displeasure.

We rode the members-only elevator down to the Senate dining room and found a table at the back. After we had ordered, Eastland fell silent. For twenty minutes, I said nothing, waiting for him to speak. He just sat there, puffing on his cigar and sipping his soup, scowling into the distance. He never even made eye contact.

I began to wonder whether I had misunderstood his invitation. Finally, our dinners arrived, and I started to eat.

"Hatch," Eastland suddenly snapped, looking directly at me, his face in a snarl.

"Yes, sir," I said, putting down my fork.

"Do you think we can save this country?"

This was my moment, my chance to explain to him my ideas for America's future. Smiling, barely able to contain my enthusiasm, I exclaimed, "Oh, yes sir!"

"Bullshit," he growled.

For some reason, however, he and Jim Allen of Alabama decided to help me out. They took time to explain why an understanding of the rules was so critical to legislative success, and how to pass and block legislation. They gave me practical advice on building coalitions, taking stands, and the benefits and dangers of elected office.

Allen was especially helpful, taking the time to walk me through some of the more arcane parliamentary rules that governed the floor: the order of amendments, the amendment trees and other procedures that can dictate not only when language can be debated but whether it will even be considered. He taught me that different committees had slightly different rules and traditions, and how to use these differences effectively. He went over in detail the dangers of having legislation referred back to committee and the games the majority could play with what seemed to be such an innocuous step.

Most important, he showed me that a legislative fight on the Senate floor, especially if it was close, was very much like a chess match. Without a thorough understanding of both rules and strategy, one could lose despite having a majority of the votes.

To this day, I am not completely certain why they took a liking to me. Eastland had been in the Senate most of my natural life and was the epitome of the classic old Southern Democrat. I was a young freshman Republican from the West, part of a new wave of anti-big-government conservatives.

In all probability, however, they had more in common with new-comers like me than with the young senators of their own party. Despite their party affiliation, they were very conservative on a wide variety of issues and often in conflict with the liberal views that dom-inated the Democratic Caucus. They undoubtedly saw several of the new western Republicans as potential allies who could be counted on to vote their way on legislation being championed by more liberal Democratic committee chairmen. Regardless of their reasons, they gave me an education on inside politics that was second to none.

But in the end, the only real educator is experience. No matter how much advice you receive, at some point you have to learn by putting yourself in a position to succeed or fail. For me, the opportunity came with a bill rather inaccurately called Labor Law Reform.

The legislation came at a time when organized labor's influence in the Democratic Party, and thus in Congress, was still at its apex, far greater than it is now. Oddly, this dominance was intact even though actual union membership was diminishing. By the late 1970s, union representation was growing in only one sector: government workers.

In 1977, it was politically risky for most members of Congress to cross the AFL-CIO's president, George Meany. He was shrewd, tough, unforgiving, and in many ways the embodiment of the mythi-cal power broker who operated behind closed doors in smoke-filled rooms. He was far more powerful than most senators and wielded his clout with a bluntness that left little doubt about his intentions.

Meany believed the timing was right for passing a major labor bill. With the help of the unions, the Democrats not only had kept control of the House and the Senate in 1976 but also had won back the White House, which had been controlled by Republicans for the pre-vious eight years. The federation was confident that President Jimmy Carter would sign any legislation they endorsed. It would be a well-deserved reward for their help with the last election. All they needed to do was get their bill on the President's desk.

Labor Law Reform was intended to fix the AFL-CIO's problem of shrinking membership. It would make organizing far easier, even allowing union organizers to come onto a site during working hours to talk to employees. It created an expedited election process for employees and would have stacked the National Labor Relations Board (NLRB), the federal agency in charge of enforcing federal labor laws, with two additional members. Moreover, it would have allowed the NLRB to set wages as a remedy for unfair labor practices and ban companies from receiving federal contracts, an unprecedented expansion of the agency's regulatory power.

Corporate economists predicted that if the bill passed, more than 50 percent of America's workforce would be forced to join a union to keep their jobs. Since the AFL-CIO used a significant portion of the dues paid by the rank and file on political spending, almost all of which went to Democrats, the bill would dramatically expand the union's political war chest and thus its influence on legislation. Given the clout the AFL-CIO already enjoyed, the bill would give it unprecedented power over the congressional agenda. Bills it did not favor would never be considered, and its own initiatives would always be given top priority. If the legislation became law, the union's control over the Democratic Party and Congress would have been cemented permanently.

Democrats in Congress knew that if they supported the unions, they could receive not only monetary support in their election but the help of a large army of operatives who work on federal campaigns while on the union's payroll, a practice still common today. It is estimated that the unions spend approximately $500 million in cash and subsidized personnel each two-year election cycle. These same members also understood that if they did not support the union position, they could lose more than just money and campaign workers. They would be guaranteed a primary challenge in their next race by a candidate enthusiastically supported by the AFL-CIO.

As adamantly as the unions supported Labor Law Reform, the business community opposed it. They believed that if it passed, the American economy would inexorably move toward domination by a centralized, institutional-labor government coalition, much like what happened in Europe. Regardless of intention, the legislation would begin a downward spiral into an American brand of socialism and all its economic and political consequences.

The economist Pierre Rinfret concluded in a published report that the bill would hit small business the hardest, jeopardizing the expansion of the traditional engine behind American economic growth. He also predicted the bill would result in a doubling of the inflation rate for every 10 percent of growth in union membership, at a time when the United States was reeling from an unprecedented inflation rate of 8 percent.

By 1977, the business community was in a panic. They knew the bill would easily pass the House of Representatives, so their only hope was the Senate. While both chambers were controlled by the Democrats, they operate differently. The House rules enable the majority to dictate not only what legislation will come up for a vote but also what amendments can be offered. In the Senate, there are ample procedures available to members who want to try to either block or amend a bill, including the time-honored tradition of the filibuster.

Business leaders contacted several of the more prominent Senate Republicans, trying to find a champion. Not surprisingly, everyone turned them down. No one wanted to stand in front of a runaway train.

Having run out of options, they turned to me, third from the bottom in seniority, hardly the best way to begin a major legislative battle. After being encouraged privately by several other members, and not fully appreciating the size and consequences of the commitment I was making, I agreed to take the lead on two conditions.

First, the business community would have to agree to stay united. In the past, key votes had been lost at the last minute because individual companies, and sometimes entire industries, would cut deals with the unions in exchange for their support of a particular bill. Second, if I was going to be the leader in public, the business community would have to follow my leadership, both in public and in private. I knew that we would have no chance of winning if time was wasted by debating competing strategies.

Beginning in the fall of 1977, I became the face of the bill's opponents, traveling around the country, giving speeches, doing all I could to educate the public about the legislation and the dangerous consequences if it became law. My efforts were mirrored by a massive lobbying and public relations campaign by business that targeted members of Congress and interested constituencies. We put together a truly impressive coalition of small and big companies and their trade associations, small business organizations, and conservative groups, creating a model that would be copied in future legislative battles. A letter-writing campaign was started to help local businesses contact their senators and representatives. There were countless meetings with the editorial boards of local papers to explain the issue and try to influence what they might say in an editorial. Although the legislation raced through the House of Representatives, as expected, our efforts were beginning to pay off. Senators were realizing for the first time that the bill would be controversial.

Of course, whatever the opponents were doing, the bill's backers were doing the same. The AFL-CIO was marshaling all its resources to generate support among its members and its allies in Congress. Labor operatives seemed to be everywhere, pigeonholing members inside and outside the Capitol building, holding meetings in state offices and organizing rallies and fundraisers. By 1978, the battle lines were clearly drawn, and everyone in Congress knew that the vote on Labor Law Reform would be the most important domestic issue in the coming midterm elections.

The bill easily passed the Senate Labor Committee by a bipartisan vote of 16 to 2. Only Sam Hayakawa of California and I, the only conservatives of either party on the committee, voted against the legislation. With sixty-two Democrats and only thirty-eight Republicans in the Senate, passage looked inevitable. Adding to the growing momentum, President Carter made it clear that he would sign the bill if it passed Congress.

All that was left was the Senate floor. Unwilling to take any risks given the high stakes involved, the Democrats decided that the undisputed master of parliamentary procedure, Robert C. Byrd, the Majority Leader, would manage the bill on the Senate floor. Senator Byrd is one of the most knowledgeable and creative legislative strategists in the history of the Senate. His leadership was a huge advantage to the other side.

Our strategy was simple. We could not stop the bill just by voting, since more than a majority of the Senate favored the legislation. Our only hope was to filibuster the bill, taking advantage of the Senate rules to talk it to death. Under a filibuster, a senator or a group of senators use a member's right to speak as long as physically possible, to talk endlessly about virtually anything, in order to delay or prevent a bill from passing. The key is endurance, not persuasiveness.

Once it is known that a filibuster is either happening or will happen, the proponents of a bill file a cloture motion. Although the rules are slightly different today, in 1978, once cloture was invoked, only amendments determined to be germane to the legislation could be considered. Under the rules, a cloture motion cannot "ripen" or be ready for a vote for three days, and when the vote occurs, sixty out of the one hundred members of the Senate have to agree to limit debate. Consequently, unlike procedure in normal circumstances, where fifty-one votes are needed to pass a bill, sixty votes are needed to stop a filibuster by invoking cloture.

A lot of people object to filibusters, arguing that the procedure unnecessarily impedes the passage of legislation and frustrates the

ability of the Senate to function efficiently. The practice fell into considerable disrepute when it was used so frequently in the late 1950s
and early 1960s by Southern Democrats (including, I am sorry to say,
Senator Eastland) to block civil rights legislation. New arrivals to the
Senate, especially former members of the House, often propose eliminating the procedure entirely. Senator Trent Lott raised the issue
again just a few years ago when he grew frustrated with repeated
threats by the Democrats to filibuster a wide variety of bills.

Although I have been a victim as well as a beneficiary of filibusters,
I hope the procedure remains intact. It is, in many ways, the fundamental parliamentary power available to the minority in Congress.
Unlike the rules in the House of Representatives, where a simple
majority can always force the passage of any bill, in the Senate the filibuster or the threat of one ensures that the majority must give some
consideration to the interests of the minority, or risk losing control of
the legislative process. Its presence has guaranteed that American law
does not reflect the will of only one side.

Moreover, most members have learned to use the tactic sparingly.
Unlike members of the House, every member of the Senate has the
ability, at least in varying degrees, to affect the legislative process. It
is well understood that what you do to another member's legislative
priority can be done to you.

A filibuster is a potent but dangerous weapon. Not only can it tie
up a bill but it can stop the Senate from moving on to other issues,
raising the possibility of offending not only the proponents of the bill
being filibustered but also the supporters of completely unrelated legislation. In addition, the Majority Leader, who is in charge of determining the chamber's schedule, can keep the Senate in session
around the clock, forcing those who are engaging in the filibuster to
literally be on the floor around the clock. Consequently, actual filibusters are usually far more the exception than the rule and normally
are used only in cases where the stakes are high and the opponents of
a bill have no effective alternative. Labor Law Reform was one of

those cases. It was an issue that could not be lost, no matter what the cost.

It is impossible for one senator to run an effective filibuster. I needed help, so I turned to another Republican elected the same year as I was, Richard Lugar of Indiana. The former mayor of Indianapolis, Dick is highly organized, a former Rhodes scholar, and a quiet, efficient and intelligent legislator. We quickly assembled three rotating teams of five to six senators each to man the floor and to protect against procedural moves to surreptitiously end the debate. If one or more of the team members had a conflict, I would fill in and keep talking until relieved.

I also knew that I could count on the private advice and counsel of Jim Allen, who, despite his failing health, could match Senator Byrd's knowledge of the rules. Even during a filibuster, the Senate is not static. Depending on the intentions of the Majority Leader, other issues can be considered simultaneously, and there are literally hundreds of little maneuvers that can be made to cut off or control debate. I had not been in the Senate long enough to know even a fraction of them. Without Allen's assistance, I doubt I would have been able to match wits with Byrd when it came to a knowledge of the rules.

Another key member of the team was Fritz Hollings of South Carolina, a Southern Democrat who was uncomfortable about tilting the balance so far in favor of unions. Given the political risks he was taking, it took real courage for Fritz not only to vote with us but to work against the bill publicly. A handful of other Democrats were willing to help, but only behind the scenes.

One other member helped us at considerable personal cost. The Republican Leader, Howard Baker, offered his help even though he was quite sure the bill could not be stopped. He did so knowing that by working with us, he was jeopardizing the fragile relationship he had built with the AFL-CIO. At the time, the unions considered him a moderate Republican, an assessment that was critical given his presidential aspirations.

The numbers—sixty-two Democrats to thirty-eight Republicans—didn't look good. The task was more difficult, however, than convincing three Democrats to join the filibuster. In the 1970s there was far more diversity in both parties than today. I knew I could count on some Democrats, but I couldn't count on all the Republicans. They might vote with me a few times, but at some point, they would switch sides and vote for cloture.

As I worked over probable voting lists with Jim Allen, it became clear that in the end the decision would come down to five Democrats: Russell Long of Louisiana, Lawton Chiles of Florida, Dale Bumpers of Oklahoma, John Sparkman of Alabama and Edward Zorinsky of Nebraska. All were from southern or midwestern states, and all had been able to vote against the unions in the past and survive politically.

Jim and I also went through possible parliamentary scenarios. He reminded me that provided the right steps were taken, the Senate could be forced to vote on every germane amendment filed prior to cloture being invoked. Although there would be no discussion, the amendments could be called up and voted upon one by one, a process that, depending on how many were filed, could be extremely lengthy since most votes take at least twenty minutes. This would become my fallback strategy to force a compromise if cloture was invoked to end the filibuster.

The debate began on May 16, 1978. Both sides were already hard at work, dumping literally millions of letters, telegrams and postcards on the Senate. The rhetoric flew, as it often does. Phrases such as "holy war" and "freedom is at stake" were tossed around routinely. Given the stakes involved, the vote would be very much like a war. It would be obvious who won and who lost.

We immediately suffered our first setback. Sometimes, the Senate will work on other matters while a cloture motion is ripening, eliminating much of the burden on the filibusters and protecting them from the inevitable negative reaction to shutting down the Senate.

Senator Byrd had no intention of being so accommodating. Using his power as Majority Leader, Byrd announced that the Senate would *not* run on a two-track system. The filibuster team would literally have to stay on the floor every daylight hour, and sometimes all night long, for as long as we were in session.

Byrd knew that to win he would have to schedule a series of cloture votes. He did not want to appear too eager to silence the minority and unintentionally generate sympathy for our side. Moreover, he knew that a handful of Democrats always voted against cloture, at least once or twice, as a matter of principle. Some Republicans would feel compelled to vote with the majority of their party at the beginning. For Byrd, the key to winning was to be patient and not to force the issue too early. He announced he wouldn't make us meet around the clock, which he could have done. In addition, he declared that there would be a series of cloture votes, a signal that the first couple were not critical. He let it slip that we would probably win the first and second cloture votes but that the majority would prevail on the third. The record for consecutive cloture votes at the time was four.

In addition, Byrd decided not to hold the first vote until after the Memorial Day recess week. The delay meant that senators who were undecided would not have to vote on the bill until after they returned from a week back in their states. The unions would have another week to work them over.

Consequently, over the next ten days, while the Senate was in session, Dick Lugar and I spent most of our time on the floor giving speeches, some of which lasted as long as four hours, and supporting other members of the team. The speeches were high on length and low on eloquence, although most related to the bill and employment issues and conditions that would be affected. I quickly learned that it is far easier for a southerner to engage in a filibuster. A southern accent is particularly conducive to slow speech and allows ample time for each syllable to be clearly enunciated. If someone else tries to do this, it comes across a poor, almost insulting imitation. To prove the point, Jesse Helms of North Carolina once showed me how he could take over a minute simply to stand, be recognized and say, "Mr. President."

When I could, I left the floor to rally supporters throughout the country and meet with other members and interested parties to discuss the bill and the justification for our filibuster. When the Senate adjourned for the evening, Dick Lugar and I would meet with business leaders to discuss the day's events, identify issues that needed to be highlighted when we reconvened and make sure that what we were doing on the floor correlated with what they were doing on the Hill, in the media and in the crucial states.

By this time, the business community had an unprecedented organization in place to fight the legislation. It was able to coordinate public relations and lobbying, building on the work that had been done over the previous ten months. Large and small business leaders had been identified in every congressional district and state. On literally a day's notice, they could put more than 50,000 letters and telegrams on a senator's desk, the most effective means for communicating with Congress in an era before e-mail, fax machines and mobile phones became commonplace. If we felt that a particular senator needed some bolstering, word would go out and the mail and phone calls would flood into his office. If an issue was raised on which there were unanswered questions, legal analyses were prepared overnight and distributed throughout the chamber the following day. The organization was an impressive and effective tool.

When I could get away for a few minutes, I also tried to visit privately with Jim Allen at his hideaway in the Capitol to make sure we had avoided procedural mistakes that would undermine our position. He did not want to flaunt his role in the filibuster and unnecessarily offend his fellow Democrats by meeting with me on the floor.

Sure enough, as I had feared, immense pressure was placed on heavily unionized employers to support the legislation. Strikes were threatened against weaker companies. Thinly veiled threats were made about what the Democrats, especially Russell Long, might do those who did not support the legislation. Long was the Chairman of the powerful Senate Finance Committee, which has authority over tax and trade laws. Most businesses had important issues before his committee and were in a vulnerable position. One evening, I received word that a certain company, an industry leader, was ready to switch sides. If this were allowed to happen, others would follow and the coalition would fall apart.

The next day, the entire business coalition met at the National Association of Manufacturers at my request. I began by talking briefly about the bill and how far we had come. I then got to the point. Without singling out anyone, I said I had heard that one company, fearful of angering the Democrats in general and Senator Long in particular, was going to announce its support for the bill. "Senator Long may be chairman now," I said, "but I'm going to be here for thirty years or more and whoever does that will be one sorry company." The coalition stayed intact.

We kept the filibuster going until the Senate adjourned for the Memorial Day recess. I decided to stay in Washington over the holiday to prepare for the next round of speeches and debate. So, on June 1, I was at my home in Virginia when I heard the startling news: Jim Allen had died of a heart attack.

The news was a shock, a tremendous personal loss. Jim was the one senator, more than any other, who had gone out of his way to make me feel welcome and befriended in the Senate. No one would ever take his place.

Moreover, I had lost my parliamentary trump card, the one person I knew who could come close to matching wits with Robert Byrd. I had no idea whether we could win without him.

Byrd scheduled the first cloture vote for Wednesday, June 7, so that members could attend Jim's funeral on the previous day. As expected, the motion failed, forty-two members voting in favor of cloture and forty-seven against. I was surprised by how well we had done, but it was a poor predictor of the future. There were too many soft votes in our forty-seven. And eleven had not voted, an unexpectedly high number.

The next day there was another cloture vote. Again, cloture failed, forty-nine in favor and forty-one against, but the numbers were tightening. Off the floor, the bill's supporters increased the pressure. Senator Byrd announced that several changes would be made to the bill, which sounded impressive, but they were far more cosmetic than substantive. The White House weighed in directly for the first time. Key members of President Carter's staff made phone calls to members, and they used the Vice President's office off the Senate floor, the traditional location of the White House congressional liaison operation in the Senate, to meet with undecided senators. (The Vice President of the United States also serves as the President of the Senate.)

At the outset, Fritz Hollings and I had agreed to take responsibility for working on the five Democratic fence-sitters individually. While we both would talk to all five, my primary target was Ed Zorinsky of Nebraska, who also had been elected in 1976 and was already one of my best friends in the Senate. He had originally been a Republican; but when he decided to run for the Senate, party officials chose to support someone else, so he became a Democrat.

I had thought from the outset that Ed might prove to be the critical vote, so we made a deal. He agreed to vote with us on one condition. I had to let him know the minute I knew there were sixty votes for cloture, not counting his. If that happened, if the filibuster was going to be broken anyway, he wanted to be able to vote with the majority to protect himself. Given our predicament, it was an easy bargain to make.

The reports we were hearing during our evening meetings were not good. Senator Sparkman of Alabama, who was in his late seventies and not in the best of health, was beginning to look as if he might crack. Fritz agreed to sit with him during votes to make sure he didn't get confused or misled.

It is not readily apparent on the outside how much of the Senate's business can be done during a vote. Some of the most important work on legislation—finding supporters, eliminating problems and turning around opponents—occurs during votes on other bills. It is the one time every member of the Senate has to come to the well in the front of the chamber. Despite being in public, it is one of the few places where a senator can talk directly to a colleague without interruption.

If you ever watch Senate proceedings on television, it is easy to spot these meetings. Look for the little huddles, the small groups of two and three senators having a conversation. Sometimes the discussion is as innocuous as any chat you might have with a casual acquaintance. At other times, however, substantive issues are being discussed and legislation is either advancing or failing.

On Monday, June 12, Russell Long pulled me aside. He repeated an offer he had made the previous week. In exchange for our agreeing to end the filibuster, the Democrats would modify several provisions in the bill. With such a compromise, he argued, everyone would win. George Meany would get the bill he needed. President Carter would not be embarrassed, and I could take credit for making the bill more evenhanded. And Long would avoid having to choose between the unions and the business community and would reinforce his deserved image as the consummate dealmaker.

What he left unsaid was that if I pushed the filibuster too far, I risked losing everything. At some point, the Democrats would have no choice but to vote as a party, and the bill, with all its inherent problems and dangers, would pass. If I accepted Long's offer, however, at least some components of the bill would be improved.

If I rejected it, I would lose Senator Long.

Despite his characterizations, we both knew his offer was more face-saving than substantive. The unions would never permit me to remedy the real problems with the bill. Those were the very provisions the AFL-CIO wanted and needed the most.

Once again, I refused to give Long a firm answer, pointing out that Labor Law Reform could not be improved with a handful of amendments. It would still be a terrible piece of legislation.

Long turned away, his disappointment obvious. He was not used to having his offers rebuffed by a freshman senator, let alone a Republican. I was convinced I had just made the fence-sitting quintet of Long, Chiles, Bumpers, Sparkman and Zorinsky a quartet.

The next day, Tuesday, June 13, there was a third cloture vote. Again the bill's proponents lost, but those voting in favor of cloture increased to fifty-four. Worse, I learned that the real switching would begin with the next vote. Ted Stevens, from the heavily unionized state of Alaska, pulled me aside during the vote to let me know that he could no longer hold out.

Ted is one of the most direct, forthright members of our institution, one of the few who will always let you know where he stands. In keeping with his character, he had the honesty to let me know ahead of time what he was going to do. He would switch sides on the next vote.

The Senate voted again on Wednesday. At this point, most of us were physically and mentally exhausted with the filibuster, which had already lasted nearly a month. Labor Law Reform had become a monster, dominating nearly every moment of the day. No one could escape the lobbying campaigns being run by both sides. It seemed that proponents or opponents were everywhere. Nerves were beginning to fray, and it was increasingly difficult to maintain a cordial front.

My voice had gone. It would take more than a year for it to recover to the point where I could be heard in public, and it would never completely heal. Sleep was becoming increasingly difficult. The few hours I had each evening to rest I seemed to spend wide awake, replaying the day's events and rehashing conversations both on and off the floor. Fortunately, with so many cloture votes scheduled in a row and Byrd's many procedural amendments to the bill, it was not difficult to fill the limited time for debate actually talking about the legislation.

Fritz Hollings spent the entire vote sitting next to Senator Sparkman. At one point, Robert Byrd approached the two, hoping to convince Sparkman to change sides. Before he could even begin, Sparkman pushed him away, telling the Majority Leader to leave him alone.

As we had feared, the moderate Republicans began to defect. In addition to Ted Stevens, Lowell Weicker, John Heinz and Chuck Percy switched sides, pushing the proponents' total to fifty-eight, only two short of cloture.

Percy's decision was a surprise. After the vote, I caught him on the floor, exhaustion making it difficult for me to appear cordial.

"I thought you promised to be with us," I said, unable to mask my anger.

"I promised that I would be with you," he snapped back, "but I never promised I would be with you forever."

Sensing victory, Byrd scheduled another vote for the next day. He predicted that he would prevail on the next vote, that the Senate understood the time had come to put an end to the filibuster.

Having raised the stakes, the Democrats went to work to make good on Byrd's prediction. No one was left alone, not even Maryon Allen, who had been appointed to finish her husband's term. She told me she was called to several meetings by the Democratic leadership. The message was clear. Regardless of how her husband might have voted, if she did not side with the unions, she risked losing all of Jim's committee assignments, which she had been allowed to inherit. Despite the threats, she held firm.

Surprisingly, the Democrats failed to increase their total on the fifth vote, and the count remained at fifty-eight in favor of cloture. His irritation obvious, the Majority Leader scheduled a sixth vote for Thursday, June 22.

All of us sensed that, regardless of the outcome, this would be the final vote. The filibuster had been far more resilient than anyone had imagined. No one had predicted we would survive a record-setting five cloture motions. Still, most people were convinced we were simply delaying the inevitable.

There were no surprises left. Of the five fence-sitters at the beginning, it was clear that two, Senators Chiles and Bumpers, though desperately wanting to, could not afford to switch and vote for cloture. Attempts to force Sparkman to change sides had backfired. Russell Long, who to my surprise had stayed with us through the last vote, was ready to move, but there would be no point unless one other member followed him. As I had expected from the outset, it came down to my friend Ed Zorinsky.

There were several meetings on the Democratic side as various members teamed up on Zorinsky. Over the next two days, they worked him over, first making threats and then offering him deals, the substance of which I never learned.

By the morning of June 22, it appeared they had made progress. Driving into Washington, I heard news reports on the radio claiming Byrd had enough votes to win. On *Good Morning America*, ABC's morning news show, it was announced we were going to lose. Following a meeting in my office with the filibuster team, I hurried over to Howard Baker's office to finalize the day's strategy. As I was walking in, Senator Long was walking out. He did not look defeated.

"Orrin, you know you're going to lose today," Howard said. His words were like a punch to my stomach.

Long had just told him he would change sides. Robert Byrd was going to ask for unanimous consent to return the bill to committee, with an instruction to report it back forthwith with a few minor changes. Again, Howard explained, the changes would be cosmetic, the entire process simply a face-saving gesture for our benefit. Moreover, most of our amendments would no longer be germane because they would reference language in the bill that no longer existed.

It was a good strategy. If I objected, Byrd would argue that the pending cloture vote was no longer about the substance of the bill but about his and his party's ability to control the Senate floor agenda. The Democrats would have no choice but to vote with their leader. Byrd would have cloture, and the bill would become law.

Howard urged me not to object. If I went along with the plan, at least some of the objectionable provisions would be deleted, even if they were insignificant. He was convinced Byrd had found the last vote he needed to end the debate.

You have to admire Senator Byrd. The old fox almost had us trapped. Almost. To Howard's disappointment, I refused to go along. I explained that even with the amendments, it would still be a horrible bill. It would be wrong to mislead anyone into believing that it somehow had been improved. If the proponents could make it law, everyone in the United States should understand who was responsible. Howard might have disagreed with my assessment, but he did not push further. He was a remarkably patient and restrained leader. In retrospect, I am sure it was not easy for him to let a freshman senator force our side into such a politically risky position.

Thanking him for his help and advice, I rushed out of Howard's office. It was time to put a few things Senator Allen had taught me into play.

The vote was scheduled for 3:00 P.M., and as often happens with important moments in the Senate, some of the members arrived early. I walked into the Senate chamber carrying five hundred amendments to the bill that our coalition had just finished drafting. Senator Byrd immediately understood what I was doing and glared at me as I filed them all with the reporting clerk. As Jim Allen had taught me, even if cloture was invoked, I could force the Senate to vote on each amendment filed prior to cloture, which together would take almost seven consecutive twenty-four-hour sessions to complete, not counting the time consumed on other parliamentary moves. In Senate time, the period would stretch into weeks or even months.

I went over to Fritz Hollings. He repeated what everyone else was saying, that Long was gone and we were going to lose. "What are we going to do?" he asked.

I responded by asking whether we still had Chiles, Sparkman and Bumpers. He said we did, and I talked over some strategy with him. He asked whether we still could count on Zorinsky.

"Let me handle Zorinsky," I answered, trying to appear more confident than I was.

One of the people I had contacted when I left Howard Baker's office was Ed Zorinsky. He sounded worn down. The Democrats had worked on him for three hours the night before. He had been forced to meet with Byrd, Long, Chiles and Bumpers. The latter two made it clear that they wanted to vote with the other Democrats but couldn't. They pleaded with Zorinsky to change sides, to join Long and break the filibuster.

Ed was clearly torn. He knew it was a bad bill, but he did not want to be the one responsible for making the Senate Democrats and President Carter suffer an embarrassing defeat. In the end, although he had voted against cloture every time so far, he would now admit to me, his friend, only to being a "mushy no" against cloture. He asked whether I could still hold on to forty-one votes. I told him I thought I could, but I would let him know if things changed. I would live up to my commitment.

Moments before the vote, Senator Zorinsky walked onto the Senate floor. I was sitting at a desk in the front of the chamber. Keeping my distance, I caught his eye and nodded. His face expressionless, he nodded back, his head moving up and down once. We never exchanged a word.

I sprang from my chair and raced over to Hollings. "We have Zorinsky," I said. A large smile broke across Fritz's face. He knew exactly what to do.

Senator Byrd stood up. With his usual eloquence and flourish, he spoke for a few minutes and then asked for unanimous consent to send the bill back to committee with a report back forthwith as the impending buisiness. He and the others turned toward me, ready for my response, but I said nothing.

"I object," a voice boomed, the southern drawl extending each word. Everyone in the chamber spun around toward Hollings, who stood defiant, a tremendous smile on his face.

Byrd was shocked. His strategy had just unraveled. He spoke for several minutes, trying to regain control, and then turned to Senator Long. The senator from Louisiana began an impassioned tirade, targeting his fury at me and the other opponents of the bill. He accused us of using parliamentary tricks to frustrate the will of the Senate, an interesting criticism given the plan he and Senator Byrd had just tried to implement. He finished by announcing that because he was so upset by what had just happened, he would switch sides and vote for cloture.

Senator Hollings jumped to his feet. "Well, the distinguished senator from Louisiana has always been the fifty-ninth vote for cloture," he said, "and we have always known it." His retort left hanging the unspoken question: Who was the sixtieth? For a moment, the chamber fell silent.

"If Senator Long is going to cross over, then I'm crossing back," another voice said, breaking the silence.

The Senate erupted as everyone began talking at once. I turned and realized that the speaker was Ted Stevens, a look of disgust on his face. He had had enough of Long's posturing. He knew what a tough fight this had been for Lugar and me.

Suddenly it was over. The vote no longer mattered. Labor Law Reform was finished. The sixth cloture vote was fifty-three in favor and forty-five against, but no one seemed to care about the final tally. After nearly five weeks, the filibuster came to an abrupt end. The runaway train had been derailed.

That night, totally exhausted, I decided to honor a commitment I had made weeks before and attended a fundraiser for Chuck Percy at the home of the former Kentucky senator, John Sherman Cooper. I had barely gotten past the front door when I saw the one man I least expected or wanted to meet that night. He was sitting hunched over in a chair. I decided I had to bite the bullet and walked over and introduced myself.

"I know who you are!" George Meany yelled as he stood, his voice so loud that it startled several guests. Yet to my surprise, he was gracious, almost courteous, about what had happened. He complimented our effort, then his face hardened.

"We respect you, Orrin," he said, his voice low but intense. "No hard feelings, but even if costs us $4 million in 1982, we're going to get rid of you." The sum was so astronomical compared to the cost of my previous race that he might as well have said he was going to spend a billion.

"If you spend that much money in Utah to get rid of me," I said, laughing nervously, "it will double our gross state product and make me a great hero."

Meany laughed despite himself, and we parted cordially. Despite his courtesy, I had no doubt that he would make good on his threat. And he did. Well, at least he spent the money.

My first major legislative fight had a significance that I would only later come to appreciate. Instead of being a crowning moment for the AFL-CIO, the Labor Law Reform bill actually represented the last comprehensive attempt by the unions to rewrite federal labor laws, and its defeat prevented a massive upheaval of the delicate balance between labor and management. Still, the ultimate impact of the battle reached far beyond labor relations.

For the first time in years, conservative Republicans had demonstrated that they were a political force. Republicans no longer would have to accept face-saving deals from the Democrats simply to remain involved. Moreover, by the end of the filibuster, the business community was far more organized than it had ever been before.

Ultimately, historians will decide the significance of the defeat of Labor Law Reform, but one does have to wonder. If the legislation had been enacted and, as a result, the unions had been able to dominate Congress and solidify their control over the electoral process to the degree they envisioned, what would have happened in the 1980 elections? I am not sure of the answer, but I am confident of one thing: Defeating Labor Law Reform was critical to Republicans' gaining control of the Senate only two years later, a change in power that would help us set a different course for the United States for the remainder of the century.

Chapter Three

What Happened to Your Principles?

Wisdom is the principal thing; therefore get wisdom: and with all thy getting get understanding.

—Proverbs 4:7

SOME things are inevitable when you hold public office. First, you never have to be the first one to speak in a conversation. Second, you will probably be booed if you are introduced at a sporting event. Third, you will never make as much money as people think. And fourth, at some point, an old friend will pull you aside in angry bewilderment and demand to know when you lost your principles.

What they are really asking is when you stopped agreeing either with their opinion about a specific issue or, more troubling, an opinion they presumed you shared. Their passion often flows from the common assumption that their view and their view alone is based on principle, and that adherence to a contrary position can only be the result of a hidden character flaw, stubborn ignorance, or craven submission to political expediency.

If asked, most Americans will say that in the ideal, our elected officials should cast every vote based upon principle. Yet there is no core principle or set of principles shared by all Americans, or by any individual state or congressional district. You can even find irreconcilable differences over the fundamental liberties and freedoms expressly set forth in the Declaration of Independence and the United States Constitution, such as those contained in the Second or the Fourteenth Amendment.

Each of us has certain issues or beliefs we consider inviolate, so important that their protection transcends all other considerations. For some, it is the right to life. Others are just as passionately committed to a woman's right to choose. Either way, the conviction is so fundamental that any infringement on this belief, be it real or perceived, is unacceptable. The same goes for gun control, the death penalty, school prayer, national defense, health care, education, labor and countless other issues. More often than not, these are the topics that have dominated the political landscape for decades.

Principles are also involved in issues that are by no means as universally significant. People can be passionate about topics that are neither well known nor particularly relevant to others. I have watched constituents battle, with the eloquence and fervor normally reserved for debates on the death penalty, over whether there should be home delivery of the mail. Comparable passions have been raised over the location of parking lots, the choice of state flowers, and even the official name of the residents of a state.

For these people, an elected official's failure to agree is no different from taking an opposing position on school prayer, national defense, or the environment. What others might see as a subject for reasonable compromise, they see as a stark contrast between black and white, right and wrong, principle and crass politics.

A politician can't help but violate some voters' principles because no constituency is monolithic. Virtually every state and every congressional district reflects the entire gamut of political opinion, from libertarian to conservative, from moderate to liberal to socialist. Despite our geographic stereotypes, there are Utah liberals just as there are San Francisco conservatives. Undoubtedly there are one or two exceptions to the rule. I have to admit I have never actually seen a conservative anywhere near Madison, Wisconsin.

Obviously, what differentiates one area from another are the numbers, the percentage of voters taking various viewpoints. In politics, as in baseball, the numbers tend toward the middle. The numerical difference between winners and losers is much smaller than it is in other activities.

For example, when Ronald Reagan won his landslide presidential victory over Walter Mondale in 1984, he won 54.4 million of the popular vote to his rival's 37.5 million, and nearly swept the electoral college. Put another way, even though he won by a colossal margin, two out of every five voters felt Reagan was wrong and Mondale was right. That's a lot of people prepared to be suspicious about the president's motives or to assume that he is acting on virtually anything other than principle.

Utah is considered a national bastion of conservatism, one of the most Republican states in the Union. Still, in most polls, approximately 33 percent of all voters identify themselves as Democrats and a comparable number as moderates. Again, that's a large pool presumably ready to believe that any vote I cast is for the wrong reason.

Just as no constituency is monolithic, neither are most people. Only a very few of us don't have at least a few personal opinions that might seem to be at odds with the balance of our political outlook, views that are based upon our own or our family's personal experience.

Often, these views are impossible to predict. I have met tough, conservative men and women who have spent their careers in law enforcement who strenuously object to mandatory sentencing. I have met schoolteachers who are strident advocates for abolishing the Department of Education. And I have worked with lifelong

Republicans considered to be rigid, doctrinaire conservatives who not only support but advocate legal preference for gays and lesbians.

Despite these realities, we like our politicians to speak in absolutes, where things are clearly defined as black or white, even though we realize we spend most of our lives working through issues of gray. If asked, some people will profess complete opposition to any and all tax increases, yet they are comfortable about raising taxes on behavior we wish to discourage, such as smoking. Others believe firmly that the answer to almost any problem can be solved through government control and regulation, yet they have never had any faith in government when it comes to military affairs or intelligence gathering. There are those who believe that public officials should always tell the truth, yet are willing to accept some lying. For some, prevarication is justified if it's about personal moral conduct; for others, it is acceptable, even expected, if it involves matters of national security.

Most successful members of Congress eventually come to appreciate that they were elected in part because of the values and principles they believe in and, if they were wise, explained to their constituency during the campaign. They realize that their election is proof that in general they reflect the attitudes and opinions of a majority of those who voted. They also understand that while they are expected to reflect the opinions of most voters most of the time, absolute unanimity is not necessary. Voters understand that there will be differences. Consequently, hiding or muting them is, in the long run, counterproductive. You cannot hold public office and hide what you believe. Eventually, you will be found out.

Senator Gordon Smith of Oregon is a good case in point. He is a conscientious and thoughtful member, a moderate Republican from a state well known for its moderate-to-liberal leanings. He is also a Mormon and pro-life, a position that would normally be politically hazardous in his state. Instead of trying to mask or downplay his position, Gordon has been forthright about his views, which are based both on his religious convictions and his personal experience.

His three children are adopted. He has made it clear that, as an adoptive parent, it would be difficult for him to have a different view of the sanctity of human life. To date, a majority of his constituents apparently respect his opinion and, if they disagree, they are willing to judge him based on his other considerable gifts and accomplishments.

Most problems arise, however, when people not only equate their position with principle but also engage in the correlative assumption that the opposition is not just wrong but somehow less moral or ethical. It is a mistake I certainly have had to struggle to avoid.

As improbable as it may seem today, beginning in the late 1970s, there was an impassioned debate over whether the federal government should balance the budget. For many conservatives, it was an outrage that the Democrats in Congress, who had been in control for decades, were comfortable spending far more money than the government could raise, strapping coming generations with a debt so staggering that it would be impossible to pay off over a lifetime. We conservatives believed that there could be only one effective protection: passage of a balanced budget amendment to the Constitution so that the federal government, like many states, could not allow its expenditures to exceed its revenues except in times of war. For us, the amendment not only was a matter of fiscal responsibility, it was the only principled position to take. We were not alone in our belief. Thirty state legislatures had called on Congress to convene a constitutional convention to consider the amendment.[1]

At the time, most Democrats in Congress felt that such a balanced budget amendment would have disastrous consequences, hamstringing the government's ability to meet its social obligations or to raise sufficient funds in times of war or national crisis. Moreover, it would deny them the funds needed to stimulate the economy in a recession. Consequently, blocking the amendment was not only right from their public policy perspective, it was the principled position.

Each side was suspicious of the other's motives. Liberal Democrats were convinced that the Republicans' real intention with the amendment was to undermine the statutory and regulatory safety net they had diligently built over the last two decades to provide social services, protect the environment and underwrite civil rights protection. The assessment fit their general presumption that Republicans were insensitive to the needs of the poor and preoccupied with eliminating regulatory restraints on business.

Republicans, meanwhile, saw the Democratic reliance on deficit spending as callous political pandering allowing them to throw money at any problem to curry favor without concern for the cumulative consequences of what they were promising. The Democratic opposition was not over principle; it was based on a fear that without an unfettered power to spend federal dollars, their reelection would be in jeopardy.

Consequently, during the 1980s, the successive fights over the Balanced Budget Amendment were prolonged, heated and personal. It didn't help that the votes were always extremely close. As an amendment to the Constitution, the proposal needed a two-thirds majority in both houses of Congress to pass and be sent to the states for ratification. Every time we brought the issue to the floor in the Senate, we fell one or two votes short.

Every year except one. In 1982, when the Republicans controlled both the Senate and the White House, the amendment passed the Senate by a vote of 69 to 31. Unfortunately, the Democrats were still firmly in charge of the House of Representatives, and the measure died once again.

As one of the prime sponsors of the amendment, I managed our side during most of the legislative fights. For bills that are debated on the floor of the Senate, one member from each party is responsible for leading his or her side. Usually, this is either the Chairman or Ranking Minority Member of the committee with jurisdiction over the legislation. Sometimes, however, this position is given to one of the primary sponsors of the legislation or the most active opponent. The bill manager sits at the desk in the very front of the chamber that is reserved for his or her respective leader, either the Majority Leader or the Senate Minority Leader, depending on who controls the Senate at the time. This person is responsible for coordinating the debate and the legislative strategy for either the proponents or the opponents of the bill. Moreover, if a unanimous consent agreement is in place, which limits the amount of time that can be spent on debating a bill or an amendment, the managers also control the amount of time that individual members will be given to speak.

As the Republican manager for the Balanced Budget Amendment, I was on the Senate floor for most of the debates and intimately involved in developing the strategy for our side. It was a frustrating experience, like a toothache that could never be relieved, because the position of a few members was so amorphous.

The amendment's opponents, almost all of whom were Democrats, did a clever job of rotating opposition by allowing a few of their members to support the amendment when they were up for reelection, but making sure that there were always just enough votes to block passage. Year after year, we would pick up a vote here and there and convince ourselves that we were close to victory; but in the end, one of our former supporters would switch sides, and we would lose yet again. Still, like Charlie Brown with the football, we kept trying. It often happens in politics that hope triumphs over experience.

In 1995, however, things looked different. By all counts, we finally had enough Democrats up for reelection to win. All we needed to do was hold the Republicans, all of whom had already voted in favor of the amendment. Even a victory in the House, which was still under Democratic control, began to look possible. For the first time in more than fifteen years, I let myself believe the amendment would finally pass.

As the day of the vote drew close, trouble cropped up yet again. A Republican who had supported the amendment in the past, Senator Mark Hatfield, indicated he was ready to switch sides. He would be the deciding vote for the Democrats.

I couldn't believe it. We finally had the opposition boxed in. We had worked so hard to time the debate so there would not be enough Democrats who could afford to change sides and give our opponents yet another victory. And still we were going to lose, this time because of a Republican.

Mark was a long-standing and well-respected liberal senator from Oregon. He was also the Chairman of the Senate Appropriations Committee, the committee that decides how the federal government will spend its money every year.

Senator Bob Dole, the colorful and popular Republican from Kansas and the most visible and consistent face of the Republican Party for nearly three decades, was the Majority Leader. He tried literally everything to convince Senator Hatfield to continue to vote with all the other Republicans. He stressed the fiscal and economic importance of the amendment, and the consequences to the country if it failed. Nothing seemed to work.

As the vote neared, I pushed Bob Dole to contact Senator Hatfield once more. Bob pointed out that they had already talked repeatedly on the phone, and he doubted there was much else that could be done. I suggested that he go and meet with Mark personally, that the significance of such a visit would not be lost on him. He would understand from the symbolism how important the issue must be to his leader and the rest of his Republican colleagues.

Like most human institutions, the Senate has established traditions. One is that the Majority Leader does not go hat-in-hand and meet with an individual member in his office, even a member of his own party. The mountain does not come to Mohammed, even if he is a committee chairman. Instead, regardless of who initiated the meeting, senators visit with their respective leaders in the leader's office.

The same is true with presidents. Even if it is the president who needs a favor or a vote, a member of Congress always travels to the White House for a meeting with the president, regardless of party affiliation or rank.

Dole broke with tradition and went to see Hatfield; the vote was that important. Unfortunately, the meeting was as unsuccessful as their other discussions. Hatfield became so exasperated at one point that he asked, "What do you want me to do—resign from the Senate?"

When Bob told me about the conversation, for a moment I thought about what would happen if we could actually take Senator Hatfield up on his offer. If he resigned or simply walked away, there would be only ninety-nine members voting. With sixty-six votes in favor of the amendment, we would finally have the necessary two-thirds needed to win.

The moment passed. Once again, we ended up losing by one vote.

A lot of people were angry about the outcome. The Democrats who had voted with us were obviously irritated. They had to face the wrath of their own leadership and were now under heavy criticism from the liberal wing of their party. Several of the new conservative Republicans were just as angry. They could not reconcile losing the Balanced Budget Amendment because a Republican had switched positions. They felt betrayed, convinced that a member of the Senate's old boys club had hijacked principle to protect the status quo.

A few began agitating to strip Hatfield of his Appropriations Committee chairmanship as punishment for his disloyalty.

I, too, was angry and upset about what Mark had done. In some ways, I felt I had been deceived. Mark told me that his vote was a matter of principle. He had decided to change sides because he was now convinced that the amendment would undermine the authority and role of the appropriations process in Congress.

Even though I never did learn exactly what had changed his mind—why it was now a matter of principle to oppose the amendment when it wasn't before—I still felt I had to respect his decision. I had no choice but to assume that his vote was just as sincerely cast as mine, regardless of my inability to understand his reasoning, let alone concur with it. I joined several others who came to Senator Hatfield's defense, and the effort to punish him quickly lost steam.

Lately, it seems that the debate over principles is most often associated with two distinct topics: campaign finance reform and party switching. Neither debate has exactly been dominated by clear thinking.

Since the nation was founded, there have been concerns that politicians were providing favors in exchange for financial support and votes. It is almost a national assumption that no matter how idealistic a person might be when first elected, he or she will quickly get caught up in a money game that has to be played in order to survive. Reelections seem to cost more money than elections. Time has to be devoted to fundraising every day one holds office to retain the position. Consequently, so the argument goes, principles are ignored as more attention is given to those who can raise large amounts of cash or deliver large numbers of votes, skewing a member's decisionmaking process in favor of the powerful, the vested money interests and the wealthy.

It would be naïve to pretend that this doesn't occur. Some members keep lists of contributors in their offices and have been known to review them when meeting with a visitor. For the most part, however, these are the rare exceptions, far less common than many people think. In fact, the way money is actually raised testifies to its real role.

Most fundraising starts with individuals who have already supported a candidate or an incumbent. These tend to be friends, business associates and people who over the years have developed a strong faith in the person because of past activities. Put another way, actions preceded the money. These contributors are the individuals who believe it is important that the person be elected or stay in office. They serve as the core of most fundraising efforts and normally provide the largest percentage of financial support.

A second category is made up of constituents who wish to show their support for what a member has done or what a contender promises to do. Individually, they contribute small amounts of money raised through direct mail and similar types of solicitations. Their real value is in their votes and their willingness to encourage others to support a candidate. They play perhaps the most significant role in determining whether someone wins or loses. Again, what usually attracts their support is what has been done more than what is being promised.

The third category of potential donors consists of those with vested interests in issues before Congress. These tend to be organizations such as the trial lawyers, company or industry associations, unions, or similar special interest groups. They provide assistance to those with whom they agree, or to ensure access, the chance to make their case on a specific bill or issue. Sometimes they give money to competing candidates to preserve their options. Often, they give to an individual knowing their opponents have already made contributions. Their impact is thus harder to determine in part because they can cancel one another out.

The difficulty for the ethicists is divining what role the money played in how a person votes. Some believe members vote exclusively because of contributed money, an easy but not instructive assessment. For example, did a member vote for a particular bill because of the campaign contribution or because the company that made the contribution employs several thousand workers in the senator's state and without the bill they would lose their jobs?

Take another common occurrence. A senator helps a constituent who has a visa problem and subsequently the constituent sends in a small contribution to the campaign. Did the senator provide the help in expectation of the money, or did he or she simply provide assistance because the individual was from the state? It is almost always the latter, but some will believe it was the former. How do you determine the "real" motive when a member votes after receiving contributions from competing sides of a controversial issue? Was one group's money better than another's?

The reality is that just as it is impossible to determine what an entire constituency wants, it is impossible to identify how all of one's donors feel about a particular bill or amendment. More often that not, there is no single opinion. Consequently, the vast majority of Congress will vote the way they would have voted without the contributions. The contributing base is too complex and too contradictory to be controlling. All of us have voted against the interests of a contributor. You can't avoid it.

Another set of "ethical" issues is often overlooked. I have known colleagues who refuse ever to discuss money or contributions and frown when a visitor tries to broach the subject. They enjoy a reputation of being more ethical and honest than the rest of us. Yet, the minute the member leaves the meeting, the chief of staff steps in to talk about fundraising. Does separating the solicitation from the member make it more acceptable?

I have known members who have attended a fundraiser, accepted the money and then voted against the contributors later in the same day. It might be proof that the member cannot be influenced by campaign contributions, but is it fair or ethical? In the same vein, some of the biggest proponents of campaign finance reform are some of the most aggressive and relentless fundraisers in Congress. When this apparent discrepancy is pointed out, they respond that they will change their behavior once the rules change. It would be nonsensical to do otherwise.

Money also creates its own problems. Several years ago, a large corporation gave a huge sum to a national campaign committee just before the election. The amount was so large that, the following year, members were loath to support the company's position for fear the public would think their votes had been bought. Instead of winning favors for the corporation, the contributions actually cost the company votes it might have otherwise have won.

Reform legislation will neither stop campaign abuses nor equalize the playing field. You cannot impose a sense of ethics on candidates or control all behavior with regulation. If you enter a race and you don't know that renting the Lincoln Bedroom is wrong, that fundraising at religious sites is inappropriate or that taking money from foreign agents is wrong, an act of Congress won't enlighten you.

Many of the people who are excited about the latest campaign finance misadventure are the ones who once told us that political action committees (PACs) would restore decency and prevent abuse. Of course, they now argue that PACs are the problem.

The innumerable constitutional issues notwithstanding, the McCain-Feingold bill, which attempts to regulate the use of soft money, will not fix the problem. A year from now, we will learn about new ways for individuals and organizations to finance the candidates they support. This has been true since our country was founded and will continue to be a reality as long as we are a nation in which freedom of expression is a constitutional right and political participation is a universal opportunity.

Federal funding will not work, either. Limiting every candidate to the same amount of money will place far greater emphasis and power on involved third parties, such as the media. How does one candidate overcome disparate treatment in the press without the ability to get his or her message out through advertising or other media?

The only effective answer is total disclosure: quick, accurate and complete reporting of who is contributing to a campaign. We live in an age when such information can be made available to essentially the entire electorate almost instantaneously. If done correctly, disclosure will enable voters to know who is behind a campaign and, if they have questions, provide them an opportunity to demand answers from the candidate. If they don't like what they hear, they can then vote against the candidate.

For reformers, disclosure is not as appealing as other alternatives, especially public financing, government regulation of campaigning and strict limitations on expenditures and spending. It will not equalize every candidate's chances to be heard no matter how minimal their support among the public, a dubious objective at best. Still, disclosure does have one advantage over most other solutions: It's legal.

While campaign finance reform is the media's favorite test for determining whether a candidate is principled, choosing a party is arguably the key moment for identifying the values and ideals that will be most controlling in a person's political life. Consequently, switching parties always raises questions of whether the change was based upon a sincere shift in philosophy and priorities or was driven by personal convenience or benefit.

In 2001, the nation confronted this conundrum more directly than ever before. Jim Jeffords was a relatively quiet and, at the time, not a particularly well-known member of the Senate. He served as the lone Vermont member of the House of Representatives for seven terms before being elected to the Senate in 1988. Even though he was elected to the longest-held Republican seat in the country, his voting record matched the liberal reputation of the state, and he tended to vote with Democrats more than with Republicans.

Following the elections in 2000, the Republicans were on the verge of the ultimate political trifecta: They were regaining control of the White House and holding on to the leadership in the House of Representatives and the Senate. The only potential impediment was the Senate where, for only the second time in history, there were an even number of Republicans and Democrats.

Under the Constitution, when the Senate is tied, the President of the Senate, who is the Vice President, is permitted to cast a vote to break a deadlock. Since Dick Cheney was the incoming Vice President, the Republicans rightly assumed that they would be in control of the chamber.

This would not happen immediately. The Senate convenes several weeks before the presidential inauguration, so initially the President of the Senate would still be Vice President Al Gore. Consequently, for approximately three weeks, the Democrats technically controlled the Senate. Not until January 20, 2001, the day of George W. Bush's inauguration, could the Republicans finally claim control over the White House, the House of Representatives and, by the narrowest possible margin, the Senate. Unfortunately, the margin was even more precarious than we realized.

Knowing they could regain control of the Senate if they could convince one Republican to switch sides, the Democrats quietly began to target a few individuals to see whether they would be receptive to changing parties. These negotiations were kept secret for as long as possible, but by spring, it was clear that Senator Jeffords was ready to jump.

Both sides weighed in hard. In a series of private meetings, the Republicans pointed out that they had stood by Jeffords when he was worried about his own reelection. They had funneled quite a bit of money into the state the previous year to help him stave off what he believed would be a serious challenge from Representative Bernie Sanders, a Socialist who runs as an Independent but is treated as a Democrat in the House of Representatives. Moreover, despite his voting record, the Republicans had supported Jeffords's assumption of the chairmanship of the Senate Labor Committee, which he subsequently renamed the Health, Education, Labor and Pensions Committee (HELP). In fact, Trent Lott, the Republican Leader, was often criticized in private by conservatives for being too accommodating to Jeffords's concerns.

There was a personal consideration as well. After serving for more than twenty-seven years, one of Jim's good friends, Chuck Grassley, had finally assumed chairmanship of the Senate Finance Committee, a position for which he had patiently waited an entire career. If Jeffords switched sides, Chuck would automatically lose the chairmanship he had held for only months. The same was true for other committee and subcommittee chairmen, including me.

The Democrats had their own arguments. They stressed Jeffords's differences and problems with a few of the more conservative Republicans. They promised that he would not only keep his seniority but receive a committee chairmanship as well.

Harry Reid, the Democratic Whip in the Senate and thus arguably the second most powerful Democrat in the chamber, was intimately involved in the negotiations and was credited for orchestrating his party's lobbying of Jeffords. Even though he was slated to become Chairman of the Senate Committee on Environment and Public Works if his party regained control, he offered to step aside so that Jeffords could run the committee, a plum assignment for a senator from Vermont. If he switched sides, he would be the only member of the Senate not to lose a chairmanship. And, unlike the Republicans, who limit the number of years a member can be chairman, the Democrats have no such cap. Jeffords would continue to be chairman as long as the Democrats controlled the Senate.

The Democrats also made promises on several legislative issues, including the assurance that specific education and disability programs that Jeffords favored would receive adequate funding.

And they stressed the historic impact of switching sides. He, and he alone, would be able to change the political landscape to ensure a level of bipartisanship that would be impossible if the Republicans controlled the White House and both houses of Congress. The party in charge sets the agenda in the Senate. It decides which bills will be brought to the floor, the subject matter of congressional hearings and oversight, and the timing and content of committee business.

By making Tom Daschle the Majority Leader instead of Trent Lott, Jeffords would be able to rewrite the list of issues and legislation addressed by the Senate and, as a result, by Congress. By putting the Democrats in charge, he would force the Bush Administration and the Republicans to address issues and accept compromises we might otherwise have avoided.

By late May, the pressure from both sides had become tremendous. Many of us met with Jim, sometimes one-on-one, sometimes in groups, trying to influence his decision.

He and I talked on several occasions. I most remember a brief chat on the floor during a vote. Jim looked exhausted, obviously worn out by the constant badgering. He indicated that he still had not made up his mind what to do. He listened while I talked, but, as is his custom, said little.

I ended by noting that I would still consider him a friend, regardless of what he decided to do, even if I felt his decision was wrong. For a brief moment, he seemed to come alive and was genuinely appreciative of what I had said.

I still did not think that Jim would give control of the Senate to the Democrats. In the past, other colleagues had switched parties, but no one had done so at a time when they could singlehandedly overturn the power structure of the Senate. I felt that such a dramatic upheaval was more than just unprecedented. Given the timing of his decision, only a few months after his reelection as a Republican, one could argue that his changing parties would at least raise concerns about the integrity of his last election.

Obviously, I was wrong. On May 24, 2001, Jeffords announced before a cheering crowd in Burlington, Vermont, that he would leave the Republican Party and become an Independent. He explained that he was making the move in order to "best represent my state of Vermont, my own conscience, and the principles I have stood for my whole life. . . . I have changed my party label, but I have not changed my beliefs."[2]

Speaking over chants of "Thank you, Jim," he also revealed that he would vote with the Democrats for organizational purposes. The Republican trifecta was dead.

Reaction was as immediate as it was predictable. Most Republicans were outraged. Some publicly expressed their disappointment and disgust. Vague promises were made about paybacks. In some circles, Jeffords was called a traitor, a political opportunist, an unremarkable man who took advantage of a remarkable moment for his own benefit. Several conservatives predicted after his fifteen minutes of fame were exhausted, his new Democratic friends would quickly forget him.

Conversely, Democrats trumpeted his decision as courageous, historic and principled. He was compared to Cincinnatus and various saints. A variety of newspaper columnists and political pundits concluded that his defection underscored the weakness of the Bush Administration and signaled that the Democrats were well on their way to regaining control of Congress in the 2002 elections.

Things were a bit overstated on both sides. Jim maintains he has no regrets about his decision. He is convinced that it forced the White House and Congress to act in a more bipartisan manner and that members must now think about people, not party.

Some have tried to lay the blame for the switch on the Bush Administration. They point to the failure to invite Jeffords to a White House event honoring the Teacher of the Year, who was from Vermont. In fairness to the administration, it should be noted that no one from Congress was invited to the ceremony. Still, while the oversight may not have helped, Jim's decision was undoubtedly based on more than a moment of pique.

Others claim that Senator Lott should have done more. They point to his allowing two other Republicans on the HELP Committee to become the de facto Republican floor managers on an education bill, even though Senator Jeffords was the committee chairman and education was his political love. But while this might have been a bit embarrassing, it clearly was not unprecedented. It has happened to others, including me. On that particular bill, Jeffords was working and voting more closely with the Democrats than the Republicans. Lott had a responsibility to make sure that his floor manager was directly aligned with the party's position on the bill.

I believe Lott did all he could to accommodate Jeffords both personally and professionally; he even offered him a leadership position and agreed to waive the Republican term limit rules that would have ended his committee chairmanship. What he could not do was reconcile, in every instance, his own party's position with Jeffords's. Lott was willing to go some distance to accommodate differences of opinion, but not so far as compromising the principles of a majority on his side.

In the end, Jim's decision was based on the belief that the principles and concerns most important to him were more closely aligned with the majority of Democrats than with most Republicans. I can appreciate that he concluded it was time to leave the Republican Party and become an Independent. I am convinced his decision was one of conscience: wrong, but still one of conscience.

It would be hard to argue that Jeffords's decision has made him more effective in the Senate or made the issues he champions more likely to pass or be funded. While it is true that a few concerns have been given more attention, several other matters have met with mixed results, and it is unclear whether his switching of parties had any discernible impact on the education and disability measures with which he was most concerned.

Having said that, I still think the more appropriate course of action, once he decided to leave the party, would have been for him to continue to vote with the Republicans for organizational purposes, at least until the next election. If he had done so, it would have been impossible for anyone to raise questions about the real reason behind his decision. There would be no lingering suspicions or doubts about his motives.

Nonetheless, despite my personal feelings about what he should or should not have done, I do not think that I or anyone else should question the sincerity of his decision. Jim Jeffords deserves the benefit of the doubt. Otherwise, to be consistent, one would have to question the motives of Phil Gramm, Ben Nighthorse Campbell and Richard Shelby as well.

All three were sitting members of Congress when they left the Democratic Party and became Republicans. While the consequences of their switching were not as momentous as they were with Jeffords, they too went through similar introspection and public scrutiny.

It is difficult to remember that Phil Gramm began his career as a Democrat. Today, he is one of the most effective and conservative members of the Republican Party, a fixture on economic issues who deserves much of the credit for changing the attitude in Congress about budget and fiscal responsibility. Phil is also one of the Senate's most honest and forthright members, never hesitant to tell you exactly what he is thinking. On more than one occasion, Phil has approached me on bills on which we disagreed and said, in his distinct Texas drawl, "Orrin, you were one of the reasons I came to the Senate—to fight all those ridiculous liberal ideas. So I have to ask, what the hell are ya doing with this bill?"

Phil probably set the standard for switching parties. He was serving in the House of Representatives when he decided he no longer felt comfortable or welcome as a Democrat. Instead of simply announcing he was changing parties, he resigned his seat in 1983 and ran again in a special election as a Republican. He thus eliminated any question that his decision was motivated by anything other than a realization that his beliefs no longer fit within the Democratic Party. Not surprisingly, he easily won the special election, and won again the following year when he ran for the Senate.

Richard Shelby is from Alabama, a state that has been in the control of the Democratic Party since the Civil War. In 1986, he narrowly beat an incumbent Republican, Senator Jeremiah Denton, a retired admiral and Vietnam prisoner of war who had been swept into office along with President Reagan in 1980. Although a Democrat, Shelby voted conservatively. He supported the confirmation of Clarence Thomas and voted for the Gulf War resolution. In fact, from the start, Dick appeared to side more with the Republicans than the Democrats.

His falling-out with his party appeared to coincide with the arrival of Bill Clinton. He was one of the most outspoken critics of the President's flawed economic stimulus plan, as well as of Mrs. Clinton's unworkable health care plan. In 1994, when the Republicans regained control of the Senate, he switched sides. He too was given assurances about committee assignments and allowed to stay in line for a chairmanship. Still, I have heard of no Republican who doubted that his decision to join the party was based on anything other than a realization that he was more suited to being a Republican than a Democrat. I did hear complaints from some Democrats, however.

There was one party switch with which I was more personally involved. Senator Campbell of Colorado was also a Democrat when he came to the Senate in 1992. The only Native American in the Senate, Ben is a larger-than-life character, a personality more likely to be found in a novel about the Senate than the actual institution. He dropped out of high school, joined the air force and served in Korea. He was captain of the United States Olympic judo team and is still considered one of the patriarchs of the sport in this country.

After leaving the military, Campbell bred horses and became an extremely successful jeweler. Although he has been in Congress for twenty years, serving first in the House of Representatives, he has never lost his independence, nor has he made any effort to conform to stereotypes. No other senators, let alone Republicans, wear a ponytail, ride a Harley-Davidson or stubbornly refuse to wear any neckwear more formal than a western bolo tie.

We became good friends after he joined the Senate, and we repeatedly discussed his growing disillusionment with the Democratic Party. I would point out that power, its accumulation and retention, seemed to be of greater importance to some on his side than finding the right answer, that the worth of an issue should not always be measured simply by political advantage. He would disagree, but over time, his protestations grew fewer and less heartfelt.

Some might consider my assessment of the other party inaccurate or unfairly simplistic, feeling that there clearly must be Republicans who operate the same way. I admit that on this point I'm biased. Over the last two and a half decades, I have found the Democratic Party to be more captivated with the politics of an issue than with its solution. Time and again, I have seen efforts to solve complex issues derailed so that a problem could be "saved for the coming election." You may not agree, but I am, after all, a Republican.

I was surprised when Ben stopped me one day in the spring of 1995. "Orrin, you're right," he said. "I can't stand it anymore over here."

He asked whether I could arrange for him to see Senator Dole, the Republican Leader at the time. "I believe I can," I answered, smiling.

Three minutes later, we were ushered into the Majority Leader's office. Bob was exuberant, a look of pure joy on his face. He welcomed Ben literally with open arms. He repeatedly commented about the courage and principle it took to make such a decision, but he knew he did not need to make a hard sell. It was obvious Ben had already made up his mind to become a Republican.

Every Tuesday while the Senate is in session, the Republican senators have a joint lunch to discuss the legislation that will be debated on the floor that week as well as other bills and issues of importance to individual members. The Democrats have a comparable meeting of their own.

Known as the Policy Luncheons, these are private meetings where members have a chance to discuss and develop the various strategies and tactics the respective parties will use during the week. Every now and then, guests will be invited in to talk about a particular subject, but usually attendance is limited to members and a handful of the most senior staff.

Based on our discussions prior to his switching parties, it was clear that Ben had become increasingly disappointed with the direction and tone of the Democrat Policy meetings. He felt they had devolved from honest discussions of legitimate differences into angry, one-sided harangues dominated by some of the most senior and well-known members. If you didn't agree with the liberal position, there was no interest or tolerance for your viewpoint.

Our meetings, he gathered, were much more low-key. I assured him that the Republicans showed great respect for one another and that there was always considerable deference given to differing points of view.

The first Policy Luncheon Ben attended as a Republican, we sat together at the back of the room, as we have done ever since. We were having a quiet discussion when an argument broke out at another table.

One of my more colorful and emotional colleagues jumped up, his anger obvious. His face drew into a snarl as he stared at another member, a senior committee chairman, then called him an "asshole." Everyone started shouting, and it took Bob Dole several minutes to restore order.

Ben's eyes got larger and larger as he watched what was happening, then without turning his head, he gave me a quick jab in the ribs. "Gee, Orrin," he muttered, "it's sure good to see how well we Republicans get along compared to those damn Democrats."

Fortunately, there was much more behind Ben's decision to switch parties than members' decorum at lunches.

Whether it is a question of switching parties or voting on a bill, each of us in Congress ultimately has no real choice but to act or vote in accordance with our own conscience, our own set of principles. Hopefully, we were elected because of our ability to make judgments that by and large mirror the views of a majority of our constituents.

When there are disagreements, when your perception of right and wrong is contrary to that of one or even most of your constituents, you have no choice but to be forthright about the reasoning behind your decision. Over time, most will come to accept your decision even if they disagree.

They might not agree with your reasoning. They might not understand or appreciate your arguments, but at least they will have some reassurance that your vote was based on something other than a complete absence of character.

Unless, of course, for them, the issue is simply a matter of principle.

Chapter Four

Three Ways
to Pass
Legislation

You can't always get what you want.

—Mick Jagger

ONCE or twice a year, Dan Jones, the dean of Utah pollsters who also teaches a course on government at the University of Utah, invites me to speak to his students about the Senate and the process of legislating. Dan is a close friend who has worked with me on every campaign I have ever run in Utah; he is an expert on the structure of government and on the rules and procedures that are supposed to regulate the passage of legislation. It's my job to give his students a few examples about how bills actually become law.

I have never agreed with the old adage that the making of legislation is like the making of sausage—neither should be witnessed firsthand. The legislative process is a fascinating activity, an amalgam of investigative research, legal analysis, collective bargaining, group therapy and carnival.

Dan's students are often disappointed to learn that there is usually more to passing legislation than the drama of one electric moment when the entire Congress collectively holds its breath, riveted on the outcome of a single vote. The few moments of debate the public might see or the vote that is carried on the evening news are normally preceded by months and sometimes years of preparation, by countless meetings with members and constituents, all done away from the public spotlight.

Legislating is not a sprint. It is a marathon that under the best of circumstances takes years to complete. Success normally depends more on persistence than on brilliance.

Usually, bills become law because they have strong and diverse bipartisan and bicameral support within Congress, a fact too often forgotten by political party regulars. Unless one party completely dominates both chambers, legislation will not pass unless it has backing among both parties. A simple numerical majority, especially in the Senate, is no guarantee of success. Bills pass because sufficient time has been taken to build this support and to convince enough members that voting for something is better than voting against it, or what often is seen as the safest political course of action: doing nothing.

It is absolutely essential that every bill have a persuasive justification that can be explained briefly in simple English.[1] Considerable time is spent developing a concise and compelling explanation of the problem and the proposed legislative solution, which can then be used to build support among members, constituents and outside organizations.

Some congressional analysts see this as marketing, or the oversimplification of legislation, another instance of the national trend toward trivialization. In fact, distillation is essential. It forces one to identify the most compelling reasons a bill is necessary and the most salient provisions within the legislation. It requires you to lead with your strongest argument.

The distilled message is also critical for the final constituency that has to be won over, or at least neutralized—the media. Whether we like it or not, whether we think the media is fair or not, the press plays a significant role in determining how bills are perceived and the priority they will be given. If reporters cannot understand a bill or the problem it is intended to correct, or if they believe the legislation is not as important as other initiatives, its passage will be that much more difficult.

Everyone in Congress, therefore, plays to the media. News conferences are held when a bill is introduced, when there is a hearing or when some procedural hurdle has been passed. Press releases are sent out when a critical endorsement is received or a new cosponsor is added.

Given so many competing events, one must attract attention. If the sponsors are an unlikely pairing or are nationally prominent, that alone might be sufficient. Celebrities can help, as can people who are publicly identified with the issue or have been victimized by the problem being addressed.

On occasion, though, you need a gimmick or a photo opportunity. To help draw attention to legislation limiting baseball's antitrust exemption, Pat Leahy of Vermont and I had to wear baseball hats and carry a bat on our shoulders while discussing the bill. I dressed up in a ski suit and a knit hat for legislation concerning ski patrols. To generate attention about important but confusing drug legislation, I stood shoulder to shoulder with the award-winning veteran television actor Jack Klugman. Jack is a wonderful and accomplished man but clearly no medical authority. He did, however, play a doctor on the popular television series *Quincy.*

What can I say? Sometimes you do what you have to do.

Nonetheless, even with public and media support, bipartisan sponsorship and a great message, the chances that a bill will be enacted are slim. Every Congress, more than 7,600 individual bills are introduced in the House of Representatives and the Senate. On average, only about 440, less than 6 percent, become law.

Thank God.

Our nation's founders had a justifiable and prescient fear of an efficient legislature. The system they ultimately created in our

Constitution is designed more to prevent legislation than to expedite its passage. Too often, mistakes occur when bills move quickly, their provisions dictated by the passion of the moment or the particular facts of the most publicized example of the larger problem.

The best laws are those that are built, torn down and reconstructed so that each provision is both understood and intended. The process takes time, patience and an unshakable faith in the idea behind the bill as opposed to its initial content.

Often, criticism of the proposed legislation is valid, and changes have to be made. Almost every bill that is eventually enacted is different in some way from the version initially introduced.

Bills become law generally for one of three reasons. First, a member makes the bill a top priority and is willing to expend the time and effort to build sufficient support to guarantee its passage. Second, a large group of constituents in multiple jurisdictions make passing a bill more politically attractive than doing nothing. Third, Congress is forced to respond to an event so tragic or compelling that the event itself overwhelms all possible criticism.

When possible, I try to use three examples with the students: the Hatch-Waxman bill of 1984, the Dietary Supplement Health and Education Act of 1994 and the USA Patriot Act of 2001. The tactics employed were different, but all three are good examples of what it really takes to enact legislation.

Hatch-Waxman: The Drug Price Competition and Patent Term Restoration Act of 1984

In the early 1980s, major research companies were increasingly frustrated with spending hundreds of millions of dollars to develop a new product, only to see its patent life undercut by the staggering inefficiency of the Food and Drug Administration (FDA) in approving new drugs for marketing in the United States. Patents on other goods gave manufacturers as much as seventeen years of patent exclusivity.

Pharmaceutical companies, however, were looking at time frames of as little as four or five years, too short a period to recoup the cost of research, which today can run up to almost a billion dollars for a blockbuster drug. To protect against duplication, a drug has to be patented early in its evolution. Consequently, even under the best of circumstances, years of potential patent life are lost while a drug undergoes the years of testing necessary to win FDA approval. In fairness, why should a drug that saves lives have patent protection for only a fraction of the time given to protect a chainsaw or a toy?

The FDA was only compounding the problem. Congress has made the agency responsible for the safety and efficacy of pharmaceuticals, medical devices, food, nutritional supplements and other products consumed or used by Americans every second of every day. Every year, it seems that something new is added to the list. Today, more than 25 percent of all consumer products sold in the United States are either approved or regulated by this one agency.

The agency's mission would be impossible under the best of circumstances. Unfortunately, it has rarely operated under the best of circumstances. In 1984, the FDA was underfunded and understaffed, and dispersed throughout the Washington metropolitan area. It had neither the scientific equipment nor the personnel to keep pace with the rapid technological changes and improvements in the private sector.

It would be hard to conjure a scenario more likely to produce a bureaucratic morass, and the agency certainly did its part. Committee investigations revealed that important drug applications were lost. Others were ignored. One was simply stuck in a reviewer's drawer out of pique. The approval process had become a mess, ripe for abuse and misuse.

Already facing unrealistically limited time to recoup its investment, the pharmaceutical industry did not want competition from an aggressive generic industry, which could market copies of name-brand products once the patents expired. In the early 1980s, the brand pharmaceutical companies had little to worry about. The domestic generic pharmaceutical industry was realizing only a fraction of its potential. The handful of existing companies were struggling because they could not afford to replicate the same expensive and time-consuming safety and efficacy trials undertaken by the pioneer firms, as the FDA required them to do, and still sell the drug at a reduced price.

Important drugs were coming off patent, but generics were not being introduced. Moreover, in the few instances where generics were being developed, it routinely took years before the companies could win FDA approval to market their products.

In sum, the FDA's regulatory system was discouraging brand or innovator companies from investing in new research and development. At the same time, it was blocking the introduction of low-cost generic products. No one was benefiting, not the brand companies, not the generic firms and not consumers.

I had become Chairman of the Senate Labor Committee when the Republicans regained control of the body in 1980. Since the committee had jurisdiction over the FDA and the drug approval process, it would be my responsibility to decide whether this issue should become a priority.

It wasn't a hard decision. I had already had enough meetings with drug manufacturers, generic companies, patent lawyers and consumer activists to understand the problems and their consequences. What I did not have was an effective and equitable solution.

There was also the political factor. Neither the brands nor the generics could push through Congress legislation alleviating only their respective problems. Each side could stop the other's legislative initiatives. It was obvious that to be successful, the legislation would have to address the concerns of both.

Shortly after becoming chairman, I scheduled a series of hearings on the problem and began to focus public attention on the need for a solution. At the same time, I continued to meet privately with interested parties, including the industry, the FDA, medical experts, consumers and taxpayers. I used these sessions to learn the merits of the competing arguments and identify the key players who might help fashion a resolution.

It took the better part of three years, but by the spring of 1984, I had succeeded in convincing both the Congress and the public that something needed to be done. Moreover, my staff and I finally understood the positions of the various interested parties and what they really needed, as opposed to what they demanded in public. The difficulty was finding a solution that would work and that could be supported by all sides. In addition, the end of the session was approaching.

Because 1984 was a presidential election year, the Senate was already beginning to slide into the traditional partisan bickering and posturing that dominates the months leading up to a major election. For legislation to pass, it would have to be seen as a real compromise both inside and outside Congress.

I found a willing ally in Representative Henry Waxman, the liberal Democrat from California and, at the time, the Chairman of the House Health Subcommittee. From the standpoint of political ideology, Henry is exactly what you might expect of a member of Congress whose district covers Hollywood and whose constituents include some of his party's largest contributors. He is an unabashed liberal, a skilled legislator and an effective inside player. Henry is also viewed as one of the most knowledgeable members of Congress on health issues, and he enjoys the confidence of consumer groups and a wide variety of public-interest organizations.

The year before, to the amazement of our respective colleagues, Henry and I had teamed up on the Orphan Drug Act of 1983, a bill that provides a series of economic incentives for companies to develop drugs that treat rare diseases and conditions. The potential patient pool for these drugs was too small for a company to recoup the cost of development. Because of the bill, 228 new drugs have been developed, which in turn have helped more than 11 million people who otherwise would have gone without treatment. We gave various incentives to the industry so that this turnaround could be accomplished.

Henry and I understood that the only way to fashion a compromise was to bring the brand companies and the generics together in an atmosphere that allowed them both to feel they had something to gain if they cooperated and, just as important, something to lose if they didn't. The meetings would have to be small and private, so that ideas could be discussed without fear of retribution or public posturing.

I invited a handful of industry leaders to meet with me personally. The brand companies were led by Joe Williams, the CEO of Warner-Lambert, one of the largest and most successful pharmaceutical companies at the time, and Jack Stafford, the CEO of American Home Products and a tough and shrewd negotiator.

Joe was a dignified white-haired gentleman who enjoyed the respect of his peers in the industry. As might be expected for a man who began in marketing, he understood people and knew how to reach his objectives without being heavy-handed. Jack, on the other hand, was hard-driving, smart and tenacious, ready to debate any issue. They made a formidable pair, even though Jack did most of the talking.

Taking the lead for the generics was Bill Haddad. A short, passionate, rumpled man, Bill looks exactly like the liberal political operative he used to be. Before working in the generic industry, Bill had been heavily involved in Democratic politics and enjoyed strong ties to the Gores, the Kennedys and the Cuomos. He served as a top aide for Robert Kennedy, playing a significant role in his Senate election and his run for president. He also worked on Mario Cuomo's first gubernatorial campaign. What Bill might have lacked in corporate experience he more than made up for with his knowledge of Congress and politics.

We met in my office over several weeks. Not surprisingly, both sides were extremely skeptical of the other's intentions. Each thought the other's position was not only illogical but avaricious.

Jack made clear that the brand companies wanted legislation completely restoring every day of patent life lost while their approvals were being processed by the FDA. They needed a greater period of market exclusivity to recover the high cost of their research.

Bill responded that these companies were already more than adequately compensated for their research. A drug company didn't need seventeen years to recoup its investment. A drug's patent life might be shorter than that for other products, but the prices that could be charged were so disproportionate to the cost of production that immense profits could be realized in short periods of time. One only had to look at the strength of pharmaceutical company stocks to understand that these firms were far more profitable.

Bill insisted that the generics needed to be able to bring a generic version of a drug to market immediately upon the expiration of the patent, without having to go through the extremely costly, time-consuming and unnecessarily repetitive exercise of re-proving that the drug was safe. The generics' obligation should be to demonstrate bio-equivalence only, that the generic was chemically the same as the brand version of the product. Thus they could copy the pioneer company's actual research.

Jack and Joe were more than skeptical of this assumption. Echoing a long-held conviction of the brand companies, they argued that generic firms were not real pharmaceutical companies. They were just copiers, they said, and not very good ones at that. They didn't have adequate personnel, laboratories or experience. They could not be trusted to make effective products on their own and they posed a real health risk to an unsuspecting public.

I gave them a copy of a draft bill my staff had prepared, and they proceeded to argue about every word, every punctuation mark, every inclusion and every omission. I pushed and prodded, alternating between being supportive and critical. At times, I was more a therapist than a legislator, as I struggled to keep the discussion impersonal and constructive.

Like most people who are forced to work together for too long under tense circumstances, they fought. Boy, did they fight.

Jack would claim people would die if a generic drug company had only to prove bioequivalence and not safety and efficacy. Bill would object, arguing that the issue wasn't safety. It was money. The brand companies simply wanted to protect their "ridiculous" profits. Jack would fire back that the brands created the products and the generics couldn't invent a drug if their lives depended on it. All they could do was leech off the brand's research. Bill would respond that the brands didn't want just a patent life. They wanted a permanent monopoly.

So it went, day after day, accusation and after accusation. Toward the end of every session, either Bill or Jack would explode in a rage, swear off the negotiations, and stomp out of the room. Their antics were so similar that I wondered at times whether they were trying to parody each other.

One day, Bill and Jack got angry at the same time. Jumping to their feet, they rushed to the door, shouting and blaming each other for the bill's lack of progress. Amazingly, they reached the frame simultaneously. Not wanting to let the other win on anything, they both tried to jump through and smacked heads. There was a loud thud, and both stumbled back into the room, groaning in pain.

I had been dreaming about doing just that for days. I had to turn away so they wouldn't catch me smiling.

In fairness, I wasn't immune to the pressure, either. During the negotiations, one of my teeth became extremely sore, and I learned that I needed root canal surgery. Foolishly, I kept putting off the treatment, not wanting to jeopardize our chances of reaching a deal. The pain became worse, and it was increasingly difficult to sit patiently while they bickered about literally everything.

After about a week, I could no longer take it. My tooth was on fire. I tried holding my cheek, hoping the pressure would stop the throbbing, but nothing worked. Worse, their constant whining seemed to exacerbate the pain, as if each complaint struck the exposed nerve directly.

Jack was in the middle of one of his prolonged objections, refusing to let Bill interrupt to make a point. Bill just started talking. Soon, both were yelling, each trying to drown out the other.

Still holding my cheek, I leapt to my feet and slapped the table as hard as I could.

"If you guys don't stop it, I'm going to kill somebody," I yelled, the words garbled but clear enough.

The room fell silent. Both were dumbstruck. Murder was probably the only threat that they had not yet made, and they were clearly not expecting it to come from me. They stared at me in shock as I rocked on my feet, my face twisted in pain. I'm sure at that point I looked crazy enough to make good on the threat.

I know. It wasn't exactly my proudest moment. It certainly wasn't my most insightful negotiating tactic, yet amazingly, it worked. The discussion began again, but now Bill and Jack were competing to see who could be more courteous and subdued.

Fortunately, no matter how often they stormed out in anger, they always came back, in part out of respect for my position as committee chairman and in part because both were worried that the legislation might be finalized in their absence. Over time, we narrowed the issues in contention, reaching agreement on a variety of secondary problems. Ultimately, the brand companies decided they had more to gain by passing legislation than by stopping it and agreed in principle to the concept of a rapid generic approval process at FDA. Once that occurred, everything else fell into place, and we quickly reached agreement.[2]

Some might be surprised by the amount of industry involvement with legislation of this kind, but it was critical. Quite simply, only someone experienced with the industry could understand the nuances and consequences of legislative wording. Great care had to be taken because we were changing the rules for a process that was ongoing. While we were negotiating, innovator and generic drugs were working their way through the approval process. Without proper care, it would be easy to unintentionally eliminate an entire product line with language that would appear completely logical and legitimate on its face.

This is true in other areas. It is virtually impossible to draft many different kinds of legislation without the involvement of individuals who are expert in the problem or industry being addressed. Imagine writing a bill concerning nuclear reactors without an understanding of how they work, how they are constructed, what raw materials are needed or what is done with the waste. One of the realities of Congress is that despite the political benefits of bashing lobbyists, they can be invaluable in their role in providing the technical and practical information necessary to write bills that work. The difficulty, of course, is finding lobbyists who actually understand and can explain the interests they represent.

This time, each side had a vested economic interest in highlighting the inaccuracies or distortions made by the other. There was no shortage of criticism, constructive and personal.

When the deal was made public, a majority in Congress recognized the agreement for what it was: a balanced compromise that refocused federal regulatory drug policy on innovation and research while creating for the first time the real possibility of a vibrant generic industry that could save consumers billions of dollars.

Still, some were unhappy. A handful of brand companies objected, convinced they would do better in the next Congress. A few generic companies cried foul, believing they could force a more favorable compromise by holding out. Several public interest groups joined in, claiming that the bill was not sufficiently pro-consumer. Whatever the reason, they all began to lobby individual members in an attempt to amend or kill the legislation.

Making matters worse, by the time we had reached the final agreement, Congress was ready to adjourn for the coming elections.

Literally only days were left in the session. At this point, for a bill to move through the Senate, it would have to be approved unanimously. And no bill could move without being first approved by Senator Howard Metzenbaum of Ohio.

Howard lived for these days. He was a shrewd legislator, a difficult and relentless negotiator and probably the most aggressively partisan Democrat in the Senate. To move a bill at the end of a session, a member would need approval not just from the Republicans and the Democrats. He or she would also need Howard's permission.

Howard had made himself a near equal third power in the Senate through his willingness to use his rights under the rules to object to any procedural motion that required unanimous consent. He thought nothing of sitting on the floor during the waning days of a session, tying up bill after bill as he and his staff passed judgment on every amendment and every proposal. He was an equal opportunity objector. Democrats and Republicans both fell victim to his tactics. He may not have been beloved, he never passed much legislation, but during the last few weeks of a session, he was certainly powerful.

Not surprisingly, Howard objected to our compromise, after being encouraged to do so by the consumer advocate Ralph Nader. Nader felt that the legislation was too protective of the brand companies and would cost consumers far too much money. Naturally, he preferred federal price controls.

Bill Haddad agreed to help, and, teaming up with several liberal allies, he worked on Howard and Nader. Eventually, he convinced them both to withdraw their opposition, but we knew that their acquiescence was temporary.

Armed with Howard's consent, I raced to the floor and had the legislation called up. I did not want to give either Metzenbaum or Nader a chance to reconsider their decision. In fact, I had even less time than I realized.

While I was making a statement about the bill and asking for unanimous consent for its approval, Howard walked off the Senate floor. I learned later he had been given a note telling him that Ralph Nader was in the Senate reception area and needed to see him. I cut my statement short, had the balance of my remarks inserted in the record and asked that the bill be approved.

The minutes seemed to drag on endlessly as a few parliamentary niceties were addressed. Every few seconds, I glanced at the chamber door, fearing that Howard would return and, despite his earlier promise, object.

Sure enough, that is exactly what Nader was persuading him to do. Fortunately, Nader, who rarely does anything with dispatch, took too long. Before he could finish making all his points to Howard, the bill was called up and approved. Since everyone had already signed off, it was adopted without a recorded vote by unanimous consent.

Howard rushed back on the floor just moments later. When he learned it was too late to object, he looked crushed, then quickly recovered and moved on to the next issue. My bill was not the only issue he was juggling that day.

President Reagan signed the act a few days later, in a ceremony in the Rose Garden.[3]

Despite the initial concerns, the Drug Price Competition and Patent Term Restoration Act of 1984 is now considered to be one of the greatest pro-consumer bills of all time. It has been credited with revitalizing research and innovation in the pharmaceutical industry, enabling these businesses to become one of the most successful sectors in our economy. Generics benefited as well. Today, the generic industry provides the medicine that fills approximately 47 percent of all prescriptions issued in the United States, even though it accounts for less than 10 percent of the money spent annually on drugs.

The real beneficiaries, however, have been consumers and, since many drugs are purchased by federal and state health programs, taxpayers. Despite the dire predictions of Ralph Nader and others, according to the Congressional Budget Office, the legislation has saved Americans an average of more than $8 to $10 billion in pharmaceutical costs every year since its passage, a total in excess of more than $150 billion. It is true that after twenty years, creative lawyers have been able to take advantage of a few portions of the legislation, a problem that must be addressed. Nonetheless, more drugs are available today at far more reasonable prices than at any time in the history of our nation, and the predicted savings for the next ten years are even greater than the savings already seen.

The Dietary Supplement Health and Education Act of 1994

While Hatch-Waxman was a triumph of closed-door negotiations, the passage of the Dietary Supplement Health and Education Act of 1994 involved a different dynamic. It would be hard to find a bill where there was more direct public involvement.

By 1992, Americans throughout the United States were frustrated with the FDA's long-standing antipathy toward dietary supplements, the general term used for vitamins, minerals, herbs and similar products used to provide the nutrients we need to protect our health and ward off disease. Despite growing evidence to the contrary, the agency believed there was no scientific proof that supplements were beneficial. In the FDA's eyes, they were nothing more that the modern equivalent of snake oil.

The agency's institutional distrust led it to twist existing law to block the sale of a variety of supplements. For example, it tried to argue in court that for gelatin capsule supplements, the capsule itself was a food. The supplement inside was a food additive. Under the law, food additives had to be approved by the FDA, and since the agency had not approved any supplements as food additives, the products were illegal. Fortunately, after years of litigation, the court threw the case out. The FDA raided health food stores, carting away books and literature about the proper use of supplements and their potential benefit. Even statements by the federal government were taken.

In 1991, the Centers for Disease Control (CDC), another federal agency, issued a statement encouraging women of childbearing years to take folic acid to help prevent certain types of birth defects such as spina bifida. In one raid, copies of this statement were confiscated.

The FDA would not finally agree with its sister agency until October 1993, a week before a congressional hearing on its treatment of supplements. The CDC estimated that as many as 2,500 babies a year were born with spina bifida or neural tube defects because of their mothers' deficiency in folic acid. Clearly, thousands would have been put at risk unnecessarily if the agency had been left to its own timetable.

The agency's conduct reflected an important institutional flaw: its own hubris. The FDA has long believed that until it decides a particular product is safe, it is not only illegal but dangerous, regardless of any evidence to the contrary. Opinions of other agencies or other governments do not matter. And unless the evidence is comparable to the information needed to market a drug, the product should not be sold in the United States. As far as supplements were concerned, the FDA claimed that Americans could obtain all the nutrients they needed simply by following a proper diet.

The FDA's attitude was not only impractical, it was poor public policy. First, while it is theoretically possible for a person to eat the foods needed to meet accepted nutritional standards, almost no one's diet comes close to the theoretical. One study of the eating habits of 21,000 people revealed that none got the daily recommended allowances for ten key vitamins and minerals.[4] Supplements are an obvious bridge between what we should eat and what we actually consume.

Second, the FDA knew that supplements would never be marketed if they first had to satisfy the same safety and efficacy standard as drugs. Today, a pharmaceutical firm can afford the average $800 million it costs to bring a drug to market, because the patent provides the company with a period of market exclusivity to recoup the cost of its investment. Supplements, however, are natural products and thus cannot be patented. Without a comparable period of exclusivity to recover the cost of research, a manufacturer would never have the chance to recoup the cost of satisfying the FDA's drug standards.

Third, the FDA has never been willing to address the fact that drugs are not a suitable answer to the health problems of thousands of Americans. Pharmaceuticals are extremely powerful substances, designed to change a body's chemistry. All can cause adverse and even fatal reactions. According to the *New England Journal of Medicine,* approximately 100,000 Americans die every year from an adverse reaction to an FDA-approved pharmaceutical. While we as a society tolerate these figures because of the unquestionable benefits so many drugs provide in curing illness and treating disease, this is of little comfort for those who are on the wrong side of the cost-benefit equation.

Moreover, given the high cost of medical treatment in the United States, many Americans have a vested interest in taking steps to avoid illness and improve their health, especially if the cost is as economical as it is with vitamins and minerals. Instead of stubbornly resisting alternative approaches, the FDA should be assisting with their discovery and use.

Finally, there is evidence that supplements are beneficial and safe. Today, we better understand the strong correlation between nutritional deficiencies and a wide range of diseases, including increased risks of cancer and heart disease. Research has shown that dietary supplements can protect against heart disease and stroke, improve children's appetites, and reduce the risk of certain cancers. They can help build a child's bone mass and improve mental development.

I have taken dietary supplements almost my entire adult life and can attest to the benefits they provide. Because of supplements, I don't look too bad for a ninety-two-year-old man.

A colleague, Senator Tom Harkin of Iowa, is an avid user of supplements and shared my concerns about the FDA's hostility toward these products. Together, we began meeting with representatives from the industry, some of whom are from Utah, as well as individuals from around the United States.

After several fits and starts, we introduced legislation in 1993 clarifying that dietary supplements could not be regulated as drugs and that the burden of proving an existing product was unsafe rested with the FDA. At the same time, the agency was given additional enforcement authority, and the industry was required to meet a variety of new labeling requirements and manufacturing practices. The FDA would have the authority to pull a product from the market if it posed an imminent and substantial risk to the public. Limitations were place on the literature that could accompany a product, and companies were required to list on the label all the ingredients in a product. The agency was instructed to issue regulations establishing good manufacturing practices, and a new office at the National Institutes of Health was created to focus on supplements.

The bill, S. 784, the Dietary Supplement Health and Education Act, faced opposition the minute it was introduced. The FDA couldn't stand it.

It was bad enough that the legislation made it more difficult for the agency to ban products without having to prove they were unsafe. Worse, unjustifiably they believed, for the first time in recent history a regulatory agency's authority was being restricted, a horrible precedent for any bureaucracy.

Agency officials immediately started lobbying Congress and other organizations against the bill. The FDA commissioner, David Kessler, was vocal in his opposition, pointing out individual products he believed were unsafe.[5]

Moreover, the rules were stacked against us. The bill would have to move through the Senate Labor Committee, which was chaired by Ted Kennedy, no fan of dietary supplements who clearly loathed supporting any restriction on FDA's regulatory authority.

In the House, the bill would be handled by the Commerce Committee, chaired by the powerful and feared Representative John

Dingell, a liberal Democrat from Michigan, and another industry opponent. Moreover, it would probably be referred to the House Subcommittee on Health, chaired by Henry Waxman. Henry made it clear from the outset that he would oppose the bill.

On the other hand, we had something unique on our side: the more than 100 million Americans who regularly use dietary supplements. In general, these people are well-educated, politically involved and avid readers. They are also prolific letter writers. And they were angry with FDA's persistent campaign against products they believed improved the health of themselves and their families.

Using the Internet and mailing lists, as well as their own personal networks, supplement users throughout the United States rallied behind the bill, creating an explosion of grassroots support. They overwhelmed congressional offices with a lobbying campaign that was sparked by the industry but sustained by consumers.

This was 1994, the year Congress debated the highly controversial, cumbersome and bureaucratic Clinton universal health care plan. While this proposal may have dominated the congressional landscape as far as the media was concerned, it was a distant second to the dietary supplement bill in constituent interest. Members received more letters, calls and visits about our bill that year than about any other issue before Congress.

Buttressed by this phenomenal effort, I pigeonholed every member of the Senate during votes and hearings, and in the halls. I stressed the importance of the bill and the critical role supplements could play in maintaining and improving one's health. When possible, I pointed out how these products could be of personal help. Working from a list of senators I kept in my coat pocket, I ranked each member between 1 and 5. A "1" was willing to cosponsor the bill. A "5" was adamantly opposed. I would not leave a colleague alone until he or she had agreed to be a "1."

In retrospect, I was probably a bit of a pest. I'm sure I got a few to cosponsor the bill only because they wanted to be left alone. Still, the effort paid off. By the time the legislation came to a vote in the Senate, it had 66 cosponsors, more than enough to ensure victory.

Once it was clear we had such broad support, Tom and I were able to convince Ted Kennedy to hold a hearing on the bill. Despite Kessler's critical testimony, the hearing underscored the legislation's popularity. Kennedy agreed to a committee mark-up after we adopted several amendments designed to clarify the FDA's authority to remove dangerous products from the market and the manufacturing practices that would be required of supplement companies. Once these changes were negotiated, the bill easily moved through committee and passed the Senate.

The same bill had been introduced in the House by Representative Bill Richardson, a Democrat from New Mexico who would become President Clinton's ambassador to the United Nations, and Representative Elton Gallegly, a Republican from California. They had been working their colleagues as well and ended up with 261 cosponsors, including a majority of the House itself, the Commerce Committee, and the Health Subcommittee.

Despite this support, we were stuck. Representative Waxman held a hearing on the legislation, but it was clear he and John Dingell had no intention of moving the bill before the end of the session.

Their opposition was being supported by the FDA. As if by magic, news stories critical of the bill and of supplements began appearing in the media. Questions were raised about how such a bad bill could possibly have been forced through the Senate. Little mention was made of its unanimous approval or the grassroots support. Instead, the stories emphasized that some of the companies involved were located in Iowa and Utah, implying that Tom and I were in the pocket of the industry.

Fortunately, despite their opposition, the House chairmen were willing to permit our respective staffs to meet and, amazingly, some progress was made. Still, by the last week of the session, a handful of issues remained unresolved.

It looked as if we had run out of time. Despite all the cosponsors, all the letters and requests by constituents, which by now had run into the millions, we had failed.

Unwilling to acknowledge defeat, I sent a final letter to Dingell and Waxman outlining what I needed in the bill. I thought that if nothing else, the letter would memorialize the negotiations and what was left to be done. To my amazement, they called back later that afternoon and asked to meet. Something had happened.

That same day, Senators Kennedy, Harkin and I sat down in a room in the Capitol building with our House counterparts, John Dingell, Henry Waxman and Bill Richardson. It was immediately clear that John would be doing the negotiating for the House. To our amazement, it was also clear that he wanted to work out a deal.

The son of a distinguished House member, John has been an effective legislator for decades, respected for his accomplishments but also feared by those who have been the subject of one of his legendary investigations. He can be a wonderful ally or a ferocious opponent. We have always worked well together, and this day was no exception. We are friends. We spent more than an hour discussing labeling requirements, limitations on health claims and the potential for consumer misperception. Henry emphasized that he and John needed to add language requiring product labels to make clear that any claims made about the product had not been approved by FDA.

Again, proposals were made and modified, but this time, the objective was to reach a compromise. Both sides made concessions, and after only another hour, we had an agreement. Our respective staffs rushed the deal to the House Legislative Counsel, where they then spent almost five hours preparing the amended bill for a final vote.[6]

There have been several theories about what triggered the change of heart, what had happened during several secret meetings the House Democratic leadership held before they called me. I will never know for sure, but I like to think that, in the end, the bill's grassroots supporters made the difference. Every step we took inside Congress was mirrored on the outside. The bill's supporters didn't stop once the legislation passed the Senate. If anything, they became even more energized and continued to flood House offices with letters and calls, demanding that the Democrats, who controlled the House, schedule a vote on the bill.

By October 1994, we all knew that for the first time since 1952 the Republicans had a chance of seizing control of the House of Representatives. There were several liberal Democrats and Republicans in close races who did not want the controversy over dietary supplements left unresolved. They understood that the millions of Americans who supported the legislation were not only writing letters but prepared to vote. Some races and, since the election was expected to be so close, even control of the House appeared to hinge on this one issue.

Whatever the reason, the amended Dietary Supplement Health and Education Act passed the House later that night, and the Senate the following day. Both votes were unanimous. Days later, President Clinton signed it into law. Public opinion had triumphed over media indifference, bureaucratic opposition and powerful committee chairmen.

Unfortunately, the story didn't end with the passage of the bill. To this day, the FDA remains bitter about the legislation. In the nearly eight years since the law was enacted, the agency still has not published regulations establishing good manufacturing practices as called for by the statute. It still has not taken action against the products former Commissioner Kessler indicated were unsafe almost a decade ago. And it still permits a small handful of rogue operators to misrepresent the benefits of their products.

The agency's lack of enforcement has been matched by its frequent complaint in the press that dietary supplements are now unregulated. Yet when the last few commissioners have been asked on the record whether the agency has sufficient authority to regulate supplements, the answer is always yes. The problem is not a lack of authority. It is a lack of interest combined with, perhaps, a hope that some of the unsavory few in the industry will someday step too far and create a public relations disaster the agency can exploit.[7]

The USA Patriot Act of 2001

There is another way legislation is enacted—when an event or crisis so galvanizes the nation that potential criticism is drowned out by the chorus demanding that something be done. The horrible attacks of September 11, 2001, were just such an event.

It was a day when the United States realized the world we actually live in is far different from the one we thought we inhabited. Collectively, we learned it is a far more dangerous place than we ever imagined. We came to face-to-face with people and countries committed to our destruction, with individuals fueled by such profound hatred that they were eager to sacrifice their lives to damage our country.

Suddenly, we learned how much of the rest of the world lives. Activities such as flying on an airplane, riding an elevator or welcoming a stranger could no longer be taken for granted. There was a risk to simply leaving the house. And once letters containing anthrax were discovered in the mail, even the home was no longer completely safe.

Interestingly, what had changed was not the truth. For years, specialists at the FBI and CIA had understood what we faced, even if they did not know in advance about the specific terrorist acts that would occur. What was different was our collective grasp of a danger many of us had preferred to ignore. With that realization came another. Battling terrorism would be a war fought at home as much as abroad. It would involve an unidentified enemy, one that did not have its own government or country and related infrastructure that could be the target of retaliation.

To fight this war effectively, we would not only have to change how we lived but also reconsider some of the rights and privileges we have come to presume are guaranteed to us as Americans, or that are willing to bestow on visitors to our country. We would have to find a way to balance our constitutional liberties with the need to be safe and secure from those whose only purpose was our destruction.

The legislative challenge was daunting. It was obvious that the tools law enforcement had to combat terrorism were insufficient to address the level of sophistication, financing, and planning now evident among terrorist organizations such as al Qaeda. Laws written in the age of rotary phones were insufficient to deal with the complexities of information-sharing and communication over cell phones and the Internet.

Moreover, defending against the threat was not solely a criminal justice endeavor. It involved the defense of our nation, the first responsibility of the federal government. No one wanted to wait for another terrorist attack in order to begin an investigation. We wanted a government that could prevent first and prosecute second.

Within days after the attack, as the country struggled to regain its balance, the administration began to meet privately to discuss what the law enforcement and intelligence communities needed to be effective. They had been built in large part to prosecute organized crime and drug lords and to spy upon the Soviet Union, respectively. New tools were needed. Conversations were also held with several of us in Congress.

On September 19, 2001, the Justice Department shared its first draft. It was a lengthy, ambitious bill addressing a wide variety of issues. Complicating matters, it touched upon topics that were under the jurisdiction of not only the Judiciary Committee but also the committees on Banking, Commerce, Foreign Relations, and Intelligence. Additional powers would be given to the FBI, the Immigration and Naturalization Service, and the Border Patrol. The Department of Justice would have new authority for electronic surveillance, for tracing information moving over the Internet and through international banking channels. Information-sharing between the intelligence agencies and law enforcement was made easier.

Normally, passing such a mammoth bill would have taken years, if it was possible at all. In addition, much of the justification was classified. The legislative language might have been public, but the reasons for a particular section or the justification for making changes to what was proposed could be discussed only among those with adequate security clearances. Fortunately, two factors facilitated the bill's acceptance. First, many of the provisions were not new. They had been discussed for years, only to be stopped for a variety of reasons in previous sessions of Congress. Now, with the events of September 11 so vividly in people's minds, they seemed legitimate and justified.

Second, it was clear that the American people had no interest in watching Congress squabble. For several months after the attack, the country experienced a refreshing change of attitude. There was unanimity of purpose and a corresponding intolerance for the posturing and fighting that traditionally dominates modern American politics. No member could afford to block the government from the tools it needed to fight terrorism. While some may have had concerns over specific provisions, the pressure to move the bill was intense.

For the next month, every day of the week, including weekends, both the House and the Senate held hearings, debated specific language and conducted separate negotiations with the administration. Members and staff, as well as representatives from the administration, worked literally around the clock. Between meetings, I gave myself a refresher course on federal criminal procedure by rereading the code and recent court cases. Much of what was being discussed did not make sense without a fresh understanding of the law.

To complicate matters, many of us could not use our offices or access our files when anthrax was discovered in letters sent to several members on both sides of the Hill. We were literally locked out of our rooms. Staff and members ended up sharing space, crammed on top of one another. Visitors' chairs became permanent workstations, and people had to sign up to use a computer. There weren't enough monitors for every staffer or member.

Consequently, many of the negotiations were conducted in small rooms around the Capitol. I remember one particular meeting. At one break in the conversation, I looked up. Several people were talking at the same time. Some members were talking to one another, sharing pieces of paper on which were amendments drafted in longhand. Others sat back in their chairs, listening to staff. Officials from the administration hovered around the table, using code books and copies of case law to make their points. It was a moment from another era, when Congress was smaller and more intimate, devoid of television cameras. If someone had captured that moment, but for the dress, it would have resembled one of the paintings of the early Congresses in the late 1700s.

Wary that the negotiations with my committee colleagues might break down, I engaged in parallel negotiations with the Democrats. On one track, I worked with the committee chairman, Pat Leahy from Vermont, an impassioned defender of civil liberties who was extremely concerned that the bill could result in a massive intrusion of personal privacy. On a separate track, I met with Joe Biden, Dianne Feinstein and Charles Schumer, who shared many of the same concerns as Leahy but were more willing to accept the arguments being raised by the Justice Department. This way, if the negotiations with Leahy broke down, we would still have a compromise acceptable to a majority on the committee. Fortunately, we were able to reach an agreement we could all support.

One could easily assume that, given the abbreviated time frame, the legislation was moving too quickly not to be seriously flawed. In fact, given the amount of time expended on the bill and the number of people involved, negotiations that would normally have taken months or years to complete were telescoped into weeks. I doubt that there is a single word in the bill that was not discussed or debated. By mid-October, different versions of the bill had passed both the House and the Senate, and the lead negotiators began to meet before the conference took place.

In the end, the debate seemed to boil down to one critical issue: whether the bill would contain a sunset provision, which would limit its operability to a finite period. The House had agreed on five years. The Senate bill was silent, but there was interest in a much shorter period.

These negotiations included representatives from the leadership of both chambers, and it quickly became clear that there was considerable interest among some House Republican leaders to change the provision to only two years. This theme was picked up in the Senate by an interesting coalition of liberal Democrats and very conservative Republicans, both of whom were concerned about giving the government too much power.

The administration was clearly worried. It would be impossible for law enforcement to do its job if it was worried that investigations would have to be called off because the provision authorizing the inquiry had expired. Terrorists were not subject to a time limit. Why should law enforcement have one? The proponents of the idea countered that the sunset provision could always be extended if necessary. Its inclusion ensured that the government would not take unnecessary advantage of its new powers.

I pushed back, and was by myself at first. In addition to the concerns raised by the administration, I feared that passing new legislation to keep key provisions operable would be much more difficult in future years. The cooperative attitude in Congress, which was already beginning to crack, would soon be gone, and it would be far easier for one member alone to block the extension. I pointed out that if there were legitimate problems, we could easily pass legislation revoking the new powers given law enforcement. In the end, we settled on a four-year sunset provision, creating a serious and potentially dangerous problem for the future.

There is another critical problem that the legislation does not resolve. The Foreign Intelligence Surveillance Act (FISA), which was passed by Congress in 1978, regulates the gathering of intelligence on international terrorists and other targets operating inside the United States. Among other things, it requires the FBI, CIA and the National Security Agency to obtain an order from the Foreign Intelligence Surveillance Court before engaging in surveillance, wiretaps and physical searches when investigating foreign spies. In its current form, the statute applies only to individuals known to be agents of a foreign government or affiliated with a known terrorist group.

This limitation had a direct role in the investigation of Zacarias Moussaoui, who is now being described by some as the twentieth hijacker in the September 11 attacks. He was arrested on August 17, 2001, on a passport violation. Efforts to search his computer and tap his phone were delayed because he did not have strong links to any foreign government or terrorist group. When the FBI finally did receive a court order, they found information on piloting, crop dusting and a flight simulator on his computer.

Attempts to expand the scope of FISA to cover foreign individuals who are not known to be agents or affiliated with a terrorist organization were rejected, however. This too will need to be fixed.

On October 25, 2001, approximately one month after its introduction, Congress passed the legislation, renamed the USA Patriot Act, and it was signed into law by President Bush the following day. The bill will not stop every future violent act, but it will help the government conduct the war against terrorism. It will take time to determine whether the bill is as effective as it should be or whether specific provisions are unworkable. If we are fortunate, we will never have to find out, but I fear there is little reason to be so optimistic. Terrorism will continue until its practitioners decide that it is no longer an effective means for imposing their beliefs on the rest of the world.

The Drug Competition and Patent Term Restoration Act of 1984 was enacted because a majority of those who understood the legislation, as opposed to the millions who would ultimately benefit from it, supported its passage. The parties to the bill understood that getting what they needed was more important than holding out for everything they wanted. The Dietary Supplement Health and Education Act became law because the very people it affected most were willing to demand that it be enacted. Most members of Congress simply voted with the majority of their constituents, not exactly a revolutionary concept. The USA Patriot Act passed Congress because the American people and extraordinary circumstances demanded it.

All three bills had bipartisan and bicameral support. Justification for the bills was relatively easy and, in all three instances, the media was neutralized. In the first, the bill moved too quickly for the press to play a role. In the second, the grassroots support was so overwhelming that it drowned out the negative reporting. In the third, the media was as interested in getting the legislation passed as the rest of the country.

Every now and then, though, a bill is introduced even though there is no overwhelming support behind it. There are no polls pointing to the safest or most popular position, no advantageous news stories. Instead, a member will champion an issue, because he or she is convinced that the legislation reflects what is right, what the American public will come to want, once the problem is understood and the need realized.

It is in these often solitary, politically vulnerable moments that real political leadership can occur.

Chapter Five

Tilting at the Right Windmills

One man with courage makes a majority.

—Andrew Jackson

Some politicians are like water—they always take the path of least resistance. They may be conservative, centrist, or liberal. Regardless of their labels, they almost always make the safe vote according to the conventional wisdom of the moment. They never put themselves in a position where they can become a target. Consumed by their own reelections and the fear of causing offense or generating criticism, they studiously avoid supporting an idea, bill or policy that does not already enjoy wide support.

One of the telltale signs of this political style is a disproportionate reliance on public opinion surveys to dictate one's legislative positions and agenda. Over the last twenty years, I have watched this disturbing trend grow within both parties, in Congress and the White House.

The Clinton Administration seemed to use polls not only to determine what position to take but also to decide what issues it would champion and when it should abandon a former priority. Polling was even used to assist with the development of defenses and explanations when questions were raised about the President's private conduct.

Recently, there have been reports in the media that former President Clinton regrets he didn't have the chance, as George W. Bush has, to lead the country through a national crisis, something akin to the tragedy of September 11. If Clinton feels he lacked leadership opportunities, part of the reason may be that he was reluctant to champion issues that may not have been popular initially but were important for the country.

There is a fundamental flaw with the concept of deciding how to vote or what to prioritize simply by relying upon polls. If done correctly (and many unfortunately are not), a poll can provide an accurate snapshot of public opinion at the time the survey was taken. What a poll cannot do, however, is predict the effects of leadership. It cannot measure the impact someone in the public eye can have by focusing attention on a problem and championing a solution. Presidents, members of Congress, the media, and individual Americans can change public opinion when they ignore the safe and easy answer and instead make people think of what could be. It is in these rare moments that real leadership occurs.

There is another danger to being limited by conventional wisdom: Always doing the safe thing is not the best way to stay safe. People who never take a stand, who never go against the grain or get out in front of an issue, tend to be forgotten. Even their supporters often see them as dull, unimaginative and replaceable. Worse, they are unreliable. Constituents have to wonder: What if my issue shows up on the wrong side of the polls? Will I be jettisoned at the first sign of trouble?

Despite considerable criticism from the media, academia and members of Congress, Ronald Reagan never faltered in his quest to reduce taxes, stimulate the economy, rebuild the military, restore confidence in the United States and end the Cold War. He accomplished all these objectives even though the Democrats either controlled or shared control of the congressional budget and tax programs for his entire administration.

President Reagan never wavered in his fight against communism. During his administration, the Soviets increased their threats against the North American Treaty Organization. They challenged our allies and interfered with inspection trips in East Germany by our Military Liaison Mission, even though the trips were authorized by treaty. Instead of seeking to accommodate the Soviets, Reagan decided in 1983 to put Pershing II missiles in Europe, creating an immediate nuclear shield for our allies. There was an instant uproar. Condemnation rained in not only from Europe and the press but even from some of his own friends.

Reagan was completely unfazed. He refused to budge, and instead began referring to the Soviet Union as the "Evil Empire," an appellation that horrified the foreign policy establishment in Washington and many liberal Democrats. They thought it was imprudent, undignified and dangerous. Reagan's objective, however, was not to maintain a cordial diplomatic front. He wanted to precipitate the downfall of the Soviet Union.

Today, a growing number of analysts credit him with accomplishing precisely that. They cite four critical factors. First, the Soviet economy was too weak to match Reagan's rebuilding of our military, which had suffered greatly under the budget austerity of the Carter Administration.[1]

Second, by putting the Pershing II missiles in Europe, Reagan made it clear that he would neither be intimidated nor tolerate the intimidation of NATO partners.

Third, Reagan announced that he would make the Strategic Defense Initiative a top national priority. Again the Soviets cried foul, even though it was well known in Western intelligence circles that they had been working hard on an antimissile defense system of their own. The Soviets were convinced they could not keep pace with

American research and development once we had made the system a national priority.

Finally, Reagan decided at a critical point in the conflict to provide Stinger-Post missiles to the Mujahedin in Afghanistan, who were fighting a bloody war against the Soviets.

I had a role in this last effort. In 1985, with the administration's blessing, I led a congressional delegation, including Senator Bill Bradley, on a trip to Pakistan to gain a personal perspective on the war between the Afghans and the Soviets. We visited a refugee camp near the Khyber Pass. It was a dry and exposed spot, and a thick layer of brown dirt and dust accentuated the desolation of the camp and its inhabitants. When the men had gathered to listen to us, it was an incongruous moment: a couple of American politicians, dressed in western-style slacks and shirts, speaking to three hundred guerrilla fighters in front of a large, open tent. They were dressed in worn jackets and loose-fitting pants. Most wore colored turbans and had thick dark beards. Their faces were creased and darkened by a hard and difficult life in the sun.

Their physical condition was a testament to the war's brutality. Some were without legs. Others were missing hands or had facial scars that seemed to glow in the sunlight. Several of them, still wary despite being in Pakistan, clutched rifles.

As the delegation leader, I was introduced and asked to say a few words. To my amazement, when I stood, the men began to chant. Their voices built steadily as the chanting turned into a roaring cheer. I told them that the United States stood with them, that we would do all we could to make sure our government supported their cause. I told them we wanted to make sure they had the weapons they needed to drive the Soviets out of their country. The men roared in approval.

From our meetings in the camps, it was clear they didn't want American soldiers fighting their war. What they needed were the resources to fight a modern enemy. They were battling helicopters, tanks, armored personnel carriers, fighter jets and missiles with guns that dated from before the First World War. They were losing men to land mines. Children were being killed and maimed by toys that had been booby-trapped. The Mujahedin could hide forever in the hills and mountains, but they needed food and medical supplies to survive.

It was also clear that they had the one thing that could not be given by someone else: the collective faith that no matter how terrible the odds, no matter how many people were killed, one day they would defeat the Russians and watch the Soviet army crawl back over the border.

We left the camps and met with Pakistan's president, Mohammed Zia ul-Haq, as well as with the twelve top rebel leaders who were running the war against the Soviets, to hear their concerns. Zia made clear his fear that the Soviets would not stop with Afghanistan. Once that country was overrun, they would push on into Pakistan, hoping to gain the warm-water port that has been the dream of the Russian military since the days of the czars.

Our delegation shared what we had learned with the Reagan Administration and pressured top officials to provide Stingers, the highly portable handheld missiles, to combat Soviet superiority in the air. I stressed the Mujahedin's inability to combat MI-24 gunships, the Soviets' deadly attack helicopters. Nothing in their arsenal could penetrate its armor and decoy systems. The Soviets could hover in the air, methodically picking off one target after another, without fear of coming under attack themselves.

Finally, six months later, the American government sent both Stingers and Sidewinder air-to-air missiles, but only to Pakistan. Arming the Mujahedin was still considered too great a political risk. The administration feared losing control over such a potentially lethal weapon. What would happen if the wrong person got hold of a Stinger and used it against an American target?

Later that year, the Reagan Administration again accommodated my travel to Asia to see whether additional military aid could be raised on behalf of the Afghan fighters.

This time, I stopped in Beijing, where I met with the chief of China's intelligence service. I had been told by our intelligence analysts that sending the Stingers to Afghanistan was a potentially inflammatory step that could not occur without Chinese support, or at least consent.

It was an unlikely meeting—a ruthless and dedicated Chinese communist who had spent his entire career trying to destabilize Western democracy, and a senator from Utah who believed that the greatest foreign policy achievement in his lifetime would be the elimination of communism as a viable force in the world. I'm not sure who was more skeptical.

I was accompanied by two representatives from the Central Intelligence Agency. After we had exchanged some perfunctory comments, I asked whether China would support greater U.S. involvement in Afghanistan. He looked at me, puzzled.

"We would like your acquiescence to arm the Mujahedin with the Stinger-Post missile," I said.

His eyes lit up. His face hardened. "We acquiesce," he barked out.

That night, there was a flurry of top secret cables between Washington and the American embassy in China as news of the meeting spread.

We then traveled to Pakistan, where we again met with President Zia. He too concurred with supplying Stingers to the Mujahedin to combat the Soviet helicopters, but observed they would not be enough. He went on to suggest targeting a variety of so-called hard sites, military installations and critical infrastructures such as bridges and supply bases.

Encouraged by the trip, I returned to Washington and renewed my pressure on the administration. It took far too long but eventually, in the summer of 1986, almost a year after we had begun, the first shipment of 150 Stingers arrived in Pakistan and was distributed to Mujahedin units. By October, these weapons were deployed in the field.

In December, the State Department reported that the Mujahedin were shooting down an average of one helicopter or jet fighter every day. By the following spring, the Soviets had stopped flying over several rebel-controlled regions of Afghanistan. A year later, the Soviet army was forced to leave.

The defeat in Afghanistan was the Soviet army's Vietnam, only worse. It came at a time when the nation itself was demoralized and weak. The military that had beaten back the Nazis in the Second World War and brutally suppressed democracy in Hungary and Czechoslovakia had been undone by a disorganized, lightly armed group of tribesman. Fear of Soviet might dissipated, and the country lost the ability to impose its will on its neighbors without question. The Soviet Union would never recover.

A year later, in 1989, the Berlin Wall was torn down. Two years later, the Soviet Union itself fell. Communist governments toppled like dominoes, and the once-powerful Eastern bloc disappeared. Today, several of these nations are members of the North Atlantic Treaty Organization, once considered the primary enemy of the Communist Bloc in Eastern Europe.

Historians will continue to debate the cause of this unforeseen change, but it is undeniable that Ronald Reagan's vision, his refusal to accede to the conventional wisdom of the experts, and his willingness to use his own political capital played a decisive role. He believed that communism, despite being a dreaded force in world politics, could be not only contained but defeated, and he acted on that belief at a time when few shared it.

It was common among Washington's so-called intelligentsia to dismiss Reagan. They saw his conviction as a lack of intelligence, his singleness of purpose as naïveté about world politics and the intricacies of international diplomacy. He did not have an Ivy League education. He didn't socialize in the right circles in Washington or New York. To these people, he was just an actor who read lines written by someone else.

Yet he was able to perceive what they could not. It was Ronald Reagan, and not all the experts, who saw that the Iron Curtain was ready to crack. He was the one who instinctively understood that the Soviet Empire could be felled by the most fatal capitalistic condition: bankruptcy.

Today, these same experts who considered Reagan's challenging of the Soviets a dangerous fantasy now claim the collapse of communism was inevitable. Reagan was simply lucky, they insist; he was in the right place at the right time. They will never admit that the end of the Soviet Union had anything to do with the conviction, courage and persistence of Ronald Reagan. But it did.

Naturally, others were involved as well. One of the front-line soldiers in the Cold War was Irving Brown, the AFL-CIO's representative in Europe. Unbeknownst to most Americans, the union, especially under the direction of Lane Kirkland, played a critical role in combating the spread of communism throughout the Cold War.

A former minor league baseball player, Brown was drafted during the Second World War and sent to France to work with the underground. He stayed on, working with the CIA to combat the Soviet attempts to organize the French dockworkers into a phony labor union which could then join its camouflaged communist labor organization. His success ensured that French ports were not closed to products from democratic countries, including the United States.

Building on that success, Brown traveled throughout the world as a lead soldier in the battle over free trade unionism. His life was in constant danger, but he stayed in the middle of the fray for more than five decades, basing his operations out of Paris. Eventually, he became so widely respected that he served as the primary voice of the U.S. delegation to the tripartite International Labor Organization (ILO), the largest United Nations affiliate agency in the world. Each member country sends a three-person delegation to the organization's annual meeting—one representing labor, one for management, and the third on behalf of the government. The ILO has the authority to ratify conventions, which are comparable to international treaties. In the United States, they must be ratified by the Senate before they are enforceable domestically.

Brown enjoyed an unusual circle of friends that included Left Bank intellectuals such as Simone de Beauvoir, John Paul Sartre, and Raymond Aron, the conservative political scientist. Brown had a compelling and fierce intellect, yet he could make anyone comfortable in his presence.

He spent much of his career searching for and nurturing sparks of democracy in Eastern Europe. In the late 1970s, he came to see me, even though I had recently led the opposition in defeating his organization's top domestic priority, Labor Law Reform. Noting my interest in combating communism, he asked me to help find support for a young electrician in Gdansk, Poland, who was challenging the Polish communist government. I had never heard of Lech Walesa, but I agreed to do what I could. Working with House Democrats, such as Sid Yates, we were able to find $2 million to pay for books, paper, printing materials, mimeograph machines and other materials Walesa needed for his fledgling organization, Solidarity. Over time, Solidarity's quest for free trade unions captured the world's attention and became an international symbol for freedom and dignity.

In the 1980s, when I was chairman of the Senate Labor Committee, Brown asked me to come to a meeting in Switzerland of the ILO to help combat an Arab-nation-sponsored resolution that condemned Israel. If it passed, the United States would have no choice but to withdraw from the organization, giving the Soviets and other communist countries free rein to use it as a political springboard into trade unions throughout the world.

Over the next two days, Irving and I met with representatives from countless countries, as well as with several ambassadors, stressing why the resolution was really a subterfuge for a much larger political agenda. I emphasized the concerns of the U.S. Congress, and Irving provided real-life examples about the economic and social consequences if the international trade union movement fell under communist control.

Lane Kirkland joined us and was invaluable working his counterparts from other countries. Our work eventually paid off. A week later, in a secret ballot, the resolution was defeated. Noting the victory, Lane commented later, "Orrin, if only you were as good in domestic affairs as you are in foreign affairs."

"You know, Lane," I replied, "I was thinking the same about you."

Irving's final achievement was the creation of the National Endowment for Democracy. Funded initially with less than $15 million in public funds, it was charged with combating the more than $3 billion the Soviets were spending every year on disinformation. Irving believed that the truth and democratic principles, coupled with free trade unionism, could defeat not only communism but most totalitarian nations as well. His life was proof he was right.

Working with Irving, I helped pass the legislation to create the organization and served on its first board of directors. Today, the endowment continues to provide small grants to support pro-democracy activities throughout the world and has had an impact on every continent.

One grant has helped changed public opinion about Castro's Cuba. For decades, most liberals in the United States have used a variety of excuses to cover up a horrible, repressive regime that has trampled the human rights of thousands. Critical coverage was dismissed as the work of right-wing fanatics, and the oldest living dictator in the world was praised for his courage in standing up against the United States.

Armando Vallardares had a different story. He was imprisoned by Castro at the age of twenty-two for being philosophically opposed to communism. A poet and intellectual, he was beaten, tortured and starved for twenty years. He survived, using his own blood to write his poetry. After his release, he asked the endowment for a grant to write his memoirs. The board of directors, a delicate balance of political opinion in the United States, split down the middle. Many feared supporting a document critical of Castro. I pitched a fit and was able to shame them into giving Mr. Vallardares a small grant that enabled him to publish his remarkable and powerful memoir, *Against All Hope*. Released in 1983, it began to turn public opinion and forced the United Nations Human Rights Commission to finally condemn the continuing violations of human rights in Cuba.

None of this would have been possible without the vision and courage of Irving Brown. As with so many true statesmen, his faith in the power of freedom and truth caused ripples that have reached into every corner of the world and have had an impact on lives and nations beyond his wildest dreams.

Not everyone has the foresight or the opportunity to change history. Nonetheless, many people have used their political or personal capital to change public opinion.

One such person was Elizabeth Glaser, who turned her own tragedy into a blessing. A tiny, pretty, exuberant woman, Elizabeth was an elementary school teacher who loved her job. Her husband, Paul Michael Glaser, was the famous one in the family, a star of the popular television show *Starsky and Hutch* and a successful movie actor and director.

In 1981, Elizabeth had trouble with the birth of their first child, a daughter named Ariel. Elizabeth hemorrhaged badly after the birth and was given a transfusion of seven pints of blood. Several weeks later, she read an article about the risk of contracting a new, highly contagious and fatal disease, AIDS, through blood transfusions. Panicked, she called her physician and was told her fears were unnecessary, that everything was fine.

And so it seemed to be. Three years later, she gave birth to a son, Jake, and this time there were no similar medical problems. Everything was perfect.

By 1985, Elizabeth was worried once again. Ariel was in pain, easily tired, and often sick. For the next year and a half, she underwent a battery of tests, but the doctors had no idea what might be wrong.

It wasn't until May 1986 that doctors decided to test for HIV. To her horror, Elizabeth learned that not only did Ariel have AIDS, she and Jake were HIV positive. Only Paul was not infected.

Elizabeth had been infected by the blood transfusion she was given during Ariel's birth and had unknowingly passed the disease to her two children. As a parent and a grandparent, I cannot imagine the agony Elizabeth must have felt. It is literally every parent's worst nightmare.

Despite all Elizabeth's efforts, Ariel died in 1988.

Elizabeth had a choice. She could give in to the inevitability of the virus and let it take control of her mind as it had her body. Or she could use her own fate and position to save others, maybe even her own son, although it meant exposing her own condition.[2]

Elizabeth decided to fight. In her struggle to help Ariel, she had learned that physicians knew little about pediatric AIDS and even less about drugs and treatments to combat the disease. Medical research on the impact of AIDS on children was virtually nonexistent. Most of us in the federal government did not even know there was a problem.

With two friends, Susan De Laurentis and Susie Zeegan, Elizabeth formed the Pediatric AIDS Foundation. Its purpose was simple: to create a think tank on pediatric AIDS and to work with the government on research. They wanted to focus on understanding how the disease affected children, how it was transmitted from mother to child, and what drugs could be used to treat it. In 1989, they came to Washington seeking federal money for research and help from the FDA.

They quickly learned firsthand the difficulties surrounding the expenditure of federal money for medical research. All existing funds were targeted at adult AIDS. Every dollar spent on children would be a dollar diverted from adults. Moreover, for pediatric research to occur, it would have to be authorized and then appropriated, a process that may take one or two years. Once the money was available, grants would have to be solicited and proposals reviewed and accepted and funded. Only then could research begin. The results would then be subject to peer review and analysis before the studies could be released. New federal research is better measured in decades than in months or years.

When I met with her, Elizabeth explained the objectives of her organization and that the children suffering from pediatric AIDS didn't have five or six years to wait for research to begin. They needed help immediately. The only practical answer was that the research be privately funded. But there was no way private citizens could match the resources of the federal government.

Over the next several days, Howard Metzenbaum, my frequent liberal opponent in the Senate, and I came up with the idea of hosting a fundraiser for Elizabeth's foundation. We hoped that by raising enough money, we could jump-start private sector research to fill the gap until federal dollars were available.

Elizabeth never thought small. Fueled by her seemingly endless energy, her group took our nugget of an idea and turned it into a remarkable bipartisan event. I made literally hundreds of calls on their behalf and helped raise nearly $1.3 million. Other fundraisers followed, including a second one I sponsored with Senator Barbara Boxer that generated over $2.5 million. Over the last twelve years, the Pediatric AIDS Foundation has been able to finance more than $130 million worth of research. Among other things, their work has led to the discovery of how to protect against mother-to-child transmission of AIDS, helped to provide treatment to pre- and neonatal women in developing countries, and sponsored an education program for pregnant women.

Elizabeth died on December 3, 1994, but her work lives on. None of her organization's remarkable achievements would have occurred without Elizabeth's courage and dedication. Until her arrival in Washington, most of us considered AIDS to be an adult disease. We didn't realize that babies were being born with AIDS, that small children were becoming infected and that mothers could pass the disease to their children. Elizabeth helped set the record straight. Children are alive today because she refused to concede to the inevitable consequence of her infection.

Everyone in politics wants to help children. The difficulty is finding the most efficient and effective way to provide the assistance.

In 1997, I met with two families from Provo, Utah. The parents were humble and hardworking, gracious, and respectful to a fault. In each family, the husband and wife both worked outside the home, struggling to pay the cost of raising six children. They didn't waste their money on frivolous purchases or gamble it away on get-rich-quick schemes. They were frugal, able to put food on the table and provide a good home for their kids; they were much like my own parents, who sacrificed so that their children would have a chance to do better.

The one thing these parents could not afford, no matter how hard they tried, was medical coverage.

Their situation was not unique. At the time, more than 7 million children of the working poor lived beyond the reach of our nation's health care system, more than 30,000 in Utah alone. Their families earned too much to qualify for public assistance and too little to pay for insurance themselves. They were left out in the cold, overlooked and forgotten. Their kids were the only ones left out of the system. The children of the truly poor were covered by Medicaid.

Although at the time the Republicans were in charge of both the Senate and the House, I knew it would be impossible to create a Republican program to help these children. Many in my party would object to creating what they viewed as a new federal entitlement program.

The Democrats, meanwhile, had nothing to gain politically from passing a Republican solution to a problem that traditionally would be a priority of their own legislative agenda. It would be in their political interest to block any initiative and then turn around and blame Republicans for the failure, claiming we lacked the compassion and interest to help the poor. Even if a bill somehow made it through Congress, the Clinton Administration would have no interest in giving a Republican Congress such a big win. The President would veto the bill.

Consequently, legislation would have to be more than bipartisan. I would have to find a Democrat partner who could not be ignored by his own party.

To my amazement, Senator Ted Kennedy was having the same thoughts. He had introduced legislation in the past to address the issue, but it was so expensive and unwieldy that it fell under its own weight. Ted came to me and asked whether I was interested in working with him. It would appear on its face to be an unlikely alliance. The issues on which we disagree are surpassed only by our personal differences.

Ted is a passionate liberal, an East Coast Democrat. I'm a Rocky Mountain compassionate conservative. He is Catholic; I'm Mormon. He was raised in a world of privilege that normally produces Republicans. My kind of childhood normally creates Democrats. Ted was educated at some of the nation's most prestigious private schools, including the Milton Academy, Harvard University, and the University of Virginia Law School. I went to public school, Brigham Young University, and the University of Pittsburgh Law School; I survived by working nights and weekends and winning the occasional scholarship.

Kennedy's personal life has been rife with controversy and well-publicized problems. Until recently, he has been a constant target of the tabloids. Other than making the *National Enquirer*'s list of possible space aliens in Congress, my personal life has never been of public interest.

Each of us is the embodiment of almost every political viewpoint the other has spent his career fighting.

Because of committee assignments, we were forced to work together. For almost two decades, we had alternated as Chairman and Ranking Member of the Senate Labor Committee, which meant that we had to sit next to each other during countless hearings and committee meetings. In the past, before the practice was banned, Ted smoked cigars during committee sessions. You could normally tell whether we were fighting by the amount of smoke he would send my way. If our differences were great, I would have to sit there, my head enveloped in cigar smoke, as we worked through amendment after amendment. Ted would lean back in his chair, puffing away, knowing he was giving me a headache that was more than just political. I would try to plow my way through without giving him the satisfaction of seeing my irritation.

To our mutual surprise, despite these differences, we have become good friends. Moreover, we have stayed friends in both good times and bad, when it was beneficial and when it was inconvenient.

We still don't agree on most issues. In fact, we almost always take opposite sides. Every now and then, however, we have been able to find the common ground that is essential to passing legislation. This has been especially true on health issues, where the disagreements tend to be over how best to achieve a common objective and not over whether something needs to be done. Not surprisingly, once we are able to reach agreement on a bill, the legislation generally passes. If Kennedy and Hatch can agree, there's not much left uncovered on the political spectrum.

Ted likes to say in public, usually when a lot of reporters are listening, that if the two of us are together on a bill it's clear one of us hasn't read it. In typical Kennedy fashion, his timing is impeccable, and I have no choice but to sit there and smile during the inevitable laughter.

One year, however, I was prepared. After Ted had made his comment and the laughter had subsided, I pulled out a dog-eared copy of the bill, heavily highlighted and notated.

"Here you go, Ted," I said as I tossed it to him, "you can have my copy. The key parts are already underlined." I don't know who laughed louder, Ted or the reporters.

We agreed to introduce legislation on health care for children of the working poor that was far more moderate than Ted's original bill, but still too liberal in several areas to withstand Republican objections in the Senate. He agreed to work on the liberal special interest groups, while I did the same on my side.

As often happens, our personal predictions were different. I knew that for the legislation to pass, it would have to offer a conservative, economically realistic structure. I was convinced that at the critical time, Ted would have no choice but to agree to changes to the bill for it to pass.

He, on the other hand, assumed I would probably not be able to convince enough Republicans to pass the bill through the Senate, let alone the House of Representatives. If the bill was stopped, he would be in the perfect position to blame Republicans for its failure.

The legislation, known as the Children's Health Insurance and Lower Deficit Act, or the CHILD bill, provided $20 billion over five years for health insurance for the children of the working poor. An additional $10 billion would be set aside for debt reduction. The assistance would be in the form of block grants to the states to be run through existing programs, eliminating the need for a federal bureaucracy to operate the program. Participation would be voluntary and the aid would not be an entitlement, which meant it would not require new federal monies if there were insufficient funds to cover its cost.

The entire program would be paid for with a 43-cent tax increase on cigarettes. We were convinced that this funding mechanism would have the added benefit of discouraging smoking by raising the cost of a pack of cigarettes. There are more than ample studies that show a correlation between increased costs and smoking cessation.

Our bill upset everyone. Republicans were furious about my collaboration with Kennedy and were convinced I had been duped. Conservatives outside of Congress were also angry. For them, any tax was a bad tax. They accused me of betraying my principles, of forgoing the wisdom of supply-side economics. No matter what the bill actually said, they were convinced it simply created yet another federal entitlement program that would eventually be foisted on taxpayers. And, naturally, the tobacco companies were less than thrilled.

Ted didn't fare that well at first, either. Concerns were raised about his working with me, of giving up so much from his original position without even a fight. Some of his supporters worried about what the bill would look like once it had made it all the way through a Republican Congress. A few of his Democratic colleagues complained that, by making the bill bipartisan, he had made it more difficult for them to capitalize on its inevitable failure.

Almost immediately, the attacks began. Citizens for a Sound Economy, a conservative group based in Washington, D.C., began spending an estimated $30,000 a week to run ads on Utah radio stations. The ads featured a voice mimicking Kennedy's distinctive Boston accent, thanking me "on behalf of the citizens of Massachusetts" for the liberal Children's Health Insurance bill. The state governors were almost unanimous in opposition. Only Governor Dean of Vermont came out in favor. The governor of Utah, Mike Leavitt, led the fight inside the National Governor's Association that resulted in a formal declaration of opposition.

We knew this would happen. Undeterred, Ted and I spoke to any group that would listen to us. Gradually, we began to win over those in the health care field, along with a variety of liberal organizations.

Kennedy was in his glory because he could use Republican opposition to the bill as an excuse to attack the party at every opportunity. His own side's initial concerns were forgotten as coverage of his criticism increased. Within weeks, he had returned to his traditional position as the voice of the liberal opposition.

I, on the other hand, was getting pounded. When we introduced the bill, I had seven Republican cosponsors. The Republican leadership was able to mute their enthusiasm and to discourage others from adding their names to the legislation. Instead of gaining in the Senate, it looked as if we were actually losing support.

In May, at the Utah State Republican convention, the bill came under attack. A resolution was passed condemning the legislation and my role with it. During the discussion, the criticisms were so ridiculous and personal that I raised a point of personal privilege and asked for time to speak. For more than thirty minutes, I explained why I had introduced the legislation and why it was the right thing to do. I rebutted the arguments against the bill and ridiculed some of the more outrageous personal attacks leveled at me.

It was a futile effort. My response ended up alienating a good number of delegates, many of whom were already thinking about underwriting a primary challenge when I ran for reelection in two years. In retrospect, I probably should have just lived with the public criticism and taken the attacks for what they were. But at the time, I was too angry to keep quiet.

I also felt it was important that my critics understand I was not going to be intimidated. If they beat me in the coming election, so be it. But until then, I would not change my position simply because I might lose my Senate seat. That was a decision for the voters, not the self-appointed activists.[3]

I continued to work on my Republican colleagues in the Senate and we began to see some progress. Sixteen billion was added to the budget resolution, the device used in Congress to establish in the most general terms the budget for the coming fiscal year. Still, the pertinent language in the resolution did not specify how the money would be spent. It was presumed that most of the money would be used on Medicaid, the federal medical program for the poorest of the poor. Only $2 billion would be targeted at the children of the working poor, too little to accomplish the job.

Nonetheless, the mere mention of these children in the budget resolution indicated that our efforts were beginning to have an impact, that public opinion about the issue was shifting, and that recognition of the problem and the merits of our proposal were increasing. Unfortunately, it also created a usually fatal political dynamic most often associated with the battles over the minimum wage.

In the past, Republicans had routinely opposed increases in the minimum wage. More often than not, despite our objections, the wage increases had passed, and the Democrats would pummel us on the campaign trail for being insensitive to the needs of working families.

These accusations were given great coverage in the press despite their questionable relevance. According to the United States Census Bureau, only 14 percent of minimum wage jobs are held by a single parent or a single wage earner in a couple with kids. More than 40 percent are held by people living with a parent or relative, which is consistent with its intent of being a means for unemployed workers to gain some experience and then move up the wage scale.

It is not supposed to be a wage for an entire career, nor is it an effective way of helping the poor. Studies by Stanford University's Thomas MaCurdy and Frank McIntyre have shown that while one in every four of the poorest workers gain from an increase in the minimum wage, three out of every four lose because of the increase in costs that result from the wage increases. Similar studies by researchers at Ohio University revealed that there was no statistical relationship between the minimum wage and the poverty level. Wage mandates are simply not an effective way to reduce poverty.

None of that mattered, however, because the minimum wage has become a political symbol, a way to measure congressional compassion for the working poor. Voting against an increase, regardless of the reason, is thus risky and susceptible to demagogic criticism.

Moreover, now that Republicans controlled both houses of Congress, our position on the minimum wage was no longer monolithic. There were now enough Republicans in Congress who supported increases to ensure passage. In fact, the last time the bill had come up for a vote, in 1996, Republicans provided the necessary margin for victory, but the Democrats got the political credit.

It now looked as if the CHILD bill would be a repeat of the minimum wage fight—enough Republicans would vote for the legislation to ensure its passage, and the Democrats would still be able to get the credit while blaming Republicans for not doing more.

On the evening of June 19, 1997, the Senate Finance Committee met behind closed doors to finalize an overall tax and spending package for the coming fiscal year. One Republican and one Democrat recommended diverting the new cigarette tax to pay for a variety of corporate assistance programs. I was incredulous.

I immediately started talking. How could we be so stupid as to slap a tax on cigarettes, then turn around and give all the money to corporate special interests? There would be nothing left for kids, even though everyone knew the new cigarette taxes were supposed to be targeted for children's health insurance. I promised that if their proposal passed, Kennedy and I would "eat your lunch" on the Senate floor.

I then suggested a new compromise. Instead of spending the money on companies, why not add an additional $9 billion to the $16 billion already in the budget resolution and spend it on children's health insurance?

Everyone started arguing. I leaned back in my chair, still upset. Alfonse D'Amato, a Republican from New York, leaned over. Alfonse is a consummate New York politician—shrewd, tough and always political. He agreed with my observation and expressed amazement at what he called the stubborn stupidity of some of our colleagues. He then spoke to the entire committee. He called my proposal fair and urged its adoption. Two other Republicans joined in as well, Frank Murkowski of Alaska and Chuck Grassley of Iowa.

Support for my suggestions was growing, but it was not unanimous. Phil Gramm of Texas and Don Nickles of Oklahoma were livid, and glared angrily at me. I'm not sure which offended them more: my characterization of their proposal or the growing support for mine.

Not wanting the moment to slip away, I turned to Pat Moynihan of New York, the Ranking Democrat on the Finance Committee. "Where are the Democrats on this?" I asked, already knowing the answer.

Grinning, Moynihan said, "All who are in favor, raise your hands." Every Democrat raised a hand.

Gramm and Nickles objected, arguing that the budget already contained sufficient money for child health insurance, but the moment had passed. To accommodate the committee chairman, Bill Roth of Delaware, I offered to reduce my proposal to the compromise figure of $24 billion over five years and $48 billion over ten years. The amendment passed by a vote of 18 to 2. The impossible had just become the obvious.

With the extra $8 billion added to the $16 billion already in the budget resolution, the CHILD bill was now funded at $24 billion over five years, $4 billion more than the legislation Kennedy and I had initially introduced. It may not have fixed the entire problem, but it certainly was a magnificent beginning.

Moreover, the provision, now renamed the State Child Health Insurance Program, or SCHIP, became the glue that held together the balanced budget package, the first balanced budget in forty years. By including the SCHIP program in the legislation, suddenly both Republicans and Democrats had a reason for supporting it. Now, neither side wanted the other to claim credit, and the bill was enacted, enabling Congress to pass the first balanced federal budget act in twenty-nine years.

As I was leaving the committee room, I was told I had a phone call from Ted Kennedy. I rushed over to the phone, anxious to share the good news.

"Orrin," Ted barked before I could say a word. "I've never been so betrayed in all my time in the United States Senate."

"Oh?" I answered, trying to stay calm. "Why is that?"

"Because of what you just did."

"Well, Ted," I said, my irritation rising, "this bill is for $24 billion over five years, and $48 over ten years. Our bill was for $20 billion over five years. It appears to me that if only you and Phil Gramm seem to be against what I've done, I must have done something right."

I slammed the phone down and walked out.

I couldn't believe it. We had just won, and Ted was complaining. My mind raced. Was he upset because I had cut a deal without him? Had he been given the wrong facts? Neither possibility made sense. I thought of the public attacks by my colleagues, the criticism during the Republican Party policy lunches, the ridicule by conservative pundits, and the snide jibes on the Senate floor. I thought of the condemnation in my own state, the radio ads, letters and telephone calls complaining that I had become Kennedy's puppet. What I had done guaranteed me a Republican challenger in a year. How could Ted be so blind, so unappreciative, so damn dense?

As my mind filled with all the reasons why I should be mad at Kennedy, I also started to remember why I shouldn't be. I remembered the Ted Kennedy who had come to my office uninvited when the press was reporting I was under investigation, a false allegation that had been fomented by several anonymous Democrats. He had listened while I vented, and then quietly reminded me that things would work out, that I had done nothing wrong. He was the only one, Republican or Democrat, who did so.

I remembered the Ted Kennedy who had come, with his wonderful wife, Vicky, to my mother's funeral. Again, he was the only one of my colleagues from out of state who did, and he helped me through that difficult and emotional period.

I remembered the Ted Kennedy who called me from his boat, after he had finished playing the song I had written for Vicky for their fifth wedding anniversary.

As I calmed down, I started to laugh, knowing what would happen in the morning.

Sure enough, first thing the next day, there was a knock on my door. I looked up from my desk and there was Ted. "Orrin," he said smiling broadly, his hand outstretched, "that really was something you did last night. That was historic."

He continued in this vein for several minutes. I stared at him as he talked, waiting patiently, but he made not one reference to the call the previous night. Finally, I couldn't help myself and started to laugh. Ted did as well. It was his way of apologizing.

Today, despite all the dire predictions and the almost uniform political condemnation, the SCHIP program is an unqualified success, roundly praised by members of Congress and state governors alike. Despite their initial objections and their considerable attempts to kill the bill, almost every governor who was up for reelection in 1998 and 2000, including the governor of Utah, claimed the SCHIP bill as his or her own.

On the day the Senate passed the SCHIP bill, one of the members of the Republican leadership stood next to me in the Senate well, grousing.

"It's a good bill," I assured him as the clerk called the roll. "It's good policy and smart politics, and it's going to help us get a bipartisan, balanced budget. It's no longer a risk."

"I hate this bill, Hatch," he groaned. "I hate this damn bill."

The clerk called his name. It was his turn to vote.

"Aye," he said.

Chapter Six

A Judge Becomes a Verb

Those who want political judges
should reflect that the political and
social preferences of judges have
changed greatly over our history and
will no doubt do so again. We have
known judicial activism of the Right
and of the Left; neither is legitimate.

—Judge Robert Bork

No one can even agree when the rancor over judicial nominations started. Republicans and Democrats point with equal indignation to completely different episodes. I'm sure that if you went back to the early 1800s, you could find reports that the Federalist Party was unfairly blocking President Jefferson's nominees. Senate confirmation of a presidential nominee is, after all, a political exercise and always has been.

Nonetheless, the blocking and disparaging of nominees, and judicial nominees in particular, is conducted with a frequency and an anger today that would surprise even the most hardened political partisans of the past. The confirmation process has devolved from a constitutionally mandated responsibility to provide "advice and consent" into a political gauntlet that even the mostly saintly would find terrifying.

To serve in a senior position in the executive branch or to be placed on the federal bench, nominees must risk exposing themselves to a modern-day witch-hunt in which no mistake is petty enough to be excused, no past oral or written statement sufficiently ancient to be ignored, and no personal fact or family issue too private to be exposed.

Worse, this trial is often conducted through the press, where anonymous sources secrete a constant venom of rumor, innuendo and falsehood. Confirmation can take months, even years. Nominees are forced to put their careers on hold indefinitely, knowing that at any moment their reputations may be permanently tarnished. It is an absolute wonder anyone is willing to serve.

Approving nominees is a responsibility peculiar to the United States Senate.

In my experience, the overt politicization of the nomination process began or at least became greatly aggravated during the Reagan years, when a conservative Republican president was elected by a landslide, giving him a mandate for change. Moreover, the Republicans were given control of the Senate for the first time in twenty-six years, creating an alignment that had never occurred under Nixon and Ford.

It was a terrifying and liberating moment for Senate Democrats. They would no longer be able to dictate the Senate agenda, conduct oversight hearings, and ensure that the issues they considered important were given prime time. Conversely, being in the minority, they were no longer responsible for managing and passing the array of bills, such as appropriations legislation, that must move through Congress every year. As one Democratic operative observed, they could "just sit back, pick their targets, and throw hand grenades." And there were no easier pickings than presidential nominees.

Every president must appoint literally thousands of people to run the administration. These positions range from cabinet positions, such as the Secretary of State or the Secretary of Defense, to thousands of low-level political appointees spread over the federal agencies and departments. Approximately half of these need Senate confirmation. In addition, presidents have the authority to nominate candidates to fill all vacancies in the 760-person federal judiciary, as well as countless commissioners and similar positions at a wide variety of independent agencies and commissions.

The Democrats quickly realized that one of the more effective ways to impede the Reagan Administration was simply to block or delay the confirmation of those nominated by the president. No one was immune. Over time, cabinet officers, assistant secretaries, even low-level agency appointments, all became political fodder. As long as a person needed Senate confirmation, a price could be extracted for a vote.

So there were bitter fights over nominations for positions such as the Assistant Secretary of Labor for Mine Safety and Health and the Occupational Safety and Health Act Review Commission. A nominee for Solicitor of Labor was held up for months by a Democratic senator on the Labor Committee, who was trying to pressure the Reagan Administration to agree to several bills in exchange for his confirmation. Commissioners of federal regulatory agencies, subcabinet positions, ambassadors and even U.S. attorneys all have become pawns in various legislative games.

Instead of abating at the end of the second Reagan term, the tactic became the norm. Today, votes on nominees are often traded like commodities—ten judges in exchange for a vote on this, two commissioners for a vote on that. This objectionable practice is so common and accepted that it has become as important in keeping the Senate functioning as unanimous consent and other key parliamentary rules.

Nonetheless, the cost to the Senate has been great, and nowhere has the damage been more evident than in the treatment of judicial nominations. Rarely does a day go by without one side accusing the other of partisan delays, procedural abuse and other ignominious tactics in considering the president's selections for the federal bench. The only change is who plays the part of the accuser and who is the accused.

During my tenure as Chairman of the Senate Judiciary Committee between 1995 and 2000, it was my responsibility to provide an opportunity for consideration of President Clinton's nominees. Although I tried to provide an orderly process, I was routinely criticized by the Democrats and the media for delaying confirmations. This never occurred, they claimed, when the Republicans controlled the White House and the Democrats ran the Senate.

In fact, in the aggregate, President Clinton had 377 federal judges confirmed during his two terms. President Reagan, the record holder for judicial confirmations, had 382 confirmed. What makes these numbers even more telling is that President Reagan enjoyed six years when his own party controlled the Senate and thus the schedule of the Judiciary Committee. President Clinton's party controlled the Senate for only two years during his presidency. Put another way, while I was Chairman of the Judiciary Committee, the opposition did virtually as well at confirming Clinton's nominees as Reagan's allies did for his.

During the last two years of President George Bush Sr.'s administration, the Democrats controlled the Senate. At the end of that year, there were ninety-seven judicial vacancies and fifty-four nominees left hanging without a vote. Six were submitted too late to be considered. There was no press outcry. There was no steady stream of accusations in the media about political conspiracies or hoary rhetoric about partisanship at its worst.

At the end of President Clinton's second term, the Republicans were in control of the Senate. There were sixty-seven judicial vacancies and forty-one nominations left unconfirmed. Nine of those selections were submitted so late that they would have been impossible to confirm even if the Senate unanimously supported their candidacies. Several others were properly and fairly having trouble with their background checks, and five were being blocked by the Democrats themselves.

Consequently, at the end of the Clinton Administration there were only thirty-two nominations left unconfirmed. Yet today some of my Democratic colleagues contend that the Republicans blocked an unprecedented number of judicial nominations. They have leveled charges of racism and sexism, and claimed we allowed right-wing conservatism to run amok. Accuracy, of course, has never been a mainstay of political rhetoric.

Ironically, I was also attacked by members of my own party and their supporters on the right for allowing too many Clinton nominees to be confirmed. They knew that I believed that whoever is president deserves fair and prompt treatment of his or her nominees, but this did not appease my Republican critics. Their anger was so pronounced that, in 1997, several conservative senators tried to devise a method for emasculating the committee process and frustrating President Clinton's ability to appoint judges. Phil Gramm of Texas recommended that a majority of the senators from the states making up a judicial circuit should be able to veto an appellate court nomination to that circuit. Slade Gorton of Washington went even further, proposing that any senator representing a state in a circuit should have the authority to veto any nominee to that court of appeals.

These proposals would have extended to appellate nominees the rarely publicized process currently in use with regard to district court judges. Today, when an individual is nominated to be a district court judge in a particular state, the two senators from that state are sent a blue slip of paper notifying them of the nomination. If either one objects, the Judiciary Committee traditionally will give that objection considerable weight when determining how to proceed. If both object, that nomination is dead no matter how good the nominee might be.

With appellate court nominees, individual senators may be consulted or make recommendations, but the view of any one member will not be dispositive. Presidents, both Republican and Democrat, have always jealously guarded their right to appoint appellate court nominees.

I argued vehemently against both Gramm's and Gorton's recommendations. Either would drastically change the dynamic between the legislative and executive branches and further increase the gaming of nominees. One of the consequences of a presidential election, I noted, is that the winner has the right to appoint nominees to the court and to the thousands of term appointments at federal agencies and departments. This is why judicial selection should be one of the major factors to be taken into account in choosing a president. The Senate's power of confirmation is not, in my opinion, equal to the president's power of nomination. To object to every nominee is contrary to the division of responsibilities assigned in the Constitution.

Moreover, there was the issue of comity. If we expected Democrats to respect the choices of Republican presidents, we could hardly do less when the situation was reversed.

Pointing to recent history, I reminded the Republican caucus that while these proposals might seem to make political sense to some—even though I found them absolutely ridiculous—they needed to consider what would happen in the future. There was a very real chance that at some point we would again control the White House but not the Senate. If that occurred, their recommendations would be tantamount to giving the Democrats the ability and opportunity to block every nominee to a federal court of appeals selected by a Republican president.

After considerable debate, I was able to defeat both proposals, but our consideration of the ideas exemplifies how distressed we had become. Moreover, Gramm and Gorton were right in one sense. The confirmation process was dangerously flawed.

Republican anger with the judicial confirmation process can be traced directly to the treatment of William Rehnquist, Robert Bork and Clarence Thomas, all Republican nominees to the Supreme Court.

In 1986, with the retirement of Warren Burger, President Reagan nominated Justice William Rehnquist to be the next Chief Justice of the United States. Although he had been a sitting justice since 1972, when he was appointed by Richard Nixon, and had been praised by Justices William Brennan and Thurgood Marshall as the leading intellect on the Court, Rehnquist's confirmation was anything but smooth. At the time, I nicknamed it "the Rehnquisition."

His hearings focused less on the specific decisions he had made on the Court than on matters largely unrelated to his judicial temperament or ability. For days, the nominee was boxed around, forced to answer questions that ranged from the substantive to the inexplicable.

For example, he was questioned about a memorandum he had written in the 1940s, when he was a Supreme Court law clerk for Justice Robert Jackson. In the memorandum, he had explained the Court's horrible but historic position that "separate, but equal" facilities for African Americans were constitutional. Justice Rehnquist answered by explaining that he was summarizing Justice Jackson's views on the issue, as he was expected to do in his capacity as a clerk.

One would think that the decisions and opinions of a sitting Supreme Court Justice would be a better indication of his beliefs about civil rights than a memorandum he wrote as a clerk four decades in the past.

Unsuccessful on this line of attack, Senators Kennedy and Metzenbaum tried to shift the focus to restrictive covenants on two pieces of land, one of which Justice Rehnquist currently owned and the other he had owned some years before. These covenants, which preclude the sale of the land to certain races or ethnic groups, can be found in most deeds to older pieces of property. They are a distasteful reminder of our nation's discriminatory past. They are also illegal and have been found to be unenforceable by the Supreme Court. Most homeowners are unaware that these covenants even exist, because they are included at the time the deed is first written. The few who are aware of their presence often have little interest in paying the legal costs associated with removing them, since they have no legal effect whatsoever.

The deed for Justice Rehnquist's vacation home in Vermont contained a restrictive covenant precluding sale to Jews. Similarly, a piece of property the justice had once owned in Arizona forbade the sale of the land to someone other than a Caucasian. No one asserted that Mr. Rehnquist had requested that these covenants be included in the deeds. No one claimed he even knew about them. In fact, he did not. Nonetheless, the implication was made that he must implicitly agree with their prohibitions, because he had not had them expunged.

Amazingly, this ridiculously contrived issue hung over the nomination until it was discovered that the deed to former President John F. Kennedy's home in the elite Washington, D.C., neighborhood of Georgetown also contained a restrictive covenant. Once this awkward fact became public, the issue magically evaporated.

Senator Metzenbaum would continue with this vein of implication in subsequent years. For example, in the late 1980s, he asked Hal Christensen, who was nominated to be the Deputy Attorney General, how many Jews lived in his neighborhood in Salt Lake City. Before Hal could respond, I mumbled loud enough for most of the room to hear, "It's probably about the same as the number of Mormons who live in your neighborhood, Howard." Senator Metzenbaum decided to move on to another topic.

The Rehnquist nomination also marked the beginning of another destructive and inflammatory practice. During the confirmation, questions were raised about the nominee's health and his use of a drug to combat severe back pain. It was agreed that the former head of the National Institute on Drug Abuse would review Rehnquist's medical records and make a determination. The doctor studied all the relevant documents and reported back to the committee that the justice had no unresolved health problems.

That should have been the end of the matter, but Paul Simon, a Democrat from Illinois, insisted that the doctor's report be made public. I objected, knowing that its release could have no purpose but to embarrass the nominee. After some debate, the committee decided to keep the report confidential.

So what happened? Someone on the committee went ahead and leaked the doctor's report to the press. Not surprisingly, the media accounts focused more on the allegations than on the doctor's conclusions.

It was never determined who did it, nor was there a sincere effort by the Democrats on the committee to find the culprit. There was no effective way for the nominee to fight back. The more he tried to tell his side of the story, the more attention he would draw to the allegations. As my good friend Bud Scruggs often observes, it's much easier to litter a mountain than to clean up the mess.

Despite the extended campaign to discredit him, Justice Rehnquist was confirmed by the Senate Judiciary Committee by a vote of 13 to 5. After five days of debate on the floor of the Senate, he became the sixteenth Chief Justice of the United States by a vote of 65 to 33.

The treatment of Justice Rehnquist might seem tame in comparison to what would come, but it established an unfortunate precedent. All the tactics that would be employed in the future—the leaking of confidential information, the reliance on innuendo, and the magnification of the insignificant—were brought into play.

For years, the Democrats had viewed the judiciary as an equal partner in the shaping of public policy. As long as the Supreme Court's liberal majority was kept intact, there was always the good chance that a judicial decision could achieve what they could not enact through legislation. Obviously, the appointment of conservative jurists threatened this important balance.

Moreover, the Democrats had not had a chance to nominate someone to the Supreme Court since the Johnson Administration. From 1968 to 2000, there would be only two Democratic nominees to the

Supreme Court, both by President Clinton. Republican presidents had the opportunity during that period to fill nine vacancies. Consequently, for the Democrats, Justice Rehnquist's elevation to Chief Justice was cause for concern.

The nomination of Robert H. Bork, however, was reason to panic. Judge Bork was serving on the United States Court of Appeals when he was nominated to the Supreme Court by President Reagan. He is a brilliant intellect and an independent and reasoned thinker who has a remarkable capacity for candid self-evaluation—not exactly a common characteristic in the halls of Congress.

He joined the U.S. Marines when he graduated from high school, but the Second World War ended before he finished basic training. He then went to college and law school, but dropped out of the latter after his second year because he felt he lacked discipline and needed to grow up. Evidencing a remarkable capacity for the unconventional, he reenlisted in the Marines.

Whatever he felt he needed, Bork clearly received from this second stint in the Corps, because the rest of his life has been a manifestation of his intelligence and his passion for hard work. He taught law at Yale, was a remarkably successful attorney in private practice, and served as the Solicitor General of the United States during the Nixon Administration. He was appointed to the appellate court by President Reagan, where he quickly gained the reputation as one of the court's most compelling conservative intellects.

Hours after his nomination became public, Senator Kennedy rushed to the Senate floor and gave a speech that would set the tone for the coming hearings. It was a polemical screed, appalling in tone, in the number of gross misstatements, and in its reliance on indefensible distortions. According to Kennedy,

Robert Bork's America is a land in which women would be forced into back-alley abortions, blacks would have to sit at segregated lunch counters, rogue police would break down citizen's doors in midnight raids, schoolchildren could not be taught about evolution, writers and artists would be censored at the whim of government, and the doors of the federal courts would be shut on the fingers of millions of citizens for whom the judiciary is often the only protector of the individual rights that are the heart of our democracy.[1]

This was only the beginning. By the end, the treatment of Robert Bork would stand as one of the most disturbing, unproductive and inexcusable chapters in the history of the Senate.

For months, Judge Bork was subjected to a constant stream of vilification both inside and outside of Congress. He was called an extremist and a racist. It was asserted that if confirmed, he would send police on midnight raids into people's homes. He would ban the teaching of evolution, censor artists and writers, and raise the price of everything from electricity to gas.

He was portrayed as a would-be Savonarola. To accomplish a fraction of what his detractors alleged, he would have had to be a dictator instead of a Supreme Court Justice.

One prominent full-page newspaper advertisement contained a whopping sixty-two falsehoods about Judge Bork. Another ad had eighty-four mistakes and a third, ninety-nine. The liberal advocacy groups that placed these ads knew of the errors but made no effort to correct them.

Typical of these exaggerations was the claim that Judge Bork supported "sterilizing workers." This calumny was based upon a 1984 case involving a chemical company's policy that female employees of childbearing age were not entitled to hold jobs that exposed them to toxic substances at levels considered unsafe for fetuses. The company made exceptions for women who could demonstrate they had been surgically sterilized. To this end, it provided information about sterilization.

Several unions alleged that the exception forced women to be sterilized to keep their jobs. They argued that the company should simply

have stated that only sterile women would be employed in the potentially dangerous jobs. The provision of information about sterilization,
they contended, constituted a hazardous working condition under the
Occupational Safety and Health Act of 1970.

Judge Bork and a unanimous court upheld the ruling of the
Occupational Safety and Health Review Commission that the sterilization exception did not constitute a "hazardous working condition"
under the statute. The decision noted that the term, as used by
Congress, referred to processes or materials that cause injury or disease at work. Whether it should also apply to so-called fetus protection policies was an issue for Congress, not the courts, to decide.[2]

That unanimous opinion was sufficient for a well-organized coalition of liberal special interest groups, who would spend millions to
defeat Judge Bork, as well as their supporters in Congress, to claim
that Judge Bork wanted to sterilize women. The media dutifully
reported the charge over and over despite its patent absurdity.

Judge Bork's candor ironically also counted against him. He will-
ingly debated legal theory with committee members, only to see his
observations twisted and thrown back at him. He readily explained his
understanding of the law and recent court decisions, and then
watched his opponents use his answers to level new charges at him.

The attacks were also personal. He was mocked for the way he
looked. He was criticized for the way he dressed. Partisan investigators pored through his garbage, hoping to discover something that
could be used against him. Even the titles of the videos he had rented came under scrutiny. His opponents hoped he could be caught
renting or purchasing something pornographic, but found nothing.
There was simply no line of privacy that could not be crossed.[3]

What none of us appreciated at the time was that the treatment
of Robert Bork represented the irreversible merging of the constitutional requirement for advice and consent and the modern political
campaign. For the first time, the art of personal attacks, distortions
and misstatements, an unfortunate but traditional feature of

American elections, became a weapon in a fight over a judicial confirmation.

Charges were thrown around so easily, and with so little concern for accuracy, because the task was no longer to discern the truth or to assess a nominee's qualifications. As in a campaign, there was only one goal: winning. Given the makeup of the Court, apparently the stakes were too high for the Democrats simply to play within the rules. They had to win at any cost. No one was held accountable. No one was held responsible.[4]

Judge Bork's opponents believed their actions were not only justified but necessary. As Bob himself has observed, he was considered such a dangerous threat mainly because he was seen as the potential swing vote on abortion. If he was confirmed, pro-choice advocates feared there would be enough votes on the Supreme Court to permit reconsideration of the decision in *Roe* v. *Wade*.

For years, there have been strong reservations about the legal sufficiency of the Court's holding that abortion is an implied right in the Constitution. Although Judge Bork had never issued an opinion on the matter, he had repeatedly argued that courts should not invent legal privileges. This fact, coupled with his being Catholic, was sufficient for abortion activists and their supporters in Congress to declare him the enemy. In many ways, the entire campaign against Judge Bork was really just a cover for his real flaw: He flunked the Democrats' most important judicial litmus test.

Unfortunately, in the end, the smearing was successful, and his nomination to the Supreme Court was rejected by a vote of 58 to 42. The Democrats' treatment of Robert Bork was so infamous that his name has become part of the political vernacular. Today, "borking" a nominee refers to the continuous use of ad hominem attacks to destroy an individual's character when no such attacks are warranted or justified.

It is difficult to reconcile Judge Bork's treatment with the confirmation of Antonin Scalia to the Supreme Court just a year earlier. If the treatment of Judge Bork was an example of the Democrats at their worst, the confirmation of Judge Scalia demonstrated a milder brand of cynicism.

If anything, Scalia was slightly more conservative than either Judge Bork or Justice Rehnquist. Like Bork, Scalia had been a judge on the United States Court of Appeals in Washington, D.C. He had a well-deserved reputation as an outspoken conservative thinker. He was, and is, an engaging, passionate man with an excellent sense of humor. He is also a brilliant scholar and has proven to be an articulate, persuasive conservative justice.

In many ways, Scalia and Judge Bork were judicial soul mates. They voted together 98 percent of the time. The slight difference was due to Judge Bork's more liberal reading of the scope of the First Amendment.

Scalia was an outspoken critic of *Roe* v. *Wade,* yet his confirmation could not have been briefer, more cordial or less controversial. Member after member sang his praises. Kennedy, Metzenbaum, Simon and Leahy found no problems with his record. Interest groups never raised a single question about his personal life, writings, video rentals or the contents of his garbage. He was confirmed unanimously.

There were, however, two fundamental differences between the two nominees. First, Judge Scalia was the first Italian American ever to be nominated to the Supreme Court. No Democrat was ready to offend such an important and powerful constituency by exposing Scalia to the kind of treatment given to Justice Rehnquist. It was no secret that New York Governor Mario Cuomo, a perennial presidential favorite among Democrats, made it clear that he would look poorly on anyone who interfered with the confirmation of his fellow Italian American.

In addition, there was the issue of timing. When he was nominated, Justice Scalia did not represent the potential swing vote on abortion. Judge Bork did.

Moreover, every nomination is always affected by the nomination that precedes it. Justice Scalia's followed immediately on the heels of

the grueling confirmation of Justice Rehnquist. No one was interested in fighting another battle so soon after the last.

The issue of timing would also come into play after Judge Bork.
Following his defeat, President Reagan nominated Anthony Kennedy,
then a federal judge on the Court of Appeals for the Ninth Circuit.
Kennedy is a well-established conservative, but his record on abortion
was mixed. The Democrats on the committee were exhausted from
the Bork battle and still reeling from the political fallout. They
believed they had made their point—that a president could never
again nominate an outspoken and presumably conservative pro-life
candidate and expect a courteous reception.

Judge Kennedy was a quiet, deliberate nominee. He was treated
with marked courtesy, moved through the committee quickly, and was
confirmed unanimously by the full Senate.

In retrospect, the Reagan Administration probably should have
reversed the order and submitted Judge Bork's nomination before
Scalia's. But the White House was unsure whether it would be able
to nominate two people to the Supreme Court. Consequently, when
the opportunity arose, they chose to go with the younger, healthier
jurist. Bob, who is stout and a heavy smoker, was considered a greater
physical risk.

Even with Bork already on the Court, Justice Scalia's heritage
would have been sufficient to overcome the concerns caused by his
opposition to abortion. If President Reagan had nominated him first,
Bob Bork would be on the Supreme Court today alongside Antonin
Scalia and he probably would have been confirmed easily.

Some assert that what was done to Robert Bork is no different from
what Republicans have done to Democratic nominees to both the
Court and to federal office, individuals such as Bill Lan Lee. There is,
however, a fundamental difference.

Mr. Lee was one of President Clinton's more controversial executive branch appointments. He was nominated to be the Assistant
Attorney General for Civil Rights, and he would be responsible for the

federal government's enforcement of federal civil rights laws. Consequently, how he intended to interpret these laws was a legitimate question to raise during his confirmation.

Before his nomination, Mr. Lee was an effective advocate for the NAACP Legal Defense and Educational Fund. While there, he frequently championed the use of race-based preferences and classifications, which he saw as consistent with his view of the principles of affirmative action. He clearly disagreed with the Supreme Court rulings that such remedies were unconstitutional in all but very limited and exceptional circumstances.

Advocating a position at odds with the holdings of the Supreme Court is a valid activity for a private attorney, but it poses a problem for a person charged with enforcing the law on behalf of the United States. Unfortunately, Mr. Lee did little during his confirmation hearings to assuage concerns that he would not use his federal position to pursue his own agenda. It was not a surprise when he was not confirmed.

The Democrats, fearing that they lacked the votes for confirmation, prevented the Judiciary Committee from holding a formal vote on Mr. Lee. Although Lee was never confirmed, President Clinton used the lack of a formal rejection to justify putting him in the position as a "recess appointment," a device that allows a president to fill positions for a short period when the Senate has not yet acted. Clearly, the intent of this procedure was bent in order to place Mr. Lee in the position.

The primary difference in the fight over the Bill Lan Lee nomination was his treatment during the confirmation process. The Republicans were very public in explaining that their opposition to Mr. Lee was based on his unwillingness to enforce the law as it was interpreted by the courts. Changing the law is a function that should be reserved for the legislature and not law enforcement. But despite the strongly held views about the nominee on both sides of the aisle, Mr. Lee was not attacked personally. Disparaging rumors about his personal life were not floated by anonymous sources, and investigators were not sent out to sift through his garbage. There was no attempt to demonize him personally. He was not "borked" by third-party surrogates.

Unlike questions raised in many of these debates, what Mr. Lee would or would not do if confirmed is no longer hypothetical. Despite the negative Senate vote, President Clinton broke with tradition and recess appointed Mr. Lee twice. As a result, Mr. Lee served as the de facto assistant attorney general for approximately three years, and his record of promoting race-based policies is well documented.

He repeatedly sought the imposition of consent decrees—court-enforced hiring and promotion formulas—designed to lock state and local government, as well as businesses, into statistically based racial preferences. One of the lawsuits he championed actually resulted in the Justice Department's being forced to pay more than $2 million because the court found the lawsuit was frivolous and without foundation, a highly unusual result for the department. He even rushed through the filing of seven more questionable suits in the final month before President Bush took office. This time, the concerns over the nominee were well-founded.

The time has come for the Senate to reconsider its treatment of judicial nominees. Unfortunately, there is no easy way to put the genie back in the bottle.

After Judge Bork was defeated, one of my Republican colleagues, who had a well-deserved reputation for voting on candidates according to their qualifications rather than their politics, told me he had changed his mind. He was so angry about what had happened that he vowed never again to follow the rule of giving the presumption to a president's nominee. From now on, he would base his vote to confirm or reject nominees on their political preferences.

It is an understandable but dangerous attitude. Activist judges are a danger to everyone, an equal threat to conservatives and liberals alike. If judges are free to create new laws and enforce new rights, a conservative judge could create, for example, a "right" to a balanced federal budget. A liberal judge could create a "right" to homosexual marriages or drug use. These are issues that should not be resolved by a court but by an elected legislature.

Moreover, trying to judge a person's political views is a less-than-accurate science. Judicial appointments are for life. You may think you know what a person believes today, but there is no guarantee that these opinions will remain intact over the course of a career of perhaps several decades. David Souter, John Paul Stevens and Earl Warren, to name a few, all defied expectations.

Politicizing the confirmation process also undermines the constitutionally required separation of powers. Our framers wisely determined that if the people wanted new rights or authorities, they had to rely upon the legislative process: The participants stand for reelection and can be held accountable for their actions or failure to act. Once put in place, however, a political judiciary is virtually immune, answering only to themselves.

Similarly, the politicization of the confirmation process undermines the independence of the judiciary by eroding its quality. A litigant is entitled to a judge who is free of any taint of political prejudice, bias and personal agenda. The more politically partisan the nomination process, the more likely its only survivors will be either political partisans or persons adept at nonanswers.

The Senate was granted the advice and consent power to prevent the appointment of "unfit characters." This authority was not intended to authorize a single-issue litmus test for nominees.

There are several immediate steps the Senate could take to help depoliticize judicial confirmations. First, there should be an agreement to stop treating the nomination process like an election. Nominees are not political candidates. They do not have the same privilege or opportunity to debate their opponents or to combat false allegations with advertisements, press conferences and public statements. The Senate must recognize that hopelessly one-sided hearings are neither fair nor conducive to discerning the truth. Nominees need to be treated differently than an opposing candidate in an election. The confirmation process needs to be returned to an inquiry about judicial qualifications instead of the permanent game of "gotcha."

Second, we must reach an understanding about efforts to force nominees to pledge in advance how they will vote on issues that will come before the court. The pattern of litmus testing of nominees will ultimately paralyze the confirmation process as the number of issues to which these tests are applied increases. They reflect a fundamental misunderstanding of the role and necessary independence of the judiciary.

Third, the committee must stop tolerating the leaking of information about nominees. The leaking of confidential material, particularly FBI reports and similar documents, is a felony. Moreover, access to most of this information is limited to the senators themselves and a few confidential staffers working for the Chairman and Ranking Member. It is impossible to explain how a leaker could not be identified if every member of the committee were genuinely interested in stopping the practice.

Fourth, the committee needs to stop relying on third-party organizations to combat nominations. One of the most unfortunate legacies of the Bork confirmation fight was the formation of a loose coalition of left-wing special interest groups whose sole purpose is defeating Republican judicial and administrative nominees. While these groups obviously have a right to engage in any congressional process, the reality is that their tactics have played a major role in the polarization of confirmations. They were responsible for many of the false rumors spread about Judge Bork, the repeated misrepresentation of fact, and a level of hysteria that undermined the committee's ability to carry out its responsibilities dispassionately.

They have also had the unintended consequence of making it much more difficult for Republicans to vote against a Republican nominee. When the confirmation process becomes so partisan, every individual nomination becomes a party issue. Because the confirmation is a test of political will rather than a hearing on the merits of the nominee, disapproval of the nominee is tantamount to disapproval of the party.

The time has come to stop coordinating attacks on nominees with these organizations and to begin giving their concerns no more weight than is afforded the opinions of other special interest groups having no responsibility for balance or moderation. A judicial nomination should not be lobbied as if it were a bill.

Finally, nominees, especially appellate court and Supreme Court nominees, should be afforded the right to a timely hearing and consideration by the full Senate. Both sides deserve some blame here because we both have delayed hearings, committee votes and floor consideration. No nomination should be kept before the committee indefinitely. Confirmation should be measured in months, not years.

Making these changes would require both Republicans and Democrats to be forthright about the blocking of nominees that now goes on in relative anonymity. Adoption of such a standard would also diminish the use of nominations as bargaining chips in other matters before the Senate.

Moreover, adoption of these ideas would dissipate some of the current animosity that is poisoning the Senate. We need to recognize that the constant haggling over judicial nominees has not only impaired the ability of the Judiciary Committee to function effectively, it also has undermined the chamber's constitutional responsibility to provide advice and consent. Today, this phrase might be more aptly described as advice and dissent.

If these basic standards had been honored in the past, the degeneration of the confirmation process that began with Justice Rehnquist would not have continued with Judge Bork, nor reached rock bottom with Clarence Thomas.

Chapter Seven

A High-Tech Lynching

He jests at scars that never felt a wound.
—William Shakespeare,
Romeo and Juliet

WHEN President George Bush nominated Judge Clarence Thomas to replace retiring Justice Thurgood Marshall on July 1, 1991, no one thought it would be an easy confirmation. But no one thought it would turn into the most controversial confirmation in modern history.

I had known Clarence for more than a decade and had either presided over or been involved in all of his four previous nominations. He is a thoughtful, exceptional man whose life is a tribute to his remarkable abilities, perseverance and courage.

He grew up near Savannah, Georgia, experiencing firsthand the physical and mental torment of segregation. He was raised primarily by his maternal grandparents, and his grandfather was the son of a freed slave. The household was poor, but the preparation for life was invaluable. The family believed in God, hard work and self-sufficiency. There were no shortcuts. There would be no free rides.

After briefly considering becoming a priest, Clarence attended Holy Cross University and graduated with honors in 1971. He went on to law school at Yale University and graduated near the top of his class. He then moved to the Midwest to take a job in the Office of the Attorney General of Missouri, who at the time was the moderate Republican John Danforth.

After a brief stint in the private sector, Clarence joined now Senator Danforth's staff in Washington, D.C. In 1981, following the election of Ronald Reagan, he was nominated and confirmed as an Assistant Secretary of Education. It was there that he met and hired another graduate of Yale Law School, Anita Hill.

In 1982, Clarence was nominated to be Chairman of the Equal Employment Opportunity Commission (EEOC), the lead federal agency charged with combating discrimination in the workplace. His public positions on racial issues, preferential hiring and quotas were already raising eyebrows among the civil rights establishment.

Clarence seemed to revel in the controversy, but he took his job at the commission seriously. The agency he inherited might have been acceptable politically, but it was an administrative nightmare. The backlog of unresolved cases exceeded 12,000, even though many complaints were being summarily settled as if they were car insurance claims. Financially, things were even worse. For several years, the agency had been lying about the state of its debts, which ranged from $27 million in unliquidated obligations to more than $1.2 million in unpaid travel advances for staff. The financial situation was so dire that staff lawyers had to bring their own copy paper to work. Office supply companies were tired of never having their bills paid.

Under Clarence's stewardship, the agency received full approval of its accounting system for the first time, obtained record amounts of monetary damages for victims of discrimination, increased the number of cases going to litigation, and significantly reduced the backlog. Clarence made the EEOC a functioning enforcement agency and not just a source of rhetoric. He accomplished this remarkable turn-around even though he was fought every inch of the way by civil rights leaders, the Democrats in the House and his critics in the media, all of whom deplored his refusal to accede to their philosophy of civil rights enforcement. Almost every year, the House Democrats slashed President Reagan's proposed budget for the EEOC, and it would fall on the Republicans in the Senate to restore the monies. Despite all this, Clarence succeeded to the point where even the *Washington Post* editorial page was forced to acknowledge his accomplishments.

None of that mattered to his critics. When he came before the Labor Committee after being renominated as the commission's chair-man, he was attacked again for his refusal to endorse quotas and to automatically equate any statistical disparity with discrimination. According to his critics, these were opinions African Americans should not have and were evidence of an insufficient commitment to civil rights.

Clarence bridled at the notion that there was only one right way for an African American to think about discrimination. As he repeatedly testified, the courts demanded something more than just a difference in the numbers. He argued that to eliminate discrimination, we need-ed to understand what caused the disparity and not focus exclusively on statistics. Otherwise, the real problems would never be corrected.

Moreover, he made clear that he believed more in self-help than in quotas, and that the problem with preferential treatment was twofold. First, if it was given, it could always be taken away. Second, it tended to benefit the black middle class more than those most in need. He wanted to refocus attention on what he perceived to be the real impediments to advancement, such as a lack of education, teen preg-nancies, and alcohol and drug abuse.

Outside of Congress, Clarence was called an "Uncle Tom," a sell-out and a traitor to his race. He also came under attack by several organizations on the right, as well as by some within the Reagan

White House, who objected to his criticism of several administration policies he felt were discriminatory. Not surprisingly, there were rumors that he might quit, but Clarence was determined to stay. His grandfather had taught him when he was a child that you always finish what you start.

It was a lonely, embattled course he set for himself. Yet, amid a level of personal invective that would have crippled or exhausted most of us, he not only persevered but seemed to flourish. As he once commented to me, being the only black at his Catholic high school for two years was good training for a career in Washington.

Despite the criticism, before being selected for the Supreme Court, he was nominated four times to posts that required Senate approval, and each time he was confirmed by a larger majority than necessary. This included his appointment in 1990 to the United States Court of Appeals for the District of Columbia, ironically to take the seat vacated by Judge Bork.

In 1991, President Bush nominated Clarence Thomas to the seat on the Supreme Court vacated by the retirement of Justice Thurgood Marshall, a legendary attorney and jurist who also had served as the legal director of the NAACP, an appellate court judge, and the Solicitor General of the United States. Among his many achievements was winning the landmark decision in *Brown v. Board of Education*, which declared the segregation of public schools illegal.

The nomination got off to a rocky start immediately. Introducing his nominee, President Bush described Clarence as "the most qualified man for the Court at this time." It was the kind of compliment that begs to be challenged and contradicted no matter who is the nominee. Clarence was targeted immediately.

Moreover, for some, the description had a different meaning. Clarence was only the second African American ever nominated to the Court and had been selected to replace the only African American who had served as a justice. Liberals suspected Bush of creating a "black" seat, the very kind of quota that Clarence supposedly abhorred. Moreover, they considered it a slap in the face that Bush would choose to replace Justice Marshall with a conservative, especially one who did not share their view of the law. Apparently, they believed that while it was offensive to treat the seat as if it were subject to a racial quota, it clearly was controlled by a political quota.

Things got ugly quickly. The groups and associations that had led the campaign against Bork four years earlier quickly went public with their threats. Feminist leaders vowed to "bork" him and to "kill him" politically. I have always been amazed by the double standard in Washington and with the media. It is not hard to imagine the reaction if a Republican or a conservative organization had used this kind of terminology about a Democratic nominee to the Supreme Court.

The Bork blueprint was implemented again. Stories accusing Clarence of a variety of terrible things began to appear in the press. Rumors were recounted as facts. Again, allegations were more important than accuracy.

Questions were raised about whether, as a Catholic, he would be controlled by the Pope. Then it was "discovered" that there was a lien for failure to pay taxes. In fact, the taxes had been paid, but the lien had never been quashed. Rumors were spread that he had beaten his first wife. These sleazy but always anonymous slanders were also put to rest. Not only did Clarence and his former wife get along, she permitted him to have custody of their only child, Jamal. Clarence is a devoted father who has an unbridled pride in his son.

Jack Danforth, one of the Senate's most respected members, was relentless in his public defense of Clarence. In private, he counseled his former staffer every step of the way. In public, Jack and I rebutted every charge made in the media. We responded to every allegation raised during the hearings. We spoke repeatedly on the Senate floor in Clarence's defense and often met with the press to answer their questions.

Jack put his considerable reputation on the line for Clarence. It is a tribute to his character and his understanding of friendship that he never wavered even when it looked as if his support for Clarence might endanger his own political career. He proved that there are some members who still value loyalty and friendship more than their own reelection.

When his hearing opened in September 1991, most of the committee began by noting how much they respected the nominee's personal accomplishments. The Democrats then began to find fault.

A member of the committee announced he would oppose Clarence unless he promised to always vote in favor of abortion rights. Another claimed Clarence was undistinguished; yet another that he lacked experience. One observed that he was a radical who would apply theories of natural law to overturn the language of the Constitution.

This last charge was based on Clarence's assertion that one had to look to the natural law of the Declaration of Independence to justify his belief in equality, because the Constitution had been interpreted by the Court to permit slavery.

Clarence repeatedly refused to take the bait, knowing that anything he said would be turned against him. The Democrats made a big issue of his reticence, accusing him of undergoing a "confirmation conversion," of being evasive to hide his real opinions. This criticism would persist throughout the hearings, even though Clarence was really following the advice of Senator Ted Kennedy. When Thurgood Marshall was being confirmed, Ted had argued eloquently that nominees to the Supreme Court should defer making any comments about issues that might come before the Court, and that their deference had to be respected.

Nonetheless, the Democrats continued to pressure him to say something about a raft of topics likely to come before the Court, especially abortion. There were more than seventy questions on this issue alone. Clarence dodged their requests, saying repeatedly that he had not yet made up his mind on the issue. Questions were asked about whether he had ever discussed *Roe* v. *Wade,* for instance among classmates in law school. Choosing his words carefully, he responded that he had never *debated* the case.

The Democrats howled in anger. How could anyone, especially someone in law school, not have "discussed" the case? He had to be lying. Every time the Democrats made this charge, I would remind them that his answer had been worded very carefully. Clarence had testified that he had never "debated" the case, not that he had never "discussed" it. My defense fell on deaf ears.

Obviously, Clarence's answer was very carefully worded, but that was because he and the Bush White House understood that the rules had changed. After the Bork nomination, the administration realized that there was no longer any benefit to having a nominee engage in an open and forthright discussion. Anything he or she said would not be judged on its merits but used instead to validate predetermined positions and complaints. Confirmation hearings were no longer about discerning judicial temperament; they were simply about winning and losing.

The one issue the Democrats did not raise was Clarence's attitude toward preferences and quotas. It was clear they had little interest, given his knowledge and expertise in the area, to debate employment discrimination policy with him in such a public forum.

There was another reason for the Democrats' reluctance: Clarence was no stranger to congressional hearings. He had testified before Congress more than fifty times and not only understood but no longer feared the process. He was used to the loaded questions, the constant interruptions, the whispering of staff in a member's ear. He was not cowed by the verbal taunts and ridicule that often pass for questions. In fact, he was known to relish sparring with members. And he had learned to wait for the right opportunity.

Several years before, he had undergone a lengthy grilling by Senator Kennedy about employment law. The questions had been a mix of inquiries, prepared observations, public criticisms and cross-examination. Clarence had taken it all, answering every question with the same deliberate, moderated tone. Senator Kennedy concluded by stating that Clarence should be ashamed of his opinion of the law and his lack of commitment to combating employment discrimination.

Clarence asked for permission to respond. He spoke slowly, choosing his words carefully. In his grandparents' small house where he had been raised, there had been only three pictures. One was of Jesus Christ; one was of Martin Luther King; and the third was of President John F. Kennedy. Each was revered, he said, his voice booming. "Senator," Clarence snapped, his face rigid with anger, "if your brother were here today, he would be the one ashamed."

During another hearing, a member of the House had challenged Clarence's discomfort with the legal theory of comparable worth, asking whether he had any idea how difficult a job such as nursing was for women.

As a matter of a fact, Clarence answered, he was aware of their difficulty. For years, his mother had worked as a maid to a couple of nurses. "I know exactly how hard they had it," he observed. The congressman quickly moved on to another point.

No one on the Judiciary Committee wanted to risk a similar exchange in front of so many cameras and reporters.

After the Judiciary Committee had finished questioning Clarence, seventy-five witnesses gave their views on his nomination. Some supported confirmation. Not surprisingly, given that the Democrats controlled the committee and thus the witness list, most opposed it.

The committee voted on September 27, 1991. Dennis DeConcini, a Democrat from Arizona, joined the six Republicans in support of the nomination. All the other Democrats voted against. With the vote a tie, the committee sent the nomination to the floor without recommendation. This action followed the tradition that the entire Senate should vote on a Supreme Court nominee, regardless of the outcome in the Judiciary Committee.

It seemed clear that, despite the divided committee, Clarence would be confirmed. Several Democrats were so worried over the inevitability of a favorable vote that they began to discuss mounting a filibuster to the nomination. The historic irony was apparently lost on them. After years of decrying the use of filibusters to derail or impede the passage of civil rights laws, they were ready to use the same parliamentary procedure to block a vote on only the second African American ever nominated to the Supreme Court. Moreover, filibusters had never been used against Supreme Court nominees. It simply wasn't done.

Fortunately, wiser heads on the Democratic side prevailed, and the idea was dropped. Nonetheless, floor action was delayed to give the opponents additional time to find anything that could be used to derail Clarence's confirmation. It was only after Senator Dole and I refused to clear the Family and Medical Leave Act, a Democratic legislative priority, that they relented and scheduled a vote for October 8.

As the vote drew near and more members made their decision public, it became evident that the Democratic objections to his confirmation boiled down to two issues. First, he did not promise in advance to always vote in favor of abortion rights. Second, his opinions on a variety of issues were not consistent with the views many Democrats normally expected from someone of his race. Neither would be sufficient to stop his confirmation.

Suddenly, on Saturday, October 4, 1991, everything changed. According to *Newsday*, a committee member or staffer had leaked a statement by his former assistant, Anita Hill, asserting that Clarence had sexually harassed her when she had worked for him in 1981 and 1982.

This was not news to the Judiciary Committee. When Senator Biden, the committee Chairman, had first learned about the allegation, he had informed the Ranking Member, Strom Thurmond. As was customary, they jointly asked the FBI to check out the story. The bureau completed a thorough examination, and its report was given to Biden, who shared it with every Democrat on the committee and Thurmond. He, in turn, shared it with Alan Simpson and me.

No member raised the issue. No one asked for additional information or sought a broader investigation. The charges were more than ten years old, they were uncorroborated, and Ms. Hill had refused to testify. In addition, the committee understood that FBI reports are compilations of raw information. They record what has been said, not necessarily what is true. Any statement made to an investigator, no matter how outlandish or slanderous, is included in the report. For this reason, the Judiciary Committee normally goes to great lengths to protect the confidentiality of these documents.

Ms. Hill agonized for several months about submitting a statement, talking at great length with several Democratic staffers, at least one senator, and other individuals intimately involved in the campaign to defeat Clarence. Apparently, she wanted the committee to learn of her accusations without being identified, hoping the nominee would then withdraw rather than have the story become public. Those in Washington knew differently. They understood that her desire to submit her allegations either anonymously or in confidence would significantly diminish the attention they received from the committee.

Now that the accusations had been printed in the media, positions changed. The committee had no choice but to address the charges publicly. Moreover, Ms. Hill's reticence evaporated and she quickly held a televised press conference in which she criticized the committee for its indifference to sexual harassment.

Upon learning the news, I called Clarence at his home. He was devastated, wondering if any position was worth the pain and humiliation he was experiencing. I asked whether there was anything upon which Ms. Hill could base her charges, no matter how obscure or remote. He said he could think of nothing.

The only point of contention had been Clarence's appointment of someone else to a position Ms. Hill had wanted. He said they had worked together for roughly two years and had maintained a cordial relationship after she left the commission to teach at Oral Roberts University. He also noted that she had called him several times since leaving. I asked about phone records, and Clarence replied that he thought her calls, like anyone else's, would be listed in the official logs.

He then asked if I thought he could still be confirmed. I assured him he would, that one day he would be considered one of the great Supreme Court justices.

I knew that the nomination would be delayed so that the committee could deal with Ms. Hill's allegations. I also realized that because of the nature of the charges and the hysteria they had generated, the normal hearing process would be woefully inadequate. This was no longer a confirmation hearing or even a political campaign. It had become a trial. Clarence's opponents were convinced they had found the smoking gun.

Early the following week, Bob Dole, Strom Thurmond, Alan Simpson, Jack Danforth and I huddled in Bob's office in the Capitol to discuss how best to handle the inquiry. I recommended that instead of having all eighteen members of the committee question Clarence and Ms. Hill for only five minutes each, one senator per side should be responsible for leading the questioning. That way, there would be a more legitimate and orderly flow to the inquiry and thus a better opportunity for the issues to be discussed.

The others quickly agreed. Now it was a question of who would take the lead.

Someone suggested that I should be responsible for questioning Ms. Hill. I disagreed, arguing instead that it should be Arlen Specter of Pennsylvania. The others thought I had lost my mind. Simpson pointed out that Arlen was the most liberal Republican on the committee. He had voted against Judge Bork and was an advocate of abortion rights.

That is exactly why he should be the Republican questioner, I responded. He was a diligent, deliberate questioner whom the media would not automatically suspect of being biased or unfair. I told them Arlen was a great lawyer who would back Clarence. Moreover, as Arlen often reminded us, he was a former prosecutor and had considerable trial experience questioning witnesses.

Strom Thurmond then seconded my suggestion, on the condition that I be responsible for questioning Clarence. The others agreed. Bob Dole called Arlen, who readily accepted the assignment.

On Friday, October 11, the Judiciary Committee reconvened. The hearing room was packed, the halls around it overflowing with cameras, reporters and onlookers. I stood outside the entrance waiting for Clarence. I wanted to wish him well.

As he came up the stairs, the stress and exhaustion visible on his face, hundreds of people began to cheer, calling out their support. His spirits seemed to lift. I stepped forward and we shook hands, then hugged. I asked if he was ready. He said he was.

Senator Biden gaveled the hearing to order. Clarence testified first and denied the charges. He then pointed out eloquently:

> I am proud of my life, proud of what I have done, and what I have accomplished, proud of my family, and this process, this process is destroying it all. No job is worth what I have been through, no job. No horror in my life has been so debilitating. Confirm me if you want, don't confirm me if you are so led, but let this process end. Let me and my family regain our lives.[1]

To our surprise, Senator Biden then announced that we could not refer to the FBI report in our questioning of Clarence. Ms. Hill had asked that the report be kept confidential until she testified.

I objected as strenuously as I could, arguing that it was a little late to be worrying about the report's confidentiality. Someone had already taken care of that. I made it clear that we intended to refer to specific portions of her statement in our questions to Clarence.

The debate quickly escalated, and Biden wisely recessed the committee. We went across the hall to Ted Kennedy's personal office to finish the discussion in private. While we were arguing, Danforth passed in a message that Clarence would be willing to allow Ms. Hill to testify and be questioned first, provided he was guaranteed the opportunity to respond the same day no matter how late the hearing ran.

Both sides felt the proposal would work. For the Democrats, the arrangement ensured that Ms. Hill would be able to testify. Since her questioning would occupy most of the day, she would dominate the evening news. We were convinced the proposal guaranteed Clarence the chance to respond to her charges immediately. Prime time was no longer an issue. The hearing itself had become prime time and would be so from beginning to end.

The United States stopped to watch. People gathered around television sets in offices, schools and homes. They wanted to see who these two people were and decide for themselves which one to believe.

Ms. Hill gave a statement that included several examples of offensive remarks Clarence had allegedly made to her, which she related with little apparent emotion. She was an impressive witness and her testimony was mesmerizing.

Senator Specter did a remarkable job of questioning her. In a methodical, matter-of-fact manner, he took her through her testimony, pointing out discrepancies between her vision of certain events and statements by others. She tried to dismiss these differences, noting:

"Well, I think that if you start to look at each individual problem with this statement, then you're not going to be satisfied that it's true, but I think the statement has to be taken as a whole."[2]

After she finished, I walked out of the hearing room and was immediately besieged by the press. One news anchor from network television pushed a microphone into my face and observed, "Well, it's all over, isn't it?"

"I've been in many trials in my lifetime," I answered, smiling as best I could. "You've only heard one witness. Wait until you've heard from him."

As I was talking, I could hear Nina Totenberg, the correspondent for National Public Radio who had been instrumental in publicizing the leaks about Ms. Hill's allegations, talking as if the hearing was all but over. Apparently, she and others in the media believed the nomination was dead. They didn't know Clarence.

Although I would be questioning Clarence, I had not had a chance to talk with him about what I would ask or how he would answer. I rushed to Senator Danforth's office, where I knew Clarence and his wife, Ginny, were waiting to return to the hearing room.

Not waiting to be introduced, I brushed past the staffers in the outer office, who had jumped up to stop me, opened the door to Jack's personal office and walked inside. Clarence was pacing back and forth, madder than I had ever seen him. We chatted briefly. Remembering his rebuke to Senator Kennedy during an earlier confirmation, I told him to be himself, to tell the truth and not to "take any crap from anyone."

When he returned to the committee that evening, he was a different man. Gone was the reticent nominee who was worried about his own confirmation, who was willing to play the ridiculous game that confirmations had become. In his place was the real Clarence Thomas: a man who had overcome every obstacle that had stood in his way, who had beaten the odds and excelled in grade school, in college, and at one of the nation's elite law schools.

The real Clarence Thomas took no shortcuts and expected no handouts or special treatment. He sat before the committee, tried, convicted, and condemned before he could say a word in his defense. Still, he was not intimidated. This day was no different from every day of his childhood. He was ready, and he was angry.

My questions were designed to let him tell his story at his own pace. He ran with every opportunity. He denied every allegation expressly. There was nothing left for interpretation, no possible room for something to be misconstrued. Everything Ms. Hill claimed, he emphatically said was false.

He faced every member of the committee, staring at each as he spoke. He was tired of the lies, he said, tired of the innuendos and false accusations. It was time for this "national disgrace" to stop.

He paused, and the hearing room collectively held its breath. And then Clarence, the anger dripping from his words, said,

> This is a circus. It is a national disgrace. And from my standpoint, as a black American, as far as I am concerned, it is a high-tech lynching for uppity blacks who in any way deign to think for themselves, to do for themselves, to have different ideas, and it is a message that, unless you kow-tow to an old order, that is what will happen to you, you will be lynched, destroyed, caricatured by a committee of the United States Senate rather than hung from a tree.[3]

The entire nation gasped in shock.

His rebuttal was powerful, convincing and complete. I knew that millions of Americans who were watching on television were convinced he was telling the truth.

Inside the room, something else was happening. The Democrats looked taken aback. No nominee had ever spoken to them as Clarence had just done. He had made it clear he would no longer silently tolerate the Senate's double standard—one set of rules for nominees and another set for senators—and he let them know he no longer cared whether he was confirmed. The implication hung in the air. If the Democrats wanted to try him, fine. He was ready to try them. Let his personal conduct be measured against their behavior. Let the truth about the allegations against him be matched against the truth about the allegations that had been made against the members of the committee.

The questioning did not last long.

When I walked out of the hearing room after Clarence had finished, Nina Totenberg grabbed me.

"You just saved his ass," she said.

"No, Nina, he just saved his ass," I answered.

"I don't know what to believe," she said. "I believe them both!"

"No, Nina, only one of them is telling the truth," I responded, "and it's Judge Thomas."

She was not alone in her confusion. Most of the country was trying to work out who was telling the truth. The statements of the two could not have been more opposite and could not be reconciled. You could believe Clarence or you could believe Ms. Hill, but not both.

The hearings continued. We heard from additional witnesses, some who supported Ms. Hill's testimony and others who repudiated it.

After reviewing all the testimony, all the documents and all the investigative reports, I had no doubt Clarence was telling the truth. To believe otherwise, one would have to assume that a large number of unrelated and unaffiliated people had conspired against Ms. Hill, some before anyone even knew she would make any allegations against Clarence.

According to the record, Clarence offered her a position at the Department of Education because she was in trouble at the firm where she was working. She denied this, but representatives from the law firm testified that they had told her she needed to find a new job.

Despite her charges that Clarence had harassed her while at the Education Department, she followed him to the EEOC. She said she had no choice and was worried about keeping her job. In fact, she held a position that could not be eliminated and she had been asked to stay by Clarence's successor.

She said that Clarence asked her out and made sexually harassing statements in his office. Clarence's secretary, a Democrat and older African American woman with a reputation for tolerating absolutely no nonsense, disagreed. She testified that she sat just outside Clarence's office and that he always kept his door open. She heard everything he said in his office, and she had never heard anything like what Ms. Hill claimed. She said, "That simply did not happen."

Ms. Hill claimed she resigned from her job because of Clarence's behavior. Why then did she continue to call him more than fifteen times after she had left the EEOC? She testified he made the calls. The phone records indicated, however, that she made the calls, and the messages indicated she was seeking his advice.

If he had been such a sexual harasser, why did she invite him to speak at Oral Roberts University on sexual harassment? Why did she offer to drive him back to the airport? She said she did not make the offer. Others who were there said she did.

Why did she tell two witnesses that it was a good thing that Clarence Thomas had been nominated to the Supreme Court?

To believe Ms. Hill, one has to believe that her coworkers at the Department of Education, the EEOC, her old law firm, and Oral Roberts University, as well as fellow attendees at the American Bar Association, FBI agents and Clarence Thomas all lied about her or misrepresented what she said.

At that point, I had known Clarence Thomas for more than a decade. I knew him to be a man of substance and honor. If he had asked Ms. Hill out or said what she had claimed, he would have admitted it.

At the end of the hearings on Saturday, Elaine and I invited the Thomases to dinner at Morton's Steakhouse, near our suburban Virginia home. I told him that now was not the time to go into hiding. We asked the Danforths to join us.

Reluctantly, Clarence agreed. When we got there, heads spun, and the restaurant fell quiet as we were seated. Then, to my surprise, people began to walk over to our table. They wanted to congratulate Clarence and offer their support. A group of young women came over. Each one told him they believed his testimony and hoped he was confirmed.

Just after we had been served our meal, I looked up in surprise to see Judge Robert Bork and Ted Olsen,[4] now the Solicitor General, approaching us. It was a singular moment. Bob was probably the only other person in the United States who could really appreciate what

Clarence was feeling. The rest of us watched mesmerized as the two men whose nominations had so radically changed the Senate confirmation process hugged and talked quietly.

When we got up to leave, the entire restaurant, the wait staff, customers and kitchen workers gave Clarence a standing ovation. It was an exhilarating moment for a proud but emotionally exhausted man. It was a reaffirmation of what he had spent his life trying to achieve. People had not just heard him speak on television; they believed what he said. I am convinced Clarence left the restaurant ready for the remainder of the ordeal. He knew he was not alone.

Several days later, the Senate confirmed Clarence Thomas by a vote of 52 to 48. We who were involved in the hearings will never be the same. In their aftermath, I have been accused of many things, primarily of cruelty and insensitivity for the way I questioned Anita Hill. In fact, I never asked her a single question. I also have repeatedly been told that the real problem was that I "just didn't get it." I am convinced I "got it" more than most.

If any good came out of the needlessly tortured and vicious confirmation, it was that the nation was forced to confront the reality, too often ignored or discounted, of sexual harassment in the workplace. My skepticism with Ms. Hill's testimony was not over the consequences or seriousness of sexual harassment. I have three daughters and thirteen granddaughters. I have absolutely no desire that they or any other woman suffer from discriminatory treatment or be forced to work in a sexually hostile environment. It would be incredibly myopic on my part, however, to believe that such things might never happen.

What I did get was that this nomination had become a trial, with all the incumbent difficult, unpleasant and messy aspects of litigation. Questions were asked that normally never would have been raised in a congressional setting. Answers were examined and dissected. Inconsistencies were highlighted and witnesses were cross-examined, just as they are in court.

Ms. Hill's testimony was not treated like the statements of other witnesses, and neither was Clarence's. The members of the Judiciary Committee did not comport themselves as they normally do. We were no longer senators. We were forced to become prosecutors, defense counsels and judges.

And the question before us was not simply the seriousness of the alleged acts, or whether such behavior if true should weigh heavily against a nominee's fitness to hold a position in the federal judiciary. The question was whether the allegations were true.

In the end, like my colleagues, I had to pass judgment. Based on the evidence, I believed Clarence. For me, it was not a difficult decision.

Every Republican who sat on the committee has paid a price. We have all been permanently tagged for what we did or for what people are convinced we did. Alan Simpson and I have been especially singled out. On the day Clarence was sworn in, a woman screamed a stream of epithets when she saw me entering the White House gate. When I got close to her, she spit at me. Fortunately, her aim did not equal her venom.

Shortly thereafter, I fulfilled an obligation to give a speech at the Federalist Society at the University of Chicago Law School. It was supposed to be a small gathering of around 150 members and their guests. When I arrived on campus, I learned I would be speaking in a hall that seated roughly five hundred. According to the organizers, an estimated eight hundred people were already crammed inside, and there were demonstrators outside. Most held placards denouncing me and protesting my attendance.

I had been asked to speak for about twenty-five minutes and then allow time for questions and answers. At first, every time I tried to speak, the protestors would rattle the placards, and the rumbling noise would drown out what I was saying. I could only speak in short bursts. Gradually, as their arms grew tired, they began to let me speak for longer periods. One woman sitting near the front chose a different strategy. Every time I opened my mouth, she would scream, "Pig," "Swine" or "Fascist," among other epithets. It was impossible not to notice her.

One of the cardinal rules of public speaking is never let a heckler, no matter how disruptive, get to you. At first, I tried to respond humorously. It didn't work. She started cursing, so I stopped paying attention and tried to speak over her.

After an hour, I finally had enough. After one particularly offensive, epithet-laden tirade, I stopped and stared at her. The auditorium fell silent, waiting to see what I would say.

"At first, I thought you might be a student at this great school of law," I said, looking right in her eyes. "Now, I realize for two reasons you couldn't be—because, first, you are so rude and, second, you are so stupid."

To my amazement, the audience broke out in a roar of approval. Even the protestors calmed down. I was allowed to finish my remarks and was given a standing ovation, if not for my talk, at least for my patience.

To this day I encounter people who will express their support for something I have done but then observe that they cannot forgive me for the way I treated Anita Hill. It never changes their minds when I point out that I didn't question her.

I understand that this doesn't matter. My real offense was my relentless defense of Clarence Thomas, in which I clearly did not act like an independent, dispassionate observer. Simply keeping quiet or holding myself above the fray, no matter what was being said or done, might have been the safe thing to do, but in this instance it was not my role. My responsibility was to stand up for the nominee in whom I believed, to serve as a brake if I could on the relentless campaign against his confirmation.

Moreover, while some take umbrage over Ms. Hill's treatment by the committee, I was offended by what was being done to Clarence.

He did not deserve to be railroaded by his opponents, who were calling on several of the most unseemly racial stereotypes of our not-so-distant past: a black man who was not very smart, who had gotten his jobs because of the color of his skin rather than his abilities, and who was a sexual predator. For Clarence, it would be hard to imagine a more vicious set of accusations. They not only represented a repudiation of his efforts to break free of the bigotry of his past, they tried to make a mockery of his belief that what you earn is far more important than what you are given.

Not everyone will agree with what I did or my reasons for doing it. Some claim I was too willing to overlook a serious allegation purely for partisan, political reasons. Obviously, I disagree, although I have found this accusation rather ironic given the thunderous silence from these very same critics when reports of President Clinton's assorted misuses and abuses of women came to light. Apparently, when the accused is a Democratic president, critics are more than willing to attack and blame the accusers.

Many will continue to let me know about their displeasure. I don't mind. If occasional discomfort is the price I have to pay for helping Clarence Thomas become a Supreme Court justice, it is still a bargain.

The consequences are not always unpleasant. Years after the hearing, I was talking with a good friend, the highly successful and brutally honest novelist Patricia Cornwell. We started talking about Clarence Thomas. Patsy cautioned that although I had been able to change her mind about a great number of things, I would be wasting my breath defending Clarence.

I pointed out that he was an exceptional and courageous person who had been treated more unjustly than any other nominee I had known. Even if you put the worst spin on what Anita Hill claimed, he never touched her. He never made demands or threatened her job. At most, if you believe her, what he said in her presence was crude and insensitive but on the whole rather tame in comparison to more recent developments. I again explained that Clarence is so forthright that if he had done anything even remotely comparable to what she claimed, he would have admitted it.

Patsy said that I would never be able to convince her that Ms. Hill was not telling the truth, either consciously or unconsciously.

"I might not be able to," I said, "but I'll bet that if you spoke to Clarence for ten minutes, he could change your mind." She laughed dismissively. I told her to call me the next time she came to town, and I would see if Clarence had time to meet her.

Well, as luck would have it, an opportunity did arise, and Clarence agreed to stop by. It was like two thunderbolts crashing together when they met. Neither is shy or hesitant. They began to argue immediately. The conversation flew back and forth. I sat to one side, like a spectator at a tennis match, my head bobbing back and forth.

After about ten minutes, Patsy turned to me in exasperation and said, "Okay, you win. He couldn't have done what she accused him of doing."

If only Clarence had the time and interest to meet all his detractors.

After the fights over Rehnquist, Bork and Thomas, it will be extremely difficult for the Senate to avoid another confirmation debacle. Until the members decide that both sides have more to gain from eliminating the political trial than perpetuating it, nominees will continue to risk being sent through the gauntlet, where they will be picked and prodded in a prolonged game of "gotcha." The vast majority will continue to be confirmed, but some good people, both Democrats and Republicans, will be humiliated, their reputations smeared and their personal lives unnecessarily exposed by a process that is out of control.

Chapter Eight

Did I Really Do That?

*Everybody has an innate talent for
mistakes. Some of us just have more
talent than others.*

—Kevin McGuiness

Y ou cannot serve in public office for twenty-five years without
making your share of gaffes, mistakes, misjudgments and simply
dumb, dumb, inexplicable decisions. I certainly have my own little
pantheon of blunders and wrong votes. There have been times when
my mouth has gotten far ahead of my brain, but I won't list them all.
My critics have proven more than capable of compiling their own
lists, although I am not sure theirs would match mine.

Some mistakes come at the least expected times. Others you
march to with bold determination, only to realize, in the reflective
clarity of a new day, that you have gotten it wrong.

For those of us in elective office, our wrongs are there for all to see,
on permanent public display. Your most insightful observations may
be forgotten almost before they are out of your mouth, but your misstatements are eternal. They will be replayed in the media until they
become part of your legacy.

Some mistakes are merely embarrassing. Several years ago, during the 1992 presidential campaign, I gave a series of stump speeches for Republican candidates in five or six western states. The schedule was so tightly packed that I would give a speech and then rush to the next location, sometimes as many as eight and nine times a day.

Individual locations and even whole days began to blur together. As we all became more exhausted, ordinary tasks became more difficult and the speeches more arduous.

For my last speech, I was given an unusually gracious and laudatory introduction before a large crowd. The attendees were clearly excited and were rooting for me before I even began. Energized by their enthusiasm, I began by pointing out how important the people of Idaho were going to be in the coming election. The room went dead. The energy was gone. Puzzled, I looked to the side of the stage and saw one of the organizers scribbling on a piece of paper. He turned it around so I could see what he had written. It said, "Senator, we're in Las Vegas."

I apologized to the crowd for my gaffe and moved on. Several minutes later, I had another opportunity, so I carefully chose my words and pointed out that the country was watching Wyoming. This time, the audience groaned. Over the next twenty minutes, I had several more chances to get the right location. I missed every one as I methodically worked my way around the West, citing every city in the Rockies but Las Vegas. By the end of my remarks, I don't know who wanted to get out of the room first—the audience or me.

More recently, I was invited to be a call-in guest on the Don Imus radio show. The program, which is broadcast out of New York but syndicated nationally, is extremely popular in political Washington. Regular listeners know it as an entertaining mixture of interviews, sports, news and the persistent retelling of an endless stream of inconsequential problems associated with being a billionaire radio announcer who is married to a stunning and intelligent woman, blessed with a precocious son, and surrounded by an entourage that could teach a Senate staff lessons about fawning.

Guests are expected to make an effort at being funny, so with the help of some friends, I dutifully prepared a series of jokes to cover the topics likely to come up during the interview. For some reason, however, the minute I went on the air, I couldn't control myself. Imus barely welcomed me before I jumped in and raced through every joke and observation I had prepared. I didn't wait for laughter. I barely paused to catch my breath. Imus didn't even have a chance to ask a question. I crammed ten minutes' worth of material into three, like some desperate comedian getting his first break on the Carson show. It was pathetic.

Afterwards, my chief of staff, Patricia Knight, poked her head into my office, a tight smile across her face. "What did you think?" I asked.

"Next time," she said, "I think you might want to work on one other thing."

"What's that?" I asked.

"Timing," she answered.

At moments like these, it helps to have an interest outside of work.

Other mistakes are far more serious. Bad votes affect a nation. In these circumstances, you have no other option but to correct the error if you can.

In 1988, Congress passed the Catastrophic Health Insurance bill. The bill was designed to limit the out-of-pocket costs for Medicare patients hospitalized for catastrophic illness and language was added providing Medicare coverage for drugs. It was widely endorsed by Republicans and Democrats, as well as special interest organizations such as the American Association of Retired Persons. The bill had flaws, but the problem it sought to address was so important that it was rushed through Congress before the election.

Unfortunately, when senior citizens found out they would actually have to pay for this new benefit, and sometimes quite a lot, they understandably became extremely upset. Shortly after the election, I began to hear complaints in my state from people who understood and detested the bill. The more I asked, the more widespread I found the opposition.

Many of my colleagues, from both sides of the aisle, were hearing the same thing. We all saw the televised report of angry seniors jumping up and down on the car owned by our colleague Dan Rostenkowski, the Chairman of the House Ways and Means Committee and an architect of the bill.

The next year, with our tails between our legs, we introduced and passed legislation repealing the Catastrophic Health bill. This time, we had the opportunity and willingness to collectively admit our error and correct it.

Every now and then you make a mistake that cannot be rectified, and it bothers you for the rest of your career. One of the worst decisions I have made as a senator was to vote against making Dr. Martin Luther King's birthday a national holiday. When it was proposed, the African American community was united in its support. Dr. King had ignited the cause of freedom and the constitutional right to individual civil rights with a success unmatched by any other African American leader since slavery was abolished. Even when encouraging and practicing civil disobedience, he insisted, no matter what response his actions provoked, the protests remain strictly nonviolent.

The general public perception of Dr. King was mixed. Many considered him to be one of the great men of the twentieth century, a charismatic and inspiring religious and cultural icon. Others saw him as a radical and argued that the proposed holiday was being advocated purely for partisan political purposes.

I convinced myself that there were valid and fair reasons to vote against the holiday. It would cost taxpayers an estimated $1 billion each year. Very few of our nation's greatest leaders have commemorative holidays celebrating their lives. Thomas Jefferson, Alexander Hamilton, James Madison, Benjamin Franklin, Patrick Henry,

Andrew Jackson, Theodore Roosevelt, Franklin Delano Roosevelt, Harry Truman and Dwight Eisenhower all had yet to be singled out for commemoration. The same is true for other African American leaders, such as Frederick Douglass, Booker T. Washington and W.E.B. DuBois.

What I failed to see was the emotional and spiritual bond that millions of Americans who have suffered the sting of prejudice and discrimination felt with Dr. King. The proposed holiday was not simply a testament to a remarkable man. It honored the courage, conviction and dedication of all who had sacrificed themselves and even their lives for racial freedom. I did not appreciate that the holiday was a tribute not only to Dr. King but to those who stood with him, who fought intolerance with compassion, hatred with love, and physical abuse and assault with nonviolence to ensure that America's promise of freedom and opportunity was not qualified by race or any other discriminatory factor. As Robert F. Kennedy so eloquently observed:

> Each time a man stands up for an ideal, or acts to improve the lot of others, or strikes out against injustice, he sends forth a tiny ripple of hope . . . and crossing each other from a million different centers of energy and daring those ripples build a current that can sweep down the mightiest walls of oppression and resistance.[1]

Dr. King started many of the ripples that have become a mighty torrent for the civil rights of all Americans. The consequences of what he did and the courage he displayed in the face of the worst in the human spirit are still being felt today.

Creating a federal holiday for Martin Luther King was the right thing to do. My vote against it was the wrong choice. I'm grateful I was on the losing side.

Sometimes one's mistakes are used by others to further their own agenda or protect themselves from scrutiny. These can be the most painful, and often impossible to remedy.

In February 1990, I gave a speech on the Senate floor defending a settlement that the Department of Justice had reached with a bank for money laundering by junior-level employees. The department had come under criticism for the settlement, even though the $15 million in fines included in the agreement was the largest penalty ever collected by law enforcement for money laundering. Among other points, I noted that the crimes were isolated incidents and many in senior management were not involved.

At the time, the speech seemed little different from thousands of others I had given on the Senate floor. True, my checking of the facts was a bit cursory, and I had relied heavily on a draft submitted by Robert Altman, one of the private attorneys involved in the case, but this was hardly the first time a senator had given a speech partially drafted by someone not on the staff. Both the Justice Department and attorneys representing the bank, who included former Justice Department prosecutors I knew and trusted, assured me the speech was accurate. In addition, both Altman and Clark Clifford were involved with one of the bank's American affiliates. Clifford was one of the most prominent Democrats in Washington, an attorney who served his country both inside and outside government and was a confidant of presidents from Harry Truman to Jimmy Carter. He had a well-deserved reputation for being honest and straightforward. Altman was his protégé.

The attorneys representing the bank also made it clear that the bank was being targeted because it was owned by Arabs. It was undeniable that several countries and vested private interests were worried about the consequences if an Arab-owned bank were to become a major player in international financial markets.

Like most Senate speeches, this one was given to a virtually empty chamber, and there was no immediate reaction. I really didn't give the speech much thought. I believed I was simply countering Democratic attacks on the Justice Department and assumed it was the last time I would ever think about that bank. I could not have been more wrong.

The bank was BCCI, the Bank of Credit and Commerce International, and that one speech would make me a human political bull's-eye for almost two years.

Unbeknownst to me, three separate investigations were already on a collision course. First, bank regulators were continuing their investigation of BCCI and would discover evidence that the bank not only had bilked thousands of depositors and engaged in systematic insider lending but also had worked with terrorists and drug dealers. A year later, in 1991, these investigations would culminate in BCCI's being forced to close its operations in seven countries. It had to forfeit all its U.S. assets, more than $550 million, to the federal government, and plead guilty to a series of new fraud and racketeering charges.

Both Clark Clifford and Robert Altman were caught in the net. Because of his age, Clifford was not indicted, but the scandal forever tarnished a reputation built over six decades. Altman was prosecuted but acquitted after a long and bruising trial. He, too, was left with his reputation in tatters.

To this day, I do not believe either man knew what was really going on at BCCI. I am still convinced the illegal conduct was hidden from them by the bank's officials overseas, and what they did know was limited to a local bank in Washington, D.C., First American Bankshares.

The second investigation was being pursued by Senator John Kerry of Massachusetts. He had introduced legislation, of which I was one of the original cosponsors, designed to toughen federal money laundering laws and enhance the ability of law enforcement to combat these crimes internationally. During the next year he would prepare an extensive report detailing what he believed to be the government's mishandling of its case against BCCI.

And third, the Senate Judiciary Committee was struggling through a partisan inquiry into the savings and loan scandal, a financial disaster that would ultimately cost American taxpayers and investors billions of dollars. The investigation, which was being orchestrated by Senator Howard Metzenbaum, focused less on the banks whose failures had cost taxpayers the most money and more on those with the strongest Republican ties, especially one in which Neil Bush, the president's son, had played a role.

The White House and the Republican leadership were incensed about the inquiry and insisted that it be broadened. After weeks of negotiations, Senator Metzenbaum relented and agreed to add to his investigation the CenTrust Savings Bank of Miami, which was believed to have strong Democratic ties. He requested, however, that my staff conduct the initial inquiry. Their investigation culminated in a fifty-seven-page report detailing a series of abuses by CenTrust's chairman, David Paul, and demanding a more formal investigation into why federal regulators had been unable to stop a pattern of mismanagement that resulted in a failure expected to cost more than $2 billion.

The report caused a firestorm inside the Senate. It revealed that Mr. Paul had led a life of unparalleled extravagance, using bank money to pay for airplanes, a 54-foot sailboat, homes, private parties that cost more than $100,000, and more than $30 million worth of artwork. When bank regulators tried to step in and stop the hemorrhaging, Paul threatened them with political retaliation, pointing out his connections with powerful members of Congress. The report revealed that his connections were, in fact, considerable.

While chairman of CenTrust, David Paul also served as the honorary chairman of the Majority Trust, a fundraising operation run by the Democratic Senatorial Campaign Committee. He steered more than $328,000 to Democratic candidates during this period, and several senators had used his private airplane and sailboat for fundraising and recreation. One had been a guest at the now infamous "French chefs" dinner, where Paul used more than $122,000 of bank funds to fly in six leading chefs from France to prepare a feast for fifty-seven of his closest friends.

In addition, a former CenTrust attorney had been hired by a Democratic senator who allegedly used his position to force meetings with federal bank regulators to discuss their ongoing investigation of the bank.

The report contained one other stunning revelation: CenTrust was actually partially owned by BCCI, which had been intimately involved in a fraudulent scheme to hide CenTrust's severe financial problems from regulators.

Given the report's findings, before its release I gave various senators copies of the portions of the report where they were mentioned. As you might expect, the reaction was volcanic.

Several members attacked back, describing the report as a blatant attempt to politicize the investigation of the savings and loan crisis. The media ran with this interpretation, ignoring what we had discovered and focusing instead on the propriety of the effort. Interestingly, no one disputed any of the facts in the report. They were systematically ignored, and the document itself all but disappeared from public view. By then, many of us in the Senate were preparing for a new political battle—the confirmation of Clarence Thomas.

After Clarence Thomas was confirmed, it would have been hard to find a conservative whom the more liberal members of the media held in greater contempt than me. They were in no mood to do me any favors. Anything that could be used against me was fair game and of great interest.

Sources in Congress began to leak a variety of negative stories about me, including allegations that I was intimately involved with BCCI. These culminated in a lead story on NBC's *Nightly News* on November 22, 1991. Tom Brokaw observed that BCCI was already the biggest banking scandal of the decade. He claimed my name had emerged during the investigation and described me as a Republican who had played a prominent role in the Clarence Thomas hearings. The story offered no evidence of my involvement but concluded by asserting that I was under investigation.

I was dumbfounded by the news and quickly called William Barr, the Attorney General, in the hopes of finding out what was happening and also to tell him I was ready to cooperate if the story was true. A day later, Justice Department officials let me know I was not under investigation. Not surprisingly, NBC chose not to mention this on the air.

Over the next couple of days, the accusation triggered a feeding frenzy among investigative reporters. It was alleged that I was BCCI's front man in Congress, that I was friendly with bank officers, that I had personally profited from the speech, and that I was still under investigation by a variety of different law enforcement agencies.

None of these accusations was true, but that no longer mattered. When real sharks go on a feeding frenzy they bite at anything—food, chunks of coral, each other. The media version is not much more discriminating. Any allegation about me, no matter how spurious, was given the benefit of the doubt and made public.

I stayed in ethical purgatory for almost six months until, unbelievably, things got worse. During the first week of August 1992, I rushed back to Utah when I learned my father, Jesse, was back in the hospital. He was suffering from Pick's disease, which is basically a series of small strokes that destroy normal brain function. At this point, my father had lost his memory and was dying of pneumonia.

It was a painful time. I struggled to control my emotions while trying to deal with the pending loss of the one person who personified so many of the virtues I cherish above all others. He was quiet, forthright and hardworking, a man at peace with his life no matter what difficulties he might encounter.

I was sitting in his hospital room with my mother when I was told that my office was on the phone and needed to talk to me. Irritated, I stepped outside and took the call. Several of my top aides had been tipped off that Senator Kerry's staff was trying to subpoena one of my former employees, as well as my personal and office records, in conjunction with Kerry's BCCI investigation.

I was incredulous. I couldn't believe any member could be so callous at a time like this, especially since, if he believed there was evidence of wrongdoing, Kerry was obligated to submit a complaint to the Senate Ethics Committee, which is responsible for investigating individual members of the Senate.

Kerry's staff never notified my own staff of their plans. Instead, they leaked to reporters that I was in Utah and implied I was hiding there to avoid cooperating with Kerry's investigation. Naturally, the leaks generated yet another round of stories repeating the allegations about my connections to BCCI, all of which were false.

With the help of some friends, including Senator Jake Garn and the Democratic Chairman of the Senate Foreign Relations Committee, Claiborne Pell of Rhode Island, we managed to block this unprecedented stunt to gain subpoena authority over another member. Still, the damage was done. Reporters bombarded me with calls at my home in Utah and at the hospital demanding to know why I wouldn't answer questions about the ongoing investigation. It was even reported that I was faking my father's illness.

For the next several days, my mother, my sisters and I rarely left Dad's room, as he slipped in and out of consciousness. It was a poignant, painful time for us all. Sometimes we laughed as only a family can in times of tragedy. Frequently, we cried together as we struggled to say our last words to our father when he could hear us.

On August 6, 1992, Dad died. We buried him two days later, and I gave the family tribute, the most difficult assignment of my life. Jesse's good friend, Vernon Law, the former Pittsburgh Pirates pitcher, also spoke and was a great comfort to all of us, as he has been throughout my life.

The funeral was more than a time of sorrow. It was also the celebration of a humble man who had led a remarkable life. Dozens of people stepped forward to share their memories of my father's kindness and generosity. Dad never made much money. He did not have much to give, but what he had, particularly his time and a seat at his dinner table, he was more than willing to share. I met an amazing number of people whom he had helped or fed during his life, the only connection among them being that they were in need at the time. As one of them observed, my father was a master builder of houses and people. I have never felt more proud or more alone in my life.

The funeral was a stark contrast to the reception awaiting me when I returned to Washington. My reputation was being savaged, and many of my colleagues were giving me a wide berth. I was clearly damaged goods.

One of the few who stopped by to offer his condolences was Ted Kennedy. Unsolicited, he talked about his own personal struggle to come to terms with the death of his father and brothers. He told me stories about his parents and patiently let me talk about my own.

It was amazing. Here I was at the nadir of my professional and personal life, and the one colleague who had the courage and grace to offer some comfort was probably my primary political adversary in the Senate.

The stories continued to build, so I took the unusual step of requesting an investigation of myself by the Senate Ethics Committee. If nothing else, it gave me an excuse for refusing to answer any more questions from reporters about BCCI.

In the fall, Senator Kerry released his report on BCCI and its American affiliates, and it was highly critical of the Bush Administration's handling of the case. Though nearly a thousand pages long, it barely mentioned CenTrust. The critical findings in my CenTrust report were not addressed, nor did the report cover the fact that BCCI had played a critical role in maintaining CenTrust's appearance of solvency at a time when the bank was contributing more than $328,000 to Democratic candidates.

Of course, I did little to help myself. I had made a series of mistakes that, in retrospect, gave the accusations more life than they deserved. First, despite the concerns of my staff, I did not check out the facts as well as I should have before giving the speech. Worse, I lightly edited a draft prepared by Robert Altman, one of the bank's attorneys and officials. Naturally, when it was discovered that I had used a speech prepared by someone affiliated with the bank, which while hardly unique was clearly wrong, it only added fuel to the allegations that I was in league with the bank.

Second, after the allegations began to mushroom, I gave a few press interviews in the hope of setting the record straight. Unfortunately, I did not have all the facts assembled before I talked to the media. Not surprisingly, the inconsistencies between what I said and what was ultimately discovered created another round of stories, even though the subsequent discoveries put my actions in a more favorable light.

Third, I woefully underestimated the consequences of releasing the CenTrust report and the amount of animus that would be directed toward me as a result of the Thomas confirmation. Days after the NBC piece had aired, I was interviewed by a reporter for a national weekly news magazine. He said he was ashamed he had been put on the story and asked if I knew why I was under attack. When I admitted I didn't, he explained that I was being paid back for my treatment of Anita Hill and my CenTrust report.

I had trouble believing him. I was convinced that I was being pursued by one or two unscrupulous reporters excited by the prospect of taking down a conservative. It was not until other reporters offered similar assessments that I began to believe that the grudge against me was so specific. Still, regardless of the personal motives of the media, I had become a target and my own mistakes were helping to keep the story alive. I would remain in the crosshairs until either I was run out of office or the story ran out of steam.

Eventually, it was the latter. After a nearly twenty-four-month investigation, generating more than $300,000 in attorneys' fees, I was cleared of all wrongdoing. The Senate Ethics Committee found no evidence that I had engaged in any activity that violated federal law or rule of the Senate, or that I had engaged in improper conduct.

Looking back today, while I clearly made a series of mistakes, they were not venal. I received nothing for giving the speech. I clearly didn't profit or benefit, directly or indirectly, from BCCI or its subsidiaries. I did not use any of the considerable resources available from BCCI's domestic affiliates. Not one of the serious allegations about my "relationship" with BCCI was true.

But truth often is an inadequate defense against anonymous and unsubstantiated accusations. The entire experience was a brutal lesson in the ability of the press, working with "investigators," to turn almost any set of facts into a destructive tale of intrigue and conspiracy, the target of which is left unable to confront his accusers or correct his record. Inaccurate leaks can sometimes be more persuasive than reality. Allegations are front page news. The facts, which take time to discover and substantiate, barely make the first section and are often much less sensational. Too often, they are not reported at all.

It was a tough way to learn a harsh political rule. In the United States, you are entitled to a fair trial. Unfortunately for those in public office, you are not entitled to a restored reputation.

Chapter Nine

No Lack
of Losers,
No Evidence
of Winners

There's just no such thing as truth
when it comes to him. He just says
whatever sounds good and worries
about it after the election.

—Presidential candidate
Bill Clinton describing his opponent,
George Bush.[1]

WILL all Senators now stand and raise your right hand," the
Chief Justice of the United States, William H. Rehnquist,
said to a hushed and somber Senate chamber. All one hundred of us
stood at our desks.

"Do you solemnly swear that in all things appertaining to the trial
of the impeachment of William Jefferson Clinton, President of the
United States, now pending, you will do impartial justice according to
the Constitution and the laws, so help you God?" he continued.

"I do," we answered together, and then our names were called individually and we repeated the pledge and then signed the Official Oath Book.[2]

The official trial of President Clinton had begun, only the second impeachment trial of a sitting president in the history of the nation. Select members of the House Judiciary Committee, who would be serving as prosecutors, took their seats in the Senate well. The Chairman of the House Judiciary Committee, Representative Henry Hyde of Illinois, then began to read the articles of impeachment.

It was an ordeal no one relished. Every senator, both Republican and Democrat, had hoped it could be avoided, that at some point during the previous year, President Clinton would have taken one of countless opportunities to extricate himself and the country from the mess he had created. But there would be no miracles.

The Clinton impeachment is an embarrassing and unfortunate story about the unnecessary, about chances not taken and reputations needlessly ruined. There were many victims, some expected and some not, but there was only one protagonist, the one person who precipitated and prolonged the crisis: the President of the United States, William Jefferson Clinton.

That a scandal had overwhelmed the Clinton Administration was no surprise. Modern American politics is as much about scandals as it is about elections and legislation.

Richard Nixon had his Watergate; Jerry Ford had the controversy over pardoning his predecessor. For Jimmy Carter, there was Bert Lance and allegations of attempted arms sales to Libya that involved his brother, Billy. President Reagan had several scandals, including the Iran Contra affair, the investigation of which consumed both Congress and the Reagan Administration for most of Reagan's second term, and even continued through the Bush Administration. The final report of one Independent Counsel was released only days before the 1992 election.

And then there was Bill Clinton. He and his administration

seemed to have as many scandals and investigations as the others combined.

Bill Clinton arrived in Washington already a controversial figure. Only a resolutely astute and cunning politician could survive the mistakes and controversy that swirled around him during the election, any one of which would probably have proved fatal to another candidate.

He was a brilliant and relentless campaigner, but these are qualities that do not automatically translate into success as a chief executive. Like many, he clearly found the White House a far more difficult and complicated responsibility than he had expected.

In addition to his own attitudes and style, President Clinton assembled a staff that signaled a changing of the guard, as the Second World War generation so prominent in the Reagan and Bush Administrations gave way to a group of younger men and women. These were people who had been raised in the 1960s and 1970s, when the formative political experience was not defeating Nazi Germany and Japan but fighting and contesting the war in Vietnam. Not surprisingly, they had profoundly different ideas about the role and responsibilities of government and the proper respect for tradition.

After twelve years of Republican Administrations, Congress and the Washington establishment needed time to adjust to the Clintons and their staff. The beginning was rocky, and the mistakes in policy initiatives and personnel seemed to build on themselves.

Still, many in Congress and Washington were patient, willing to give the new administration the benefit of the doubt. Over time, however, patience was replaced by concern and eventually dismay.

Despite our obvious political differences, I had several opportunities to talk privately with President Clinton about a variety of issues, especially judicial nominations. In 1993, with the resignation of Justice Byron White, he had the first opportunity for a Democrat president in twenty-six years to nominate someone to the Supreme Court.

At the time, I was Chairman of the Senate Judiciary Committee and would play a significant role in the confirmation process. Consequently, it was not a surprise when the President called to talk about the appointment and what he was thinking of doing.

President Clinton indicated he was leaning toward nominating Bruce Babbitt, his Secretary of the Interior, a name that had been bouncing around in the press. Bruce, a well-known western Democrat, had been the governor of Arizona and a candidate for president in 1988. Although he had been a state attorney general back during the 1970s, he was known far more for his activities as a politician than as a jurist. Clinton asked for my reaction.

I told him that confirmation would not be easy. At least one Democrat would probably vote against Bruce, and there would be a great deal of resistance from the Republican side. I explained to the President that although he might prevail in the end, he should consider whether he wanted a tough, political battle over his first appointment to the Court.

Our conversation moved to other potential candidates. I asked whether he had considered Judge Stephen Breyer of the First Circuit Court of Appeals or Judge Ruth Bader Ginsberg of the District of Columbia Court of Appeals. President Clinton indicated he had heard Breyer's name but had not thought about Judge Ginsberg.[3]

I indicated I thought they would be confirmed easily. I knew them both and believed that, while liberal, they were highly honest and capable jurists and their confirmation would not embarrass the President.[4] From my perspective, they were far better than the other likely candidates from a liberal Democrat administration.

In the end, the President did not select Secretary Babbitt. Instead, he nominated Judge Ginsberg and Judge Breyer a year later, when Harry Blackmun retired from the Court. Both were confirmed with relative ease.

While President Clinton and I were able to maintain a cordial working relationship when it came to Supreme Court nominees, I had significant problems, as did many of my colleagues, with the way he ran the White House. Unlike his predecessors, there was little difference between the Clinton Administration and the Clinton presidential campaign. He appeared to base every decision on the same criterion he used in his election—immediate political or personal benefit for the candidate. Tradition and the law took a beating.

By 1994, the Clinton Administration was in serious trouble, and its days looked numbered. His health care plan and energy tax had been defeated, and Congress was actively investigating a series of issues over fundraising practices and the possible exchange of political favors for campaign contributions. Probably the starkest rebuke came from the voters, who elected a Republican House of Representatives for the first time in forty-two years.

President Clinton reacted quickly. Priorities were shifted, and several policy initiatives were abandoned in preparation for the coming election. In an amazing reversal of roles, he became something akin to the nation's governor, protecting Americans from a legislature that he and the media repeatedly portrayed as having swung too far to the right.

The Republican-controlled Congress could initiate all the ideas it wanted. The President's job would be to sift the good from the bad, even if it meant letting the government shut down, which occurred in 1995.

It is a tribute to President Clinton's abilities that he was able not only to assume such a different style but also to succeed with it. Of course, there was also the economy.

The economic recovery that had begun during the last six months of the Bush Administration was turning the country back into a financial and fiscal powerhouse, fueled in no small part by the unprecedented and unforeseen explosion of the online world. A robust economy can assuage a variety of political ills and Clinton, like any other sitting president, took full credit for the nation's prosperity.

Again, he was fortunate. Several of his top legislative priorities, specifically his massive federal health care plan and an unusually punitive energy tax, were defeated by the Republicans when the Democrats still controlled the House early in his administration. If they had become law, the economic growth that marked so much of his tenure in the White House would have been impossible to sustain.

By 1996, despite a growing number of investigations into land deals, misuse of the FBI, the White House travel office firings, and illegal fundraising, President Clinton's popularity had increased significantly. The conventional wisdom switched from his probable defeat after only four years in office to the inevitability of a second term.

That November, President Clinton was reelected, again without winning a majority of those voting, as the opposition split its votes between Senator Bob Dole, the Republican candidate, and Ross Perot, who was the Reform Party nominee. Little did anyone know, however, that a series of activities that occurred leading up to the election would end up consuming the remainder of President Clinton's time in the White House.

When appointed in 1994, Independent Counsel Kenneth Starr was charged with investigating an assortment of allegations arising out of a series of financial and real estate dealings by President Clinton and his wife that occurred before the election in 1992. In 1998, Starr's office received information that Monica Lewinsky and others were prepared to perjure themselves in the sexual harassment suit brought by Paula Jones, and that Ms. Lewinsky had talked about her testimony with the President and his close friend Vernon Jordan, who was trying to find Ms. Lewinsky a job. Given the similarities to the conduct already under investigation, Starr presented the information to the Attorney General, Janet Reno, who concluded that it warranted investigation. She petitioned and was granted authority by the Court of Appeals for the District of Columbia to expand the Independent Counsel's investigation to determine whether Ms. Lewinsky and others had suborned perjury and obstructed justice.

Rumors immediately began to circulate about whether the President had broken the law and might be forced to resign. There was even talk that he might be impeached if the allegations proved true, especially given the number of individuals who were convicted as a result of Starr's investigation. Even then, I doubted that the Senate would ever vote to convict Bill Clinton; either there wouldn't be sufficient votes or, if there was sufficient evidence of wrongdoing beyond what was being discussed, he would resign before subjecting the country to such an infamous ordeal.

What is often forgotten is that this particular investigation was caused by only one person, the President. He knew about his relationship with Monica Lewinsky. He knew exactly what happened before he ever testified under oath in the Paula Jones case.

If he had truthfully answered the questions, he might have been embarrassed, but there would have been no subsequent inquiry by Ken Starr. There would have been no prolonged investigation, no subsequent grand jury testimony or impeachment proceedings. The last four years of his administration would have been about far more than his own desperate attempts at political preservation.

Instead, he chose not to cooperate. Exhibiting a defense strategy that he would follow religiously throughout the case and subsequent investigations, he used every conceivable tactic to avoid being questioned by Ms. Jones's attorneys.

He had to know the strategy could not work. He knew he was not beyond the law. In 1997, the Supreme Court rejected his attempt to delay the Jones suit until after he left office. In 1998, he was finally forced to sit for a deposition. Unfortunately, he then made matters worse. President Clinton decided to lie.

When asked whether he had met with Ms. Lewinsky, he evaded the question, implying that he had seen her only once or twice while she was at the White House and offering that there may have been another time or two when she brought him some documents.

When asked whether he was ever alone with her in the Oval

Office, he couldn't recall. When asked whether he had ever talked with her about testifying, he said he wasn't sure. When asked whether he had given her gifts, he said he didn't know, and then he asked whether the questioner knew what they were.

The only question he answered with absolute clarity was the one concerning whether he had engaged in an extramarital sexual affair with Ms. Lewinsky. He answered no, he had never had an affair or sexual relations with her.

By the end of January 1998, there was little else in the press but report after report that President Clinton had not told the truth. Every day it seemed, some new fact, rumor or allegation would be publicized, allowing the media to repeat all of the charges once again. The nation's capital was polarized and the presidency was frozen.

Desperate to stop the political hemorrhaging, President Clinton went on television. Many hoped that he would finally tell the truth and allow the country to move on. Instead, with his wife at his side, he lied yet again, issuing the now infamous denial, "I did not have sexual relations with that woman, Miss Lewinsky. I never told anyone to lie."

Compounding his false statements, he then had several female members of his cabinet buttress his rebuttal and endorse his outrage over the accusations.

Over the next several weeks, we began to see evidence of what would become the foundation of his legal defense. Instead of telling the truth and relying upon the innate forgiving nature of the American people, President Clinton and his supporters targeted everyone else involved.

Rumors were spread about Ms. Lewinsky and the other women who had accused him of sexual misconduct. Words such as ambitious, spoiled and obsessed were used to describe the White House intern. Stories were floated that she was sexually active and had engaged in a previous affair. Ken Starr came under similar treatment. He was attacked for being partisan, for operating beyond the law, and for intentionally delaying the investigation to embarrass the President, even though it was Clinton's own legal tactics that had prolonged the inquiry for so long.

The strategy was simple—destroy the personal credibility of the women and the Independent Counsel so that anything they might say would be tainted and any subsequent activity undermined. It was a surprising tactic for a man who professed to be a champion of women's rights.

There was another factor at work. The Clinton team hoped to shift the focus from the facts to the personalities involved. The former might prove problematic, but the latter was the President's strongest card. He is clearly one of the most engaging, charming people ever to have served in the White House, and he had an unprecedented ability to survive one self-created crisis after another. One colleague compared him to a rogue younger brother who breaks every rule in the house but then regales a captivated family with stories about his escapades. If the focus could be on his personality, he would survive.

The strategy was fairly successful. Ken Starr was increasingly portrayed as a vindictive, puritanical partisan who would stop at nothing in his relentless pursuit of the President. In fact, Ken is a quiet, courteous attorney, the antithesis of the Inspector Javert described by the White House and its sympathizers in the media.

Ken's record of public service is impressive. He had been appointed to the United States Court of Appeals by President Reagan, but resigned from the bench to serve as President Bush's Solicitor General of the United States. After the election in 1992, he returned to the private sector and quickly developed a very successful legal practice.

In truth, Ken is one of the least instinctively political people in a town where it seems that everybody operates with an eye on the political consequences of every action.[5] He clearly was not prepared for the vicious campaign mounted against him.

As more and more came out, however, the President simply could not escape either the facts or the lies he had told. Buoyed by a strong economy, his job approval ratings remained more than favorable, but his reputation was plummeting as an increasing number of Americans believed many of the charges against him were true. They could not help but notice that the White House certainly was acting as if he were guilty.

What Clinton and his defense team refused to appreciate was that the controversy was about more than "just sex." There was also the issue of a broken trust.

If the allegations were correct, he had broken the law. He had broken faith with the American people and violated his oath to protect and respect the office to which he had been elected.

The simple fact is that teachers shouldn't have sex with students. Doctors shouldn't have sex with patients. Lawyers are not supposed to have sex with their clients, and presidents should not be engaging in amoral conduct with interns, however you want to describe what was occurring. If caught, presidents should then not compound their error by lying under oath in a civil proceeding that has nothing to do with our national interests.

Instead of dissipating, emotions on both sides grew over the spring and summer. As the Chairman of the Senate Judiciary Committee and a Republican who had suggested that the President could avoid further problems by simply telling the truth, I began to be a much more frequent guest on the various news talk shows when the Clinton investigation came to dominate the news.

These programs are an integral part of the political culture in Washington. The Sunday shows not only wrap up the previous week's events, they are also used by guests and commentators alike to test ideas and set the tone for the coming week's coverage. Although fairly repetitive, they are religiously watched by those in and outside of government.

They have also proliferated, due in large part to the expansion of all-day cable news. What was once a function primarily reserved for

Sunday morning is now a seven-day-a-week ritual. Still, the Sunday shows are the most heavily watched and the most likely to create news that will be reported.

In July 1998, I used an appearance on the CBS's *Face the Nation* to criticize Clinton's continuing refusal to provide testimony to the Independent Counsel, simply the latest attempt to delay Starr's investigation as long as possible. I suggested if Clinton ignored the grand jury subpoena, which was issued after the White House rebuffed Starr's efforts to negotiate an opportunity for President Clinton to testify voluntarily, his refusal to cooperate with a court-authorized investigation could become an article of impeachment.

I pointed out that the President had an obligation as the highest official in the country to respect the laws of the nation and to comply with its legal requirements and proceedings. He could fight the subpoena all the way to the Supreme Court, but, in the end, he would lose, unnecessarily risking a constitutional crisis. I urged him to cooperate and to testify.

Two days later, the pressure I and quite a few others had exerted appeared to work. President Clinton agreed to testify. Whether he would really cooperate, however, was still in some question.

Consequently, I used another show to offer President Clinton some unsolicited advice. I suggested that by telling the truth and stopping his strategy of evasion, delay and obfuscation, he and the country could move forward. Come clean, I said, and if necessary apologize to the American people. If he did, we all could put the controversy behind us.

Several of my Republican colleagues in the Senate were upset by my comments. They had no interest in suggesting that there was any alternative other than Clinton's being held legally accountable in a court of law. Once again, rumors floated that I should be publicly punished and stripped of my committee chairmanship.

What they didn't understand was that my concern was not just for

Bill Clinton. I was worried about the consequences for the country, Congress and Republicans if we could not find a way to change the course on which we seemed to be so firmly stuck.

I was convinced that if President Clinton didn't tell the truth, his actions would inevitably lead to the filing of articles of impeachment. The House would have no choice but to proceed, even though very few thought there would be sufficient votes in the Senate to reach the two-thirds needed for a guilty verdict. In fact, several, including me, believed that no Democratic senator would vote to convict under any circumstances.

I had little doubt that as astute and shrewd a politician as he was, President Clinton had reached the same conclusion. Given the ultimate importance he placed on personal victory, pushing the country over the cliff of impeachment was a dangerous strategy, but it did have an effective endgame.

He probably understood better than many in Congress that, should impeachment be played out to its inevitable conclusion, he would not be convicted. Instead, he would claim victory, and the Republicans would be blamed for dragging the country through an unnecessary and unwanted constitutional crisis.

Conversely, by doing the right thing—admitting he had lied and asking for the forgiveness of the American people, President Clinton would not be able to claim vindication and his enemies would go unpunished. Given the two choices, I had little doubt which he would choose. I could only hope to be proved wrong.

On August 17, 1998, President Clinton finally testified to the grand jury via remote television. I was asked to appear on NBC to offer my reaction to a speech he was scheduled to give after his testimony.

Consequently, I was sitting at the anchor desk at KSL, the NBC affiliate in Salt Lake City, when President Clinton stepped in front of the cameras. I watched with the station's personnel and a crowd of reporters as he spoke for only five minutes, then walked away without answering questions.

He claimed his earlier assertions were legally accurate, but that he did have a relationship with Ms. Lewinsky that was not appropriate, although he refused to explain what kind it was. He then reverted to the normal White House defense: denial, obfuscation and personal attack.

Once again, Ken Starr was singled out. Clinton complained that the investigation had gone on too long, cost too much and hurt too many people. He said his actions should be of no interest to anyone but his family.

I was disheartened by the performance. Like others, both Republicans and Democrats, I hoped he would use this latest opportunity to put an end to the scandal. He had an opportunity when he testified in the Jones deposition, but he lied. He had another when he spoke to the nation about his testimony, but he lied. Once again, he had the chance to set the record straight, but instead he engaged in his pet game of parsing words, distorting phrases, and blaming everyone but himself for the consequences of his own conduct. Given the opportunity to behave like an adult, he responded like a teenager.

Knowing what he was forcing on the country and the Congress, I became angry. When it was time to comment, I pointed out to Tom Brokaw that the President had not apologized to the American people, even though he was clearly backtracking on his earlier, televised denial. While he admitted he had engaged in an inappropriate relationship, he never explained exactly what he meant by the phrase and, given his repeated reliance on word games and semantic tricks, this oversight was ominous.

By the time the interview was over, I was even more upset. I walked out of the studio, chatting with the local anchor. Summing up the President's performance, I mumbled, "What a jerk!"

My comment was picked up by one of the reporters following us, and it was quickly sent out over the news wires. I was immediately criticized for demeaning the office of the President of the United States, but my comment paled in comparison to what Clinton was doing to the institution himself.

In retrospect, I wish I had made the comment over the air. That was exactly how he was behaving—like a selfish, childish jerk.

Ken Starr's report was made public shortly thereafter, clearly delineating not only President Clinton's repeated lies but also laying the basis for potentially eleven impeachable offenses, including lying under oath, suborning perjury and obstructing justice. I felt sick. First, the report laid out in stark detail the extent of the President's misconduct and illegal activity. If true, it was both embarrassing and inexcusable.

Second, despite the collective hope for a different result, the inevitable legal process would now begin. The lives of so many would be permanently altered and an incredible amount of the nation's time and money would be wasted, and all because President Clinton stubbornly refused to tell the truth.

That evening, Larry King asked me to appear on his show. We talked about the salacious nature of the Starr report and the unfortunate fact that Clinton's lawyers had spent a significant portion of their rebuttal attacking the Independent Counsel instead of addressing the President's lies.

In response to one of Larry's questions, I argued that if impeachment was warranted, Congress had an obligation to put aside politics and the polls and do what was right. I had little confidence, however, that any Democratic senator would vote for any article of impeachment, no matter how it was worded.

We also discussed reports that Chelsea Clinton, the President's daughter, might drop out of school because of the controversy. I had been told that she was even being taunted by some of the students, which was incredibly unfair. She was not responsible for what was happening.

I expressed my support for her and my disgust for the way she was being treated. I said I hoped she stayed in school, and then observed when you looked at Chelsea, who is an exemplary young woman, you had to conclude that her parents were clearly doing some things right. Naturally, some found this observation upsetting and called my office to complain.

Larry asked if I believed the President should resign. I said that any such decision was premature. It was an assessment that needed to be voiced, given the reaction by some that he did not even deserve the opportunity for a fair hearing. Moreover, I did not think a president should resign until there was absolute proof that he had broken the law. A president should not be above the law nor should he be below it. President Clinton deserved the opportunity to hear the charges and offer a defense, even though I was concerned that the defense might be far different from the truth.

That Sunday, I was invited again to be a guest on the CBS morning show *Face the Nation*. As I was pulling into the parking lot, I was told the President was trying to find me. I called the White House and was immediately put through.

President Clinton said he just wanted to chat. He pointed out that he had followed my advice about coming clean. He was referring to a speech he gave at the annual White House prayer breakfast, where he admitted he had sinned and had repented.

I responded that it would have been better if he had made his confession clearer and earlier and had apologized to the American people.

Clinton asked what he should do now. I told him he should follow the advice he was being given by several of his top aides. Come clean, and tell the entire truth. Stop hiding behind word games and trying to exhaust the process in the hope that the nation would grow so weary of the investigation that its termination would become more important than the truth.

President Clinton claimed he had already repented. I reminded him that there was a lot more to repentance than just saying you're sorry. He not only needed to recognize what he had done wrong but also to show remorse and then refrain from ever committing the offensive conduct again. He also needed to make restitution—to his wife and daughter, to his cabinet and those he worked with, and to the American people.

It was a bizarre moment. Here I was, sitting in my car in the parking lot of a television station, on a cell phone, lecturing the President of the United States, and a Democrat to boot, on the religious obligations of repentance. At least it was Sunday.

Meanwhile, the network was getting worried I would miss the taping of the show. While I was talking on the phone, a stream of people kept coming out to the car and tapping on the window. I would nod in acknowledgment and then continue talking. Panic must have really set in at the studio, because eventually the show's host, Bob Schieffer, appeared at my car. He knocked on the window and then pointed at his watch. I smiled and tried to use various body gestures to tell him I understood. I'm sure Bob had no idea what I was trying to signal, but I did not want to cut off the President. He was asking for my advice, and I felt obliged to take advantage of the opportunity.

I pointed out to President Clinton that no one believed his word games concerning his relationship with Monica Lewinsky. Knowing he was worried about the possibility of indictment if he told the truth, I ended by arguing that if he made a clean break with the past, no one would indict him either during his presidency or when he left office.

The President indicated that he had made amends to his family and was trying to do what was right for the nation. He thanked me for defending his daughter on the *Larry King Show*.

Just before we hung up, he mentioned that during the latter part of his relationship with Lewinsky, he had stopped the physical activity and focused instead on trying to help her. It was a singularly awkward moment in an already strange conversation, and his unexpected explanation sounded particularly phony.

I appreciated what the President was probably trying to do. He knew I was appearing on a nationally televised show. I am sure he hoped that by talking to me directly and asking for advice, he would discourage me from calling for his impeachment or resignation. Of course, I had no intention of doing that. It was neither the right forum nor the time for such a momentous recommendation.

After all, Bill Clinton is, if nothing else, a shrewd man. He fully understood that it is always easier to be critical of someone when he or she remains at a distance. Familiarity encourages giving the benefit of the doubt, especially for those soliciting advice.

Nonetheless, I criticized the President on the show for not being straight with the American people and for continuing to rely upon various legalisms to avoid taking responsibility for his own actions. I pointed out that attacking Ken Starr was not the answer. He needed to tell the truth and take responsibility for what he had done.

Unfortunately, nothing I said, nor any of the recommendations so many others made, had any real impact. Opportunities continued to be missed, and the country moved inexorably toward impeachment.

In October 1998, the House of Representatives voted to begin consideration of Ken Starr's recommendations but decided to delay formal proceedings until after the November elections.

The elections indicated that President Clinton's legal strategy, while unbelievable, was not hurting his standing with the American people. The Democrats picked up five seats in the House of Representatives, putting them in a position to regain control of that chamber in the next presidential election.

When the House returned to deal with impeachment, the Republicans got off to a rocky beginning. Newt Gingrich had resigned as the Speaker of the House. A successor was selected, Bob Livingston of Louisiana, but when his own marital infidelities were revealed he resigned as well. The House then turned to Denny Hastert, a well-liked but not nationally known representative from Illinois. Denny has proved to be a stabilizing, calming influence, and deserves much credit for mitigating the poisonous atmosphere that was undermining the chamber's ability to operate when he took office.

Still operating as if they were in the middle of a campaign, the Clinton team continued to press that the impeachment was not about the President's alleged perjury. It was "just about sex." They asserted his "marital indiscretions" should be a family matter and not the nation's business.

Consequently, his conduct was no longer the real issue. Instead, it was the blatant partisanship of his Republican accusers who could never come to terms with his election and reelection.

It might have been a politically clever argument, but it was a morally inexcusable disinformation campaign. Unfortunately, it was succeeding.

By the end of 1998, the nation was comfortable with its economic success, and people were wary not only of what they perceived as political posturing but also of anything that seriously threatened the status quo. Many Americans simply wanted the entire mess to disappear. It was too embarrassing, too tawdry and, for some, downright inconvenient.

According to national polls, most Americans believed Bill Clinton had lied under oath and would probably lie again. Still, only one in four wanted the impeachment proceedings to continue. The rest preferred either censuring the President or dropping the matter entirely, so long as whatever was done was finished as quickly as possible. The American public had grown weary of the Clinton scandals, worn down by the administration's constant delays, repeated denials and torrent of accusations. Whatever they might think of Bill Clinton, most did not feel that impeachment was the right punishment.

The House Judiciary Committee did not have that luxury. Faced with no other legitimate legal alternative, it moved forward and turned Starr's eleven allegations into four articles of impeachment. Two concerned perjury in the Paula Jones case. One addressed witness tampering, and the last, abuse of power.

On December 19, 1998, after an acrimonious and, at times, less than legally enlightening debate, the House voted to approve two of the articles.

Any hope that such a tragic, historical moment as a president's impeachment would be treated differently from a routine campaign event was quickly eliminated. Right after the vote, the Democrats gathered at the White House to hold a pep rally. It would be hard to imagine a sorrier day in the nation's capital.

The inevitable had occurred, and the Senate had no choice but to take up the articles of impeachment. For a conviction to stand, two-thirds of the Senate, a total of sixty-seven votes, would have to be cast in favor of one of the articles.

Privately, the Senate was struggling with another reality. If no Democrat would vote against President Clinton, it would be impossible to meet the constitutional requirement that two-thirds of the Senate would have to vote in favor of conviction for it to be binding. If that was true, what was the point in putting the nation through a prolonged, agonizing and embarrassing trial?

Various proposals short of an outright conviction were floated. Former Presidents Ford and Carter suggested that the Senate vote to convict President Clinton but not to remove him. The idea of censuring the President instead of impeaching him was discussed, but no agreement could be reached.

Republicans were split on what to do. Some felt that even though there might not be sufficient votes for a conviction, there would at least be a majority of senators who would find the President guilty of at least one of the counts. Others believed that under the Constitution, we had only one option—to vote on the articles of impeachment regardless of the inevitability of the outcome. Given these attitudes, it was impossible to reach an accord on censure.

After more than two weeks of getting nowhere, the Senate agreed to meet privately in the old Senate chamber. Although there is a firm rule about revealing what is said during these sessions, they do have an immense institutional value. By meeting out of the public eye, we were finally able to talk to each other instead of at one another. Members on both sides rose to the occasion.

The House prosecutors had suggested that their case be limited to only three witnesses: Monica Lewinsky, Vernon Jordan, who had found Ms. Lewinsky a job in New York, and Sydney Blumenthal, who had spent much of his time at the White House defending the President. Only Ms. Lewinsky would be called to testify.

The Senate rejected the idea, by a bipartisan vote of 70 to 30. The Democrats were concerned about the public's reaction if they saw just how young and relatively naïve Ms. Lewinsky actually was. Several Republicans joined them, believing that someone with her questionable record had no place in as an important a proceeding as an impeachment trial.

I thought the decision was a mistake. If she testified, the American people could decide for themselves whether she was telling the truth. Regardless of how one might feel about what she did or didn't do, she was clearly a central character to the facts that were the basis of the articles of impeachment.

In the end, all three testified via videotape. There would be no live witnesses. It was obvious we were heading toward a result many of us would find unsatisfactory.

Despite differing opinions about the trial, many of my colleagues believed the President's perjury should not be completely excused, and there was concern that the White House would interpret a vote to acquit as not just a repudiation of the articles of impeachment but also an implicit endorsement of Clinton's actions.

Consequently, I proposed that the Senate vote to adjourn the impeachment trial on three grounds:

1. President Clinton gave false and misleading testimony under oath in a federal court proceeding and has, in many ways, impeded the justice system's search for truth.

2. He will be subject to federal criminal jurisdiction for his acts when he leaves office.

3. The Senate acknowledges, recognizes and accedes to the articles of impeachment passed by the House as Impeachment Without Removal, the highest form of condemnation other than removal.

I had reviewed my proposal at some length with the Senate parliamentarian. Under the rules, any senator had an absolute right to move to adjourn sine die to end the impeachment trial. On the other hand, including in the motion the additional precatory, explanatory language that was critical to my proposal would be subject to a point of order, which if raised by the presiding officer could be overturned by a simple majority vote of fifty-one senators, a procedure that occurs periodically during the normal course of business in the Senate.

In other words, the proposal did not violate the Constitution. It would have validated the House's impeachment vote but avoided a specific vote on the actual articles. President Clinton would not be removed from office, but his conduct would be condemned. Moreover, by voting to adjourn the trial sine die, the issue could not be resurrected at a later date, as some in the administration feared.

I had several discussions about the idea with Senator Joe Lieberman, one of the few Democrats to criticize the President's conduct publicly. He was clearly intrigued, but there was too little support for the idea on either side.

Many Democrats did not want to sanction the impeachment, not even implicitly. The Republicans were still split. Some felt obligated to continue with the trial as envisioned under the Constitution, even if it produced a result that pleased no one but the President. Others raised concerns that overruling the point of order would be an embarrassment to Chief Justice Rehnquist, who was serving as the presiding officer in the Senate, as prescribed by the Constitution. And several were still convinced that while there might not be enough votes to convict, a majority of the Senate would still find the President guilty. With so many disparate views, I was unable to build support for my idea and it was put aside.

Days later, the Senate agreed to end the trial on February 12, guaranteeing the inevitable. The Senate voted to acquit President Clinton on the article concerning perjury, with ten Republicans joining all the Democrats. We split evenly, 50 to 50, on the second, again all Democrats voting in the negative.

I voted guilty on both counts, believing the evidence could support no other position. The simple fact was that President Clinton had committed perjury. The record was clear on this point. Even his own obfuscation could not hide the truth.

Perjury is an impeachable offense, regardless of the judicial forum in which it occurs. It cannot be excused nor can the offense be diminished by the subject matter involved. Moreover, the President clearly obstructed justice. Bill Clinton engaged in a conscious, intentional campaign to hide the truth, to cover up what he had done. The evidence is even more overwhelming on this count than on the perjury. He intentionally put the nation through an unnecessary ordeal for one simple reason—he did not want to be held accountable for his conduct.

One of the hallmarks of our nation has been the proposition that our president is not above the law. We do not have an imperial presidency. Presidents, like all other Americans, are subject to the same laws, the same rules. Others who have committed the same kind of acts have been penalized and even incarcerated. The Senate vote, however, establishes a dangerous precedent that the president is in fact not subject to the law of the land.

For many, however, the votes were not about facts. They were about political outcomes and consequences. Moreover, for some of my colleagues, lying about marital infidelity was not behavior sufficient to be disqualified for holding public office.

In the end, President Clinton's legal strategy was successful, at least as far as he was concerned personally. Despite the exorbitant cost to the nation and his administration, he was not convicted. In fact, he would feel sufficiently vindicated to claim later that his defense was not only principled but necessary to protect the Constitution.

Moreover, his political strategy also seemed to work, at least initially. The Republicans, especially in the House of Representatives, were ridiculed and widely condemned for voting to impeach him. Several would end up losing their positions as a result of the vote.

Nonetheless, President Clinton did not emerge unscathed. He was held in contempt of court by the judge who oversaw the Paula Jones case and forced to pay a little over $90,000 in fines for providing "false, misleading, and evasive" answers in his deposition. The sum was in addition to the $850,000 he paid to settle the case.

In addition, he was forced to agree to a five-year suspension of his Arkansas license to practice law and pay a $25,000 fine to the state bar association. Interestingly, his conduct may not have barred him from being President of the United States, but it was enough to bar him from practicing law.

It wouldn't be until January 2001 that he would finally tell the truth. As part of a settlement with Ken Starr's successor as Independent Counsel, Robert Ray, Clinton finally made the following admission only days before he left office:

> I tried to walk a fine line between acting lawfully and testifying falsely, but I now recognize that I did not fully accomplish this goal and am certain my responses to questions about Ms. Lewinsky were false.

We will never know what his actual legacy might have been. By so stubbornly refusing to acknowledge his misconduct, by repeatedly ignoring chance after chance to tell the truth, President Clinton ensured that his administration will be remembered more for his actions as a defendant than what he accomplished as President.

He was unable to take advantage of the unprecedented economic boom that dominated his two terms and ended up leaving unsolved several of the problems that had dominated his first campaign. Some were never even addressed.

There also were a few unexpected casualties of the scandal. Among others, the feminist leaders, so prominent in their attack on Clarence Thomas, came off poorly, apparently compelled to remain silent throughout the investigation. There were no marches on the Senate by the female members of the House. There was no steady stream of public press conferences demanding accountability.

The allegations of sexual harassment by Paula Jones, the claim of forced sex by Juanita Broaddrick, and the charge of unsolicited sexual overtures and fondling by one of his White House staff, Kathleen Willey—all were met with either muted concern or skepticism about the reliability and hidden motives of the accusers.

What was the difference? This time, the accused was a prominent Democrat who was a strong supporter of abortion rights and held an important public office. Accordingly, his misconduct was a private issue not to be discussed or addressed in public.

Today, the feminists' charge that the Senate "just didn't get it" has a different meaning. Apparently, for some the weight given allegations of harassment depends on the politics of the harasser.

And there was one final casualty. During the 2000 election, the Democrats were unsure what to do with President Clinton. If they criticized his conduct, they would offend party loyalists, who were convinced he had done nothing wrong. Conversely, if they embraced him, they risked offending independent and swing voters, who believed his behavior was inexcusable for the nation's chief executive.

No position needed to be taken, however, if he stayed at the White House. Consequently, the decision was ducked. The best national campaigner in the Democratic Party spent much of the 2000 election on the sidelines.

It was a mistake, because Bill Clinton could not be hidden. He did not have to be seen to be remembered, especially since the Republicans were running just as hard against him as they were the actual nominee. He was allowed to hang over the 2000 election like a malevolent ghost, rarely visible but always felt.

If President Clinton had told the truth from the beginning, or if he had confessed that fateful day in January instead of lying to an entire nation, he might have been embarrassed but he would not have been impeached.

His administration would not have been overwhelmed by his legal problems. He would have been free to campaign in an election that was so close that his personal involvement in only a few states might have made the difference in the eventual outcome.

If Bill Clinton had simply told the truth, in all probability Al Gore would be President today.

Chapter Ten

What They Never Tell You About Running for President

You know, you could learn a few things about taking care of yourself.

—Iowa voter

A n old adage has it that if you walk onto the Senate floor and say "Mr. President," a hundred Senators turn around. I always thought that was a little unfair. The number is more like ninety-five, because there are always at least five current members of the Senate who have actually run for the presidency at some point and had their delusions brutally eviscerated by reality. I am one of them.

Every four years, a group of seemingly normal, often successful, and frequently well-intentioned people, individuals who have already demonstrated some capacity for politically successful behavior, decide to announce their candidacy for the White House. For most, the immediate response will be the same: Why?

This was the most frequently asked question about my own decision in the summer of 1999 to run for President of the United States.

The second was when would I withdraw from the race. The press seemed to have only one reaction to my decision—bewilderment. As the rumors began to build that I was contemplating a run, individual reporters would catch me off the Senate floor and, always with a tone of bemused sympathy, ask the same question, "Why are you doing this?"

One journalist caught me just after a vote. Shaking her head slightly, her pen poised over her small spiral pad, she said, "Why are you risking the reputation you've built for yourself in the Senate?"

"Why shouldn't I?" I answered. When she failed to answer, I plunged on.

"I've faced impossible odds before. In many ways, this is no different from when I first ran for the Senate," I explained. "In 1976, few people knew who I was. I certainly wasn't a well-known party player, even in my own state. I wasn't a Utah native and had only moved back to the state six years before. I wasn't part of the social in-crowd, or even considered or discussed when people started talking about politics. Yet I ran, and I won, because I was better able to represent the interests, values and aspirations of my fellow Utahns than my opponents."

"But," she said, slightly exasperated, "this is different. This time, you really could look foolish."

The night of my announcement, I appeared on *Larry King Live*. Larry and his wife, Shawn, are good friends, and I have been on his show several times over the years. He is simply one of the best interviewers on television, able to make anyone interesting and coherent no matter how unprepared or unfocused he or she might really be. He is also part showman, with his trademark suspenders and glasses, and he has one of the most recognizable voices in America since Howard Cosell. And he is part interrogator too, a fair and open questioner who never appears to be working a personal agenda. He has mastered the art of probing without causing offense. Every night he manages to create the impression that the public is listening in on a private chat Larry just happens to be having with his guests.

Larry introduced me as the latest entry in the Republican presidential field and a "real long shot." His questions came rapidly. How could I make up so much ground on the other candidates? How could I be competitive in big states, such as California? What was going to be the symbol or theme of my campaign? And what was the secret strategy that would lead me to victory?

I answered the questions as best I could in the handful of minutes I had. Larry was gracious but clearly skeptical. I was followed by another repeat guest, the medium and healer Rosemary Altea, who would take up the bulk of the program. Larry asked whether she could predict the future for my campaign. "I'll pass," she answered, as she and Larry laughed knowingly.

For both the candidate and staff, running for president is unlike any other political campaign. It is a massive, unwieldy, uncontrollable monster. In the end, it's not something you orchestrate; it's something you survive.

The best way to prepare for a presidential run is either to have run before or to be intimately involved in another presidential campaign. President Bush certainly learned much about what to do, and what not to do, on the campaign trail during his father's successful and unsuccessful runs.

For those who do not have the luxury of a presidential father yet still choose to run, there are some very basic, practical rules that can be followed. I make no promises of victory. That advice will have to come from someone else. The purpose of these rules is to give long shots a chance of surviving the experience with some shred of dignity intact.

The Media Needs a Show

There is a symbiotic relationship between the press and a presidential campaign. Neither can survive without the other, and each desperately needs the other to be validated.

Reporters have a mental image of what a busy, successful operation looks like, and when they come to check out a campaign, they want to see it. They want to visit large, unkempt rooms filled with people hard at work; they want to hear phones ringing and see folding tables piled high with posters, news releases and position papers. They want to meet the people who will be running the campaign, the individuals responsible for answering their questions and hopefully providing the anecdotes, quotes and insights that will make their stories stand out from the competition. They want to hear firsthand the strategy by which the candidate will accomplish the unimaginable and actually win.

The reporter, much like the candidate, is feeling something like desperation. Presidential races come along once every four years, and latching on to the winning candidate early can mean front-page bylines, a possible book contract, lots of face time on national television and a chance at the ultimate validation—the White House press corps. Successful presidential campaigns have made a lot of journalists' careers. To be assigned to a loser is to contemplate being back on the national desk in a matter of months, trying to make the latest Transportation Department regulations sound newsworthy.

So the first thing a reporter wants is to make sure the campaign is more than personal whimsy. They want to see that the candidate is resonating with at least some discernable segment of the population. Second, they want to know that even if the person can't win (and most don't), there at least will be a great story in the effort.

No one has understood this better than John McCain. One of the most brilliant and successful strategies of the last election was his Straight Talk Express, the bus that housed the candidate and the reporters assigned to cover him. The name itself echoed John's primary themes: that he was the only candidate willing to tell the truth, and that he was so confident and comfortable with himself that he was willing to sit with reporters day in and day out. It was the ultimate endless press conference.

That this arrangement succeeded is a tribute to John's singular talent for working the media. I can only imagine the disaster that might have arisen if other presidential candidates had provided reporters this kind of access. In John's campaign, it allowed him to shape his own coverage and repeatedly emphasize themes he wanted stressed. Just as important, it provided unparalleled personal validation for many in the press.

Good presidential campaign stories are guaranteed air time and print space. With so much face time, even the least known or experienced person on the bus had the freedom to ask a presidential candidate almost any question that came to mind. Instead of making them struggle to find something to report, McCain almost guaranteed them a story. Moreover, by spending so much personal time with their subject, the press became as much a part of the campaign as many of the staffers. The Straight Talk Express was a risky but ultimately brilliant strategy.

A reporter assigned to the Hatch campaign got much less personal validation. This was never more evident than the afternoon a reporter from the *New York Times* joined us as I was making the rounds of television stations near Des Moines, Iowa. I had just finished one interview and was running late to our next appointment. She climbed into the backseat of our "bus"—a Ford Explorer with room for five people. Wedged tightly between two staffers, she glanced around the car, the disbelief obvious on her face. I offered her part of the now cold fast-food sandwich I was trying to finish, but she wisely refused.

I could see she was sizing up the situation. She asked what to her was the obvious question. Was this all just an act to create a humble impression?

"I wish it were," I answered, laughing.

Know Thyself

At some point during almost every race, someone will conclude that the real problem with the campaign is the candidate. He or she is not coming across properly in person or on television to the mythic average voter. Suddenly, specialists will be brought in to explain to the candidate not just what to say but also how to say it, what to wear and how to behave.

Sometimes this advice is constructive, especially when the problem is a matter of semantics. What we really feel can be lost in the words we choose to use, and what voters hear can be far different from what a candidate believes he or she is saying.

For years Republican candidates would highlight issues they felt reflected the core principles of the party. They would talk about responsibility, loyalty, hard work and sacrifice. These are the qualities we believe form the bedrock of our culture and society.

Focus group testing revealed, however, that what we thought we were saying was not what some voters, especially women, were hearing. When we talked about taking personal responsibility and the need for hard work, they heard a lack of compassion and an insensitivity to the difficulties of daily life. Our message was getting lost in our semantics. By using different words, we were able to communicate our position more accurately and without unintended offense.

The key is to avoid advice that is designed to make you into something you are not. During one of my early Senate campaigns, a young campaign advisor decided I needed to dress more casually when visiting the rural districts in my state. He believed the dark suit and light shirt I traditionally wore made me look distant and unapproachable.

His concerns reflected a generational difference. I grew up during the Second World War, when people dressed more formally on almost every occasion. People wore suits to work, to church and to social gatherings. Men wore jackets, ties and hats on weekends and at sporting events. For me as a senator, dressing formally was a way of showing respect, not only for the office but for my constituents. I thought it was what one would expect from a person holding such a position.

Obviously, attitudes have changed over the decades. Today, politicians who dress formally all the time are perceived as stiff and out of touch. Casual dress is accepted literally everywhere. We are comfortable seeing a president dressed in jeans and a cowboy hat, or chopping wood in his shirtsleeves. People do not expect to see their elected officials in dress that is any different from theirs.

This staffer had gotten hold of my cowboy boots and then, on his own, purchased a pair of jeans, a pearl-buttoned cowboy shirt, a leather belt with a huge buckle, and a ten-gallon hat. He caught up with me while we were campaigning in the southern part of the state. It was a Saturday evening, and I was scheduled to give a speech to a group of cattlemen. He implored me to change into the clothes he had bought. My dark suit might be fine for Washington, D.C., he argued, but it was incongruous in the rural West.

The rest of the staff agreed, so I went into the next room and put on the new outfit. Feeling like one of those carnival attractions where you poke your head through a painted board to get your picture taken, I returned to confront my staff.

The room fell silent. No one knew what to say. Just at that moment, my campaign manager, Bud Scruggs, burst through the door, looked at me and gasped.

"What are you people trying to do?" Bud yelled. "Mock cowboys?"

I vowed at that moment never to try to dress a part or play a role when campaigning. If the public is uncomfortable with what you really are, if you have to hide your true feelings to get elected, you may not be the right person to represent that constituency.

Begin Way Too Early

You have to start campaigning much earlier than you think you should. Remember, your opponents have probably already started.

To judge from the campaign process, the one quality we value the most in our presidents is stamina. Congressional elections take months. A run for the presidency takes years.

To build the right base, the campaign should begin at least three years before the election, even if much of what is initially done is accomplished under the public radar. Presidential campaigns have to be built from the center out. Supporters have to be identified throughout the United States. The competent have to be selected from the merely enthusiastic. Surrogates have to be found, and key party officials have to be won over.

Not all of this work has to be done by the candidate. Many of the initial meetings and soundings can be taken by those who will play critical roles in the campaign and clearly are in a position of some authority. Still, campaigns are nourished by personal contact, and a candidate must be willing to invest a great deal of time in winning over party officials in every state.

This is why candidates seem to be constantly making appearances in Iowa, New Hampshire and other states with early primaries. They are quietly building the base they will need to run. Moreover, they all know that every weekend they take off to spend with their families or to have some semblance of a normal life is a weekend that their opponents have the field to themselves.

That does not mean, however, that for those who enter the contest late, there will be no one left who is willing to help. What it does mean is that there is a reason these folks are still available.

Good Senators Make Bad Candidates

Despite much evidence to the contrary, the United States Senate is still considered a logical position from which to launch a presidential campaign.

In the twentieth century, only one sitting senator, John F. Kennedy, was elected president. Of the twelve who have held office since the Depression, four have served in the Senate, but three were first elected vice president. If anything, a more direct route to the White House is from a governor's mansion. Five of the modern presidents were elected after having been successful governors.

Many people think the public and media visibility that comes with the Senate provides a perfect springboard for a national campaign. While that may be true, the Senate also imposes an almost impossible hurdle. Too often, congressional obligations conflict with the demands of a presidential run. It is impossible to satisfy both because both are full-time occupations.

A normal workday in the Senate runs twelve hours. This is especially true of members who are in leadership positions or are committee and subcommittee chairmen. Hearings alone are scheduled for every day of the working week, often several in one day, and time has to be reserved daily to meet with constituents, an obligation that often extends over the weekends. In addition, unlike many governors, senators have little control over their own schedules. Their lives are largely dictated by the leaders in the House and the Senate, none of whom are willing to inconvenience the lives of the rest of the members to accommodate one or two who happen to be running for president.

To run, therefore, a sitting senator has no choice but to miss votes and put legislative responsibilities on hold. One of the reasons John McCain's candidacy was as successful as it was is that he was willing to put his presidential run first. Even so, he too was ultimately unsuccessful.

Bob Dole may have taken the most appropriate step for a serious candidate. A frequent contender for the White House, he resigned from the Senate in 1996 to dedicate all his time to his presidential campaign.

When I ran, I told my presidential campaign staff I would not miss a vote in the Senate, nor would I jeopardize my ability to fulfill my congressional responsibilities, a decision that left them muttering with frustration. While I doubt the outcome would have been different had I resigned, I still missed out on valuable opportunities to build a strong base in the early states because I had to be in Washington for hearings, mark-ups, and votes on the Senate floor. I simply did not have enough time to satisfy the myriad commitments of a national campaign.

Currently, several Democratic senators are considering running against President Bush in 2004. One indication of whether they are serious will be their willingness to start missing votes and putting their legislative priorities on hold. Even then, history is not on their side.

Rich or Poor, It's Good to Have Money

In the fall of 1999, I flew into New Hampshire for a debate. As we were leaving the airport, I saw a group of Bush campaign workers putting up prefabricated signs on the side of the road. They were wearing matching outfits, and their jackets had a Bush logo on the front. As a veteran of campaigns, I was surprised by the amount of money being spent. It was obvious that none of the rest of us would be able to compete financially with an operation that could afford not only excess signage but signature clothing.

To his credit, Governor Bush had amassed the largest war chest in modern political elections. Six months before the first vote was cast, he had already raised $36 million.

I didn't begrudge him a penny. Raising such a sum represented a phenomenal effort on his part and was an undeniable testament to his popularity. If you don't believe me, try doing it yourself.

Of course, he was also spending at a clip that far outpaced anyone else. I remember thinking at the time that if Bush did get elected, I hoped he wouldn't govern the way he campaigned. The country couldn't afford it.

A campaign can run without money about as long as you and I can run without oxygen. Campaigns consume money, and national campaigns consume money at prodigious rates. Costs that are staggering in congressional races—for staff, travel, research, advertising, signage, telephones, computers, food and lodging—are simply unbelievable in a presidential campaign. Multiples of everything are needed to ensure a presence and an impact in all the key states.

Every campaign vows to control costs, to break even. New measures are adopted and key personnel are assigned to do nothing but restrain spending. But in the end, every campaign, especially the serious ones, breaks its vows and wastes money on expenses that make no sense outside the world of politics. To save time, rental cars are abandoned at the airport instead of being returned to the dealer. Computer hook-ups at hotels turn an evening stay from less than $100 to more than $1,000 because the press secretary, who had not slept in two days, passed out before disconnecting his machine. Planes are chartered to make sure the candidate doesn't miss a dinner with a handful of potential donors who will end up supporting someone else. As the election draws close, money is spent so frantically and by so many people that it often takes years to sort out all the costs, let alone identify the legitimate ones.

Almost every national campaign eventually has to hire an attorney simply to clean up some mess involving the raising or spending of money, or the returning of money improperly raised during a campaign. The more money raised, the more problems.

Nonetheless, to paraphrase Pearl Bailey, I've run poor campaigns and rich ones; rich is better. Not all the advantages of a well-financed campaign are readily apparent.

Early support discourages competition. The $36 million that George Bush had raised by the summer of 1999 undoubtedly warded off other potential contenders. It signaled that he had already locked up most of the resources available to Republican candidates. A rival would not be able to run a conventional race against that kind of money.

A well-financed campaign has the wherewithal to hire the resources it needs to cover every possible contingency. If there is a problem, the right people can be brought in to address it. Time is not wasted trying to determine what should be done and who should do it.

Money also enables a campaign to be better prepared. For example, the Bush campaign actually spent money preparing attack advertisements similar to ads they believed the Gore campaign would commission. They were able to test these ads with groups of prospective voters and learn how best to respond. When the Gore campaign actually fielded their negative television ads, the Bush team knew in advance how to counter the negative impressions.

A well-financed campaign also protects a candidate against becoming invisible in that dangerous period between the end of the presidential primary season and the beginning of the fall election. One of the problems that beset Bob Dole's presidential run in 1996 was that by late spring he had run short of funds and was not able to run an effective national advertising campaign to counter the Democrats' attacks. For several months, President Clinton had the airwaves to himself, a disaster for any rival presidential campaign.

Few people today remember that Michael Dukakis actually led George Bush Sr. in the polls coming out of the 1988 party conventions. He retreated to Massachusetts for a month to conserve his funds. Bush seized the initiative, and the Dukakis campaign never recovered its momentum until it was too late to make a difference. Obviously, there were other problems with his candidacy than just money, but Dukakis suffered from being absent.

This does not mean, however, that I advocate the use of public funds to finance political campaigns. It's bad enough that the American public has to live through our national campaigns. It would be an insult if they also had to pay for the privilege.

I still dream that one day a candidate will be able to run by relying upon small contributions from a large donor base. My own request for $36 each from a million donors, to match George Bush's $36 million from mostly large donors, was far more popular than many realized. Contributions came from an unusually diverse group of people, Republicans and Democrats, liberals and conservatives. Several made it clear that while they were supporting other candidates, they wanted to contribute as a way of endorsing my proposal.

I started far too late to give the idea time to come to fruition. Still, if this model is ever implemented successfully, it would represent a far more effective solution to the influence of money in a campaign than any of the legislative and regulatory proposals currently being championed.

For Challengers, Problems Win Elections, Solutions Don't

Challengers run on problems; incumbents run on solutions. Voters expect those in office to explain what they have done with the trust invested in them rather than just describe what they will accomplish if reelected. For challengers, it's different. Voters want to hear less about what they have done in some other office or capacity and more what they will do if elected.

This is true in congressional as well as presidential campaigns. It is an unfortunate political reality that having solved a problem is less beneficial for a new candidate than being able to electioneer about an issue that demands fixing.

For example, during the summer of 1999, many skilled nursing facilities in Iowa and around the country were facing potential bankruptcy and closure because the reimbursement they received from Medicare to cover the expense of treating the most severely ill patients did not come close to matching the actual cost. Instead of campaigning, I stayed in Washington on several occasions to force through a resolution and serve as the chief negotiator for the Senate in several meetings with my counterparts from the House. In the end, we were able to increase the reimbursement rates so that they would more closely resemble actual costs.

While my decision was the right one from a legislative perspective, it did not help my campaign. It would have been far more dramatic to campaign about an actual crisis, with news reports about senior citizens being denied care and nursing facilities going bankrupt, than to talk about a health care emergency that was narrowly averted. In today's world, a governmental failure is always more newsworthy than a success.

Beware the Questionnaire

Unless you have actually experienced a presidential campaign, it is impossible to imagine the number of special interest organizations that will submit a detailed questionnaire demanding the candidate answer questions that range from the substantive to the ridiculous to the unintelligible. Although I was in the race for only seven months, my campaign staff had to fill out literally hundreds of these documents.

One survey asked every conceivable question about the right to life. Another wanted to know my position on every type of health delivery service in the United States. There were questionnaires on foreign trade, defense spending, financial institutions, gun control and youth issues. One wanted to know what books I read, what movies I had seen, and my favorite color, professional sports team and tree.

There is a profound downside to the tempting option of simply ignoring these requests, especially for those who are not front runners. Most organizations will prepare candidate report cards; these are given to the press, distributed to the organization's membership and posted on the Internet.

Failure to respond is prominently displayed on the report card. Candidates who don't cooperate will be criticized for their lack of candor, and there will be the inevitable news stories about ducking issues. By failing to fill out the card, a campaign also risks alienating potential supporters or giving a voter a reason to go with another candidate, especially where the differences between opponents are minor.

The other unfortunate reality about questionnaires is that they never go away. Every answer can and will be used against you. You must consider every nuance, because your responses tend to reenter your life at inconvenient moments. That is, after all, the real point of special interest questionnaires: to lock candidates into positions for the rest of their political careers.

Don't Bet on the Debates

Debates are often the most highly anticipated moments of any campaign. Challengers love them, especially those who are competing against better-financed or known opponents. They believe debates are critical to their chances at an upset and are a proven opportunity to change the course of an election or their own status. Consequently, there can never be too many.

Not surprisingly, incumbents and front runners consider debates an exercise to be survived and kept to a minimum. They have little to gain by besting an opponent they are already beating in the polls, and much to lose if they expose themselves to the verbal equivalent of a knockout punch.

Every incumbent and every challenger remembers the same examples. There was Ronald Reagan's famous criticism of Jimmy Carter, when he observed, "There you go again." In 1984, without being mean spirited, President Reagan effectively eliminated the ability of Democrats to raise the issue of whether he was too old to be president when he jokingly promised, "I will not make age an issue in this campaign. I am not going to exploit, for political purposes, my opponent's youth and inexperience." And no one in politics today has forgotten the devastating rejoinder Lloyd Bentsen shot at his colleague Dan Quayle during their only debate in 1988. Whether it was fair didn't matter to the public. It was memorable.[1]

These are moments candidates either pray for or dread. In reality, the vast majority of debates have limited value, especially during the presidential primary season.

First, the debate is usually designed by third parties, generally either the news media or the station hosting the event. More often than not, a reporter asks a question and a candidate has a limited number of seconds to respond. Additional time may be given for a follow-up inquiry and response. Instead of focusing on a specific topic, such as foreign relations or health care or education, the questions cover several areas, eliminating any real chance to focus on what is being said or to discuss the responses. No effective opportunity exists for one candidate to disagree with another. To contest an earlier statement, one has to race through one's own answer and then use whatever time is left to return to a previous topic. It's like holding a boxing match without ever letting the contestants be in the ring at the same time.

Second, the candidates and the parties usually have no role in choosing the questions. The subject matter of the debate may be important to reporters, but too often it ignores the issues of greatest concern to primary voters. I remember commenting during one of the primary debates in 2000 that if you listened just to the questions, you would think the only two issues of importance to Republicans were the fate of Elian Gonzáles and South Carolina's state flag. The other candidates nodded in agreement, but nothing changed.

Third, primary debates are too crowded to be personal. The memorable political exchanges invariably occur between just two candidates. That electricity is dissipated when four and five people share the stage. A pointed criticism may be leveled by one candidate, but by the time the target has had an opportunity to answer, the moment has passed and the response seems either disjointed or contrived.

Finally, primary debates are not widely watched. The audiences of cable operations such as MSNBC, especially in the evenings, are a fraction of the viewers watching one of the networks. Even the best of their shows are usually dwarfed by sitcom reruns and sporting events. At best, most voters will see only an eight-second clip of the debate on their local evening news, this chosen by a reporter who then laments how political discourse has been reduced to sound bites. Unfortunately, a challenger has a much better chance of getting into the clip by doing something really stupid than by being extreme-ly clever or persuasive.

It was repeatedly suggested during the last presidential election that primary debates be limited just to the front runners. Speaking as one who would have been a victim of such a policy, I believe it would unnecessarily marginalize too many challengers and could put the media sponsors of a debate in the position of censoring some candi-dates.

Similarly, moderators should not be allowed to skew the debate or the questions toward only one or two candidates. During the last Republican primary, at least one moderator appeared to treat the event more like a Sunday news talk show with only one guest than like a political debate. Care has to be taken to ensure that all the candi-dates not only have a chance to speak but also have a chance to be heard on different topics.

Some have suggested that the "town meeting" format is the most informative, where candidates are questioned by ordinary voters rather than by pundits. They assert that this format generally yields a more interesting, varied and relevant set of questions. It could, but I still think a real debate would be more interesting and informative, one where the candidates question one another and are allowed to respond and directly question their opponents.

Perhaps there's another way to make the debates more useful. Until it's discovered, the lesson to be learned is that if your strategy for success hinges on scoring a series of knockouts in the primary debates, you may be in far more trouble than you realize. In their pres-ent form, they're greatly anticipated but much overrated.

Humor Is Essential for a Serious Candidate

Never underestimate the importance of a good laugh. One of the most critical components of any campaign is the ability to laugh at your circumstances, at the innate incongruity of the endeavor and at yourself. Sometimes humor is the only way to deflect criticism or soften a blow. As former Representative Morris Udall once observed, "Other things being equal, a droll politician will have an easier time than a dour one getting elected. Wit is an essential element of charisma, of leadership."[2] On the other hand, the memoir from which that advice comes is entitled *Too Funny to Be President.*

Obviously, humor provides an opportunity to get a little attention. During one of the Republican debates, I was required to ask a question of Steve Forbes, whose vast personal wealth gave his campaign a durability that outweighed his complete lack of experience in public office. Sincerely trying to send him a signal, I prefaced my question by noting that it would be completely straightforward, a fat pitch.

Steve took it the wrong way and responded that he had learned that anytime anyone began with that promise, he'd better hold on to his wallet.

"Don't worry, Steve," I observed, "I couldn't lift your wallet."

Having gotten into the race so late, I was often asked about my lack of funds, especially given the huge amount George W. Bush had raised and the assumption that at least some portion of my money was coming from Mormons. Instead of trying to provide a more positive spin on a desperate situation, I learned just to nod and note how difficult it was trying to raise political money from folks who were stone cold sober.

During the Republican primary season, questions were raised about whether then Governor George Bush had sufficient experience to be president. There were stories about whether one term in state government was adequate preparation for arguably the most difficult and most important job in the world, especially when it came to foreign policy. One reporter went so far as to give Governor Bush an impromptu quiz on the names of foreign leaders, a tactic I thought both unfair and a terrifying precedent. I mean, let's be honest. It wouldn't be hard to make any of us look silly trying to name various world leaders, especially if the reporter had the advantage of having a list prepared in advance. Heaven knows, most of them couldn't pull off the questions without a crib sheet.

During a debate in Arizona, I was asked about the vice presidency. I used the opportunity to raise the "experience" issue without appearing offensive or looking as if I was straining to make a point. I told the reporter that the question went in the wrong direction, that I would be willing to have George Bush as my vice president. "You should have eight years with me," I observed, "and, boy, you'll make a heck of a president."

Ironically, it was humor that enabled me to change some of the attitudes in the media about my presidential run. To my surprise, I was invited to be the Republican speaker at the Gridiron Club, where Washington's media glitterati gather to laugh at themselves and those of us in politics. One can barely imagine the number of rejections that must have occurred for such a prestigious humorous organization to get down to inviting me.

The speech gave me an opportunity to use humor to signal to the political reporters in attendance that I fully understood both the improbability and the incongruity of my presidential campaign. It allowed me to have some fun at my own expense and indicate that I could laugh at myself and their stereotype of me.

According to the reviews, the speech was a hit. More than one attendee told me later that they had no idea I had a sense of humor, let alone such a good one. Remember, these were reporters talking to a Republican. We get the rose treatment—every bouquet has to have a barb.

Interestingly, coverage of my campaign changed slightly, softening both in tone and frequency. Several stories popped up about what I was saying, and they expressed some sympathy for the fact that the pack mentality of political coverage allowed little time for anyone but the front runner. None of that would have occurred without humor.

Care has to be taken, however, that self-deprecating humor is not used too much. Otherwise, it serves only to reinforce one's stereotype.

Of course, it didn't stop nearly every news story from including the unsolicited observation that I didn't have a chance of winning. Humor can help, but it can't cure everything.

Enjoy the Unexpected Because You Have No Other Choice

No matter how hard you plan, no matter how experienced you might be, the race will be full of the unexpected. Candidates are constantly surprised not only by the mishaps but by moments of pure serendipity, by small acts of support and encouragement that are as reassuring and invigorating as a convention full of cheering delegates.

Elections often hinge on issues that would be impossible to predict or on events better suited to a political novel. No one running in the 2000 campaign predicted that its ending would be dominated by debates over hanging chads and butterfly ballots, or decided only after a ruling by the Supreme Court. I am sure there are people in both campaigns who wish they had spent more time studying Florida election law than their opponent's health care proposals.

A seemingly well-planned event can come completely unglued at the last second. One evening in Iowa, I attended an important fundraiser at the home of one of my key supporters. It was an impressive house with beautiful landscaping and a backyard large enough to hold a good-sized gathering. After everyone had eaten, my host called for the crowd's attention. I stepped forward and began to speak, explaining why I was in the race and what the challenges facing our country were. Just as I began to talk about my need for their help, there was a tremendous, deafening noise.

It was then we learned our host's yard backed up to a train track. For the next ten minutes, the longest train in the history of the United States ran over those rails, obliterating any hope of conversation, let alone a speech.

The audience was more than polite, and we all had a good laugh about what had happened. Nonetheless, I knew the evening was a loss. You just can't compete with a loud train.

Similarly, just before one of the debates, I had one of those moments we all fear when we are about to do something in public. Minutes before I was scheduled to take my place on the television stage, I stepped to one side to gather my thoughts. I noticed a loose thread coming off one of my center coat buttons and, without thinking, pulled it. Naturally, the button flew off.

There was a quick scramble as my staff and I searched and finally found the button. We then had to figure out a way to reattach it. I couldn't go on television with my coat hanging open.

All the preparation that had gone into the debate, the hours spent practicing and trying out different answers, no longer mattered. I needed a needle and thread.

To our collective amazement, Mike Bell, who traveled everywhere with me during the campaign and never seemed rattled, pulled out a sewing kit. He smiled and said, "Don't ask." The others cheered, then fell silent as they jointly came to the inevitable next question. Finally, Mike asked, "Can anyone sew?" They all shook their heads.

"I can," I answered, taking Mike's kit. I took off my suit jacket, sat down, and threaded the needle. For the next several minutes, I sewed the button back on while photographers gathered around and took my picture. I think my sewing got more coverage that night than my answers.

The most personally memorable moments of a campaign occur at the most unlikely times. After a presidential campaign speech I gave in Iowa in which I compared my record in foreign affairs to Governor Bush's, an older man caught up with me as I headed toward the exit. He was obviously upset about my remarks. "What's the problem?" I asked. "You're not being fair," he answered. "I think you're being a bit too critical, especially after all George Bush has done for this country."

"Could you be a bit more specific?" I asked.

"Well, you know, all that he did last time," the man answered. "I mean with the Gulf War and all that."

"I think you're getting yourself a little confused," I said. "I was talking about Governor Bush, not the former president. This time, it's the son who is running, not the father."

"I don't think so," the man replied. "You know, Bush looks good, all rested up and ready to go, years younger than when he left office." He paused, looked me up and down, and said, "You know, you could learn a few things from him about taking care of yourself."

What was also unexpected was the number of friends, supporters and former staff who stepped forward to help with the campaign. Most worked for no pay, often in the evening after they finished their regular jobs. Some took leaves of absence or vacation time to help, knowing full well the odds we faced.

They were tireless, giving up weekends and holidays. They traveled to primary states. They helped draft position papers and assemble briefing books for the debates. They answered mail and helped with fundraising. I never anticipated so many would help and ask for so little in return. Many later told me they not only had fun but what they learned can't be taught in school or understood simply by reading a book. It has to be experienced.

I couldn't agree more. The only way to understand a presidential campaign is to be part of one, to witness the inexplicable, to exhaust yourself on issues and problems that hours before you didn't even realize existed and, ultimately, to survive a ride through every emotion a person can experience, often in the same day. Those who joined me will always be the unexpected heroes of my campaign.

Knowing all this, one could ask again, why did I run for president? The truth is less complicated than you might think. Despite the common assessment, I actually did know what I was doing. I had not lost my mind.

I was the last Republican candidate to enter the race. I understood

I was late, and had little money and no immediate organization. I came from a small state that had a limited number of potential donors, unlike Texas, New York or California. I fully appreciated that it would take a Herculean effort or a completely unexpected chain of events to catapult me all the way to long shot.

Still, there was much we didn't know then that seems obvious now. In June 1999, it was obvious that Elizabeth Dole, Dan Quayle, Pat Buchanan and Lamar Alexander were in trouble and would probably drop out after the Iowa straw poll in August. If that proved true, by September there would be only five names in the race.

Looming large, a Gulliver in a field of Lilliputians, was then Governor George Bush. By the summer of 1999, he had more money, more endorsements and more momentum than the rest combined. He was clearly a popular and effective governor, a principled man who seemed, after eight years of the Clintons, to have a refreshing ordinariness to him. And the credential most frequently cited by Republicans was the most important: He could win in November.

Still, at that time, there was much we didn't know about Governor Bush. There were rumors about problems in his personal life, questions about his business practices, and concerns about his ability to overcome a lack of personal experience on the national and international level. If he stumbled, if one or several of the allegations proved true, or if he made a serious mistake in the debates or during the campaign from which he couldn't recover, the field would become extremely thin. If Bush was suddenly out of the race, where would his supporters turn?

There was John McCain, the liberal's favorite Republican, who had taken up unshakable and permanent residence in the "honest" candidate niche. John seemed to enjoy attacking his own party as much as the Democrats, a tactic the media found endearing but one that didn't sit well with many Republicans.

There was Steve Forbes who, by virtue of his money, was the most formidable of a trio of candidates who had never held public office.

He had sufficient personal resources to build an impressive organiza-tion in Iowa and New Hampshire, but his campaign once again seemed unable to create the excitement that surrounded McCain or Bush, let alone demonstrate how he could run effectively throughout the country.

Finally, there were Gary Bauer and Alan Keyes. Of the two, Alan was clearly the more memorable, such an instinctively fascinating and compelling speaker that he made the others seem stiff and awkward in comparison. Both were popular within a tiny slice of the Republican Party, but they were never able to appeal to a broader constituency.

Given these alternatives, I was convinced that if Bush faltered, many Republicans would look for another option, that they might be interested in a candidate such as myself who had a demonstrable record of achievement and proven conservative credentials. When I entered the race, I was under no illusions. I fully appreciated my role—a kind of election insurance for Republicans in case Bush stum-bled. I knew from that outset that if he proved to be as effective a campaigner as he ultimately did and none of the rumors proved to be fatal, there was no chance I could win and no need for me to run.

There were also some personal motivations behind my candidacy. First, I genuinely wanted to see whether a candidate could run a real populist campaign, one financed by tiny $36 contributions instead of the normal large sums from wealthy individuals and corporations. Such an effort would be the real answer to campaign finance reform and would eliminate the justification for legislative proposals such as McCain-Feingold, which will only replace one regulatory problem with another. With my campaign, anyone could participate directly in the presidential process, and at a level far under the normal bar. I fell about 985,000 people short, but I do hope in the future that someone more popular will pick up this theme.

Second, there were several issues I felt should be part of the national debate, primarily the president's responsibility for picking judicial candidates for the federal district court, the court of appeals and, depending on vacancies, the Supreme Court. In many ways, the appointment of judges is the one way a president can have impact far beyond his term in office. Despite the importance of this executive function, it is generally overlooked during elections. I felt it was important to force the other candidates to make the selection of judges as much a part of the campaign as Social Security or tax cuts. And, it is clear this objective was met.

Third, there was the issue of my religion. I belong to the Church of Jesus Christ of Latter-day Saints, commonly nicknamed the Mormon Church. Many younger Americans have forgotten that forty years ago, then Senator John F. Kennedy's Catholicism was an issue during his presidential campaign. There were persistent complaints that he would take his direction from the Vatican and not from the American people. He overcame this prejudice by addressing it directly.

Today, there are still several areas of the country that consider my Mormon faith a cult, riddled with dangerous practices and beliefs, even though it is in fact one of the five largest religions in the United States and widely accepted by most denominations as a mainstream Christian faith. Some fundamentalist Christian groups falsely believe my religion to be satanic, which obviously is not only absurd but a real challenge to a political campaign. One poll found that 18 percent of all Americans would not vote for a Mormon president. I hoped that by running a respectable campaign, I could expose and eliminate this ridiculous prejudice, making it easier for the next national candidate who belonged to my church.

There is at least one other factor: I had no fear about losing.

Several days before I announced my candidacy for president, Tom Parry, one of my former staffers and a good friend, asked to see me, hoping to talk me out of running. We met in my office and for more than an hour he reviewed a list of reasons why I should run and a much longer list of reasons why I should not. He discussed the practical, political and financial problems with mounting a last-minute national campaign and the virtual impossibility of winning.

When he finally stopped, I asked him one question: "What are you really worried about?"

"I'm afraid you'll lose and be embarrassed," he admitted.

"I'm not," I said.

"What about your reputation?" he asked.

"If my reputation is so fragile that it can be destroyed by running for president, then it's not much of a reputation, is it?"

I explained I had decided to run because I sincerely believed I had something to offer the country that was different from the other candidates. During my tenure in public life I had established a record that demonstrated not only the principles and ideas I espoused, but also the approach I would take to solving the problems confronting the nation. As a candidate, I would be able to offer not just promises of what I hoped to do but proof of what I had actually done. I had shown how to make conservatism work, how to work through the traditional partisanship in search of the best idea, regardless of origin.

It was clear that the chances of success were extremely small, yet in truth, so were the consequences of failing. If the voters disagreed with my assessment of what I could offer, which this time they clearly did, I was more than comfortable with their decision. All I really risked was a bruise to my own pride.

"So now what do you think?" I asked Tom.

"If that's your attitude, all the objections don't really matter," he said, shaking his head. "Of course, there's still one thing that should worry you."

"What's that?"

"What happens if you win?"

Chapter Eleven

"... And Start All Over Again"

The ... more and more unfolding of nature's secrets implies there was a divine healer.

—attributed to Sir Thomas More

Politics never stops, and neither does Congress. There is always a new issue, a new concept to learn and understand. Even as old battles are fought and refought, every year at least one problem emerges that is truly novel. You have to devote considerable time simply to understanding the principles and issues involved before you can even begin to make a constructive judgment.

In 2001, a constituent named Cody Anderson of West Jordan, Utah, came to see me. He had a problem and, after we had talked, I promised to do everything I could to help. Our meeting was no different from thousands of similar encounters I have had with people from my state and around the country who are looking for advice, guidance and help. Except for one thing.

Cody was four years old. Articulate, cute and courageous, he is a remarkable young man, but then his life is like that of no other child I have ever known.

At age two, he was diagnosed with a particularly virulent form of juvenile diabetes. To live, he needs a mechanical pump to maintain his daily insulin level. The spot where the pump enters his body must be changed at least three or four times a week. In addition, his blood must be drawn six to ten times a day. Every bite of food he takes has to be monitored for carbohydrates so he can be given the correct amount of insulin. Something as simple or routine as a common cold can have a devastating effect on his health. Even growing, a normal and wonderful part of a child's life, poses a risk.

For Cody's parents, the future is a terrifying prospect. He was named after his grandfather, who had the same disease and died at age forty-seven after surviving twenty-eight operations. Grandpa Cody lost his left leg below the knee, lost toes from his right foot, had a colostomy, went blind, had to have his blind left eye removed to relieve the pressure and pain, and lost kidney function, forcing him to be on dialysis for the last ten years of his life. Each of these is a well-known possible complication of diabetes. Grandpa Cody's disease was so severe, however, that he endured all the complications at a much younger age than most diabetes sufferers, who may be afflicted with only one or two.

According to the doctors, Cody faces the same fate. Unless something can be done, unless a medicine can be discovered or a new medical technique invented that can change what now appears to be inevitable, he can expect a life of pain and discomfort that will worsen with each passing year.

Fortunately, a new field of research is opening that may dramatically alter the treatment not only of diabetes but also of prevalent and debilitating diseases such as cancer, heart disease, Alzheimer's, Parkinson's, ALS and multiple sclerosis. Cody and his parents had come to see me to tell me how important it was that the government support this research, because its future may well depend more on the politics involved than its scientific potential.

The scientific community calls it regenerative medicine. Others call it human cloning.

When a complex issue of this kind is first brought to your attention, it's hard not to respond emotionally before understanding all that may be involved. Before doing or saying anything publicly, I decided to learn as much as I could about this new field of science and the recommendations and objections of the interested parties. Calling on relationships built over two decades of working on public health issues, I met with as many experts and laypeople as I could.

I sought out Nobel laureates who have been studying the issue for years. I learned about the ongoing research at Advanced Cell Technology Corporation and the Geron Corporation. I met with families who are at risk, theologians from a variety of denominations, social scientists, ethicists and political activists from both sides.

The normally cautious Harold Varmus, the former director of the National Institutes of Health, a Nobel Prize winner, and the current head of Memorial Sloan-Kettering Cancer Center, shared his excitement about the new technology. He compared the potential impact of regenerative medicine on science to that of splitting the atom and mapping the human genome. Steven Prescott, Executive Director of the Huntsman Cancer Institute, explained how this research could allow scientists to work backwards, as if they were solving a crime, to determine how a disease develops. Nothing else offers such promise. Mario Capecchi, a professor of biology at the University of Utah, told me about his research on mice and its potential impact for understanding genetic diseases such as cystic fibrosis and muscular dystrophy.

Leon Kass, the University of Chicago ethicist and current head of President Bush's Bioethics Commission, discussed the moral opportunities and dilemmas that were involved. Never judgmental, he worked through the competing opinions with me and stressed the need to consider regenerative medicine's impact not only on science but also on our future as human beings. Curt I. Civin, a nationally known professor of pediatric oncology at Johns Hopkins University, described in detail why an unfertilized egg is a human *cell* as opposed to a human *being*, and why embryonic stem cell research is so critical. Irving Weissman, a professor at Stanford Medical Center and an expert in adult stem cell research, told me that despite spending his career on adult stem cells, he believes embryonic stem cells hold unique promise and their study must be pursued.

Richard Doerflinger, the associate director of the National Conference of Catholic Bishops, provided a detailed and heartfelt explanation of his church's perception of when life begins and the inviolability of life.

What I learned from these discussions was both fascinating and a little troubling. The potential of stem cell research is truly boundless. By understanding how cells become specialized for particular functions, we can learn what happens within a cell to cause abnormal growth and division, which is often the cause of disease and birth defects. By learning how to direct or modify cell growth, eventually we might be able to replace damaged or malfunctioning cells with healthy ones.

For instance, Cody Anderson has diabetes because the cells in his pancreas that produce insulin are destroyed or disabled. Stem cell research may allow doctors one day to replace these cells with new ones that function normally, saving him from the life of pain his grandfather endured.

Moreover, this research may help solve the two biggest problems associated with organ transplantation and the use of donated tissue: shortage of supplies and rejection of transplants.

In sum, the promise of regenerative medicine cuts across all fields of medicine and touches everyone who either has a chronic disease or who may develop one or suffers a traumatic injury. If its complete potential is realized, treatments could be developed to address not only fatal and life-altering diseases but also injuries and degeneration, including stroke, burns and arthritis.

Unfortunately, regenerative medicine also raises significant problems. There is the basic question about the proper limitations of science and whether support for legitimate and needed research can be misused to fund experimentation with human creation. We are forced to confront, in far greater detail than ever before, what we know and believe about life and human creation.

To understand what is involved, you need a little basic knowledge about human biology. It is estimated that every human cell contains the same group of roughly 30,000 to 50,000 genes. This group of genes provides the blueprint for everything the cells do: how they grow and specialize, how they organize themselves into tissues and organs, and how those tissues and organs function to keep us alive. But not all cells use the same genes. Only a few of the 30,000 to 50,000 are "turned on" in any one cell.

What determines whether a particular cell becomes a blood, fat, brain or some other type of cell is the specific set of genes activated or deactivated during growth, and the pattern in which this occurs. By knowing which genes to turn on and off, researchers could theoretically grow specific types of cells and eventually specific types of tissues.

Stem cells are relatively unspecialized cells, yet they still have the potential to develop into many different cell types. They are most easily found in embryos at the earliest stages of development, in fetal tissue and in some adult tissue, although isolating adult stem cells is extremely difficult and to date they are far more difficult to grow outside the body. Moreover, embryonic stem cells appear to have a far greater plasticity—the potential for developing into different cell types than adult stem cells.

When a sperm fertilizes an egg, it creates a single totipotent cell, the term for a cell whose potential is unlimited. Out of this single cell will arise not only the embryo but also its surrounding tissues within the womb.

After roughly four days of repeated cycles of cell division, the totipotent cells form what is known as a blastocyst, which contains both an outer and an inner layer of cells. The two layers have discrete functions. Inside the womb, the outer layer will go on to form the placenta and other supporting tissues needed for fetal development. The inner layer cells are called pluripotent—their potential is large but limited—and they will serve as the basis of all the tissues in the human body. It is these pluripotent cells that can become stem cells.

Today, fertilization can occur both inside and outside the womb. I have been lucky to be the father of six remarkable children and the grandfather of twenty. Whatever I may have accomplished professionally pales in comparison to the joy I have experienced in my roles as a husband, father and grandfather. Quite simply, my life would not be complete without the happiness and challenges of parenthood. Elaine and I will always consider ourselves blessed. Sadly, not everyone is as fortunate. Through my church work, I have counseled several young couples who were experiencing difficulty in conceiving a child. Some chose to adopt. Others, using in vitro fertilization clinics, were able to have children, an opportunity they feared they had lost forever. Approximately 200,000 babies in America have been born as a result of these clinics.

These clinics can facilitate the fertilization of a human egg in a laboratory. The resulting blastocyst can then be implanted in the mother's womb to trigger pregnancy. But since the procedures normally result in more blastocysts than can be used, there are always extras, many of which are kept frozen. Some will not survive protracted storage. Others, estimated to be tens of thousands each year, will be discarded or destroyed once they are no longer needed.

Scientists recognize these unused blastocysts from in vitro fertilization clinics could provide a source of stem cells for study. Some were voluntarily donated to science and used to create privately funded stem cell lines.

Concurrently, another possible source of stem cells was identified—the use of a technique called "somatic cell nuclear transfer" or "nuclear transplantation." Here, the genetic material from a woman's unfertilized egg (i.e., its twenty-three chromosomes) is removed and replaced with the full complement of genetic material, namely, all forty-six chromosomes, from a specialized cell such as a skin cell from an individual.

This artificially manufactured cell is then electrically stimulated, and it will begin to divide and multiply within the laboratory much like a fertilized human egg. In time it will form a blastocyst, and cells from the inner layer can then be used to develop pluripotent stem cell lines.

Unfortunately, taking egg stem cells from an unfertilized in vitro blastocyst results in the destruction of the blastocyst. For many religious groups, such as the Right to Life movement, the blastocyst is not merely a group of living human cells but a living human being. They argue that its destruction is no different from the termination of a fetus, even though the blastocyst would be discarded anyway. From their standpoint, taking stem cells from an unfertilized blastocyst is simply another type of abortion.

This somatic cell nuclear transfer process also raises a different problem. By replacing all the chromosomes in the egg with the existing DNA of one person, unscrupulous scientists could use this process to clone human babies.

Consequently, any discussion of the relative merits of regenerative medicine is directly impacted, and sometimes limited, by the current debate over cloning and abortion, probably the two most controversial issues in American domestic politics.

Human cloning elicits a nearly universal negative reaction. It immediately creates images of personal duplicates, bizarre experiments and strange asexual beings, characters normally associated with science fiction and horror movies. It generates a fear that is fundamental to us all—the potential loss of our own identity—and implies that, somehow, scientists could interfere with God's sacred plan for human reproduction by a husband and a wife.

Until 1997, this concern was largely hypothetical. Then Dr. Ian Wilmut and his team of scientists announced that they had successfully cloned a mammal, a sheep named Dolly, and what was once so abstract became a distinct possibility. Later, Dr. Richard Seed announced his intention to open a human cloning clinic in the United States. Every fear suddenly seemed justified, and Republicans and Democrats quickly voiced their collective opposition.

While feelings about abortion are every bit as strong, there is no equivalent consensus. It would be hard to find a more politically polarizing issue in our nation than abortion, and it has been that way since the Supreme Court's decision in *Roe* v. *Wade* in 1973, which in effect prohibited states from making abortion illegal.

A few years ago, I learned that one of the Senate staffers with whom I frequently work was pregnant. When I next saw her, I enthusiastically congratulated her and started to talk briefly about the joys of family life. I stopped when I saw her face, which had grown uncharacteristically sullen.

I asked what was wrong. She admitted she was considering having an abortion. Her career was just beginning, and the pregnancy could not have come at a worse time. She had no idea how she could fit a child into the plans she had for herself. She observed, "After all, I should be able to choose what to do with my own body."

The real issue, however, is not whether we have the freedom to choose but what we choose to do with that freedom. To me, the question is not whether we are free to terminate a life for our personal convenience but what moral consequences the choice will have for us, our families, including the unborn child, and society as a whole. If we truly value freedom of choice, are we not also obligated to respect the other choice directly involved, the unborn's desire to live?

Almost all the rights we enjoy in this country are restricted. Some are confined by law, some by their impact on others or by the religious and moral consequences on those directly affected. Is it wrong to assume that there might be a valid restriction on this particular choice?

Since *Roe* v. *Wade,* the number of abortions in the United States has skyrocketed. Today, there are more than 4,000 abortions performed every day, the vast majority having nothing to do with the life or health of the mother. Irving Cushner, a physician and an abortion advocate, has testified that less than 2 percent of all abortions could be justified as medically expedient. Most are performed for reasons of convenience: The child is not the right sex; he or she may pose a financial burden; the pregnancy comes at an inconvenient time.

In fact, no baby is really "unwanted." In my home state of Utah alone, there are nine couples who wish to adopt for every available child. As one adoptive parent stated the other day, "placing a child for adoption is a great act of love—both for the child and for the adoptive couple who, without the child, would never know the joy of being parents." Despite this interest, the number of abortions steadily grows, including late-term abortions. These occur after the twentieth week of pregnancy, the period at which most doctors believe a child may be delivered and survive on its own. Lately, it is not uncommon to hear of a child being aborted during the seventh or eighth month of pregnancy. There also is increasing interest in "partial birth" abortions, a medical procedure so horrendous that it is nothing more than legalized infanticide.

For me, there is simply no justification for such routine taking of life. This is not a question of the life of the mother or instances of rape or incest. This is about the responsibility owed to the life we create, about our adherence to the simple majesty of the biblical command, "Thou shalt not kill." A society that is unwilling to protect its most defenseless and helpless members has lost sight of the most fundamental bond that holds it together: the right and respect of life for those who are alive and capable of defending themselves and those whose voice can be heard only through another.

Every child, both those born and unborn, is unique and capable of making a contribution to family, community and nation, a contribution that no one else can duplicate or replace. The only way to know exactly what that offering will be is to give the child the most important of all opportunities: the chance to live.

Others, however, take a different view and are as adamant and sincere in their convictions as I am in mine. They believe there are different issues involved with different types of abortion and that broad generalizations do not reflect all the personal, medical and social considerations at issue, or how agonizing the decision often is. I respect their right to hold their own opinion about abortion, but I will never understand it.

It is the passion on both sides, coupled with the absence of any plausible middle ground, that makes abortion one of the most significant wedge issues in American politics. These are issues that by themselves can motivate voters and allow candidates to draw sharp distinctions with their competitors.

Understanding this political reality, liberal and conservative strategists are always looking for ways to insert abortion into some other issue. Nothing else plays such a significant role in so many legislative battles. Abortion has come up during the consideration of bills involving foreign relations, federal appropriations, reauthorization of the National Institutes of Health, and military appropriations. As I write this book, desperately needed and widely supported bipartisan bankruptcy reform legislation has stalled yet again; this is because one member of Congress believes that the legislation should include a provision that prohibits a person found guilty of blockading an abortion facility from being discharged in bankruptcy from paying court order judgments. No comparable crime is treated this way. Other members may not agree that this one act should be singled out in a bankruptcy bill, but they cannot afford to be perceived as opposing a pro-choice amendment. As a result, the legislation remains in limbo, although I believe there is a chance we may finally resolve this problem prior to adjournment.

Abortion affects every judicial confirmation, especially those involving nominees to the various courts of appeals and the Supreme Court. One of my colleagues explained during a private session of the Senate Judiciary Committee that he would oppose any nominee who is pro-life, notwithstanding any other considerations or issues. Unfortunately, that senator is not alone.

While I obviously disagree with both that senator's position and the imposition of such a rigid litmus test, his motivation is politically understandable. Because of its importance to certain voters, abortion plays a disproportionately important role in elections, especially for Democratic candidates. A Democrat can disagree with his or her party's traditional positions on labor issues, defense spending and even taxes, but only a rare few can risk being pro-life.

Several years ago, I was on an airplane traveling to a city in the Northeast. After takeoff, a flight attendant stopped by my seat. She apologized for bothering me and expressed her appreciation for my service in the Senate. She said she wished I were her senator instead of the ones currently in office, who she felt not only were wrong on economic issues but had a deserved reputation for treating women poorly. I thanked her and said she never needed to apologize for interrupting anyone with such kind remarks.

Before we landed, she stopped by my seat again and asked where I stood on abortion. I explained that I was pro-life. She sighed and shook her head. She said she could never vote for anyone who was not pro-choice, no matter what other issues were involved.

"Why?" I asked.

"I had an abortion years ago, when it was unlawful to have one, and it ruined my life. I never was able to have children. If abortion had been legal, I would have been able to go to a good doctor instead of the butcher I had."

I expressed my profound sympathy for what happened but suggested that one issue alone should not determine how she votes. She disagreed and maintained that while she agreed with almost everything I was doing, she could never vote for me. Even if it came to a choice between a pro-life candidate with whom she agreed on every other issue and a pro-choice candidate who had a horrible record substantively and was personally abusive toward women, she would vote for the latter. She went on to explain that every one of her friends had gone through an abortion, and pointed out that most women her age either have had an abortion to save their sanity or health or know someone who has had one for those reasons.

For the rest of the flight, I thought about what she had said, wondering if we really had reached a point in this country where this one issue outweighs every other. Does abortion provide certain Democrats a free pass on other political positions or on personal behavior? Are there that many women who could never support a pro-life candidate, regardless of every other consideration?

Fortunately, the answer appears to be no, at least in general. People such as Senators Gordon Smith of Oregon, Mike DeWine of Ohio, and Rick Santorum of Pennsylvania are elected in states that are considered politically moderate or even liberal, even though they are pro-life. Still, it is clear that for at least some discernible part of the population, being pro-choice is a litmus test that supersedes all others. When this happens in politics, any consideration and discussion of the issue automatically becomes more complex and difficult to resolve. The debate gravitates to the extremes on both sides.

Consequently, it was no surprise that once people began to understand what was actually involved in stem cell research, hard lines immediately began to form. Several religious and pro-life organizations quickly made clear their fundamental opposition both to using leftover fertilized embryos from in vitro fertilization clinics and unfertilized blastocysts derived from the somatic cell nuclear transfer process.

Most of their arguments were based on the proposition that a blasto-cyst or embryo, no matter its origin or use, is in fact a human being. For these groups, the debate over stem cells was really a question of whether a person could cease having individual value and could be sacrificed involuntarily to preserve the life and health of others.

Senator Sam Brownback of Kansas, an intelligent and principled pro-life advocate, described the issue this way:

> The central question in this debate is simple: Is the embryo a per-son or a piece of property? If you believe. . . that life begins at con-ception and that the human embryo is a person fully deserving of dignity and the protection of our laws, then you believe that we must protect this innocent life from harm and destruction.

Several national pro-life organizations quickly made it clear that there was only one position they would find acceptable—embryonic stem cell research must be banned under any and all circumstances. No legitimate commercial or scientific benefit could come from what they described as the "slaughter of the innocent."

Others disagreed. A coalition of doctors, scientists, Nobel laure-ates, patient advocates and biotech executives was organized to make the alternative argument—that responsible stem cell research could provide the medical answer to a wide variety of conditions and dis-eases suffered by an estimated 128 million Americans for which there is no other solution but pain and death.

Former Senator Connie Mack of Florida, a pro-life leader, made the following observation in an editorial in the *Washington Post*:

> It is the stem cells from surplus IVF embryos, donated with the informed consent of couples, that could give researchers the chance to move embryonic stem cell research forward. I believe it would be wrong not to use them to potentially save the lives of people.[1]

Naturally, as the debate intensified, so did the rhetoric. Materials were circulated comparing the study of stem cells to the research performed at Auschwitz by the infamous Nazi scientist Joseph Mengele, and as proof that Aldous Huxley's "brave new world" was now a reality. More and more, criticism was reduced to a simplistic slogan: killing to cure.

The stridency of the opposition to stem cell research echoed previous fears raised about scientific and medical advancements considered dangerous at the time of their discovery. Some argued that the opposition to regenerative medicine was no different from the Catholic Church's reaction to the proposition by Galileo, Copernicus and Keppler that the Earth revolved around the Sun, or the fears surrounding the discovery of electricity.

It was pointed out that in medieval Europe, several different religious councils banned surgery and postmortem dissection. Not until the mid-1800s was anesthesia considered appropriate for obstetrics patients. Many religious leaders of the time taught that the practice defeated God's intention that women should experience pain during childbirth. This particular debate continued until 1853, when Queen Victoria gave birth with the assistance of chloroform.

As recently as the late 1700s, the well-known English theologian and cleric Edward Massey delivered a sermon titled "The Dangerous and Sinful Practice of Inoculation." It was given at a time when religious leaders and scientists were arguing over the use of vaccines to prevent the spread of smallpox. According to Reverend Massey, "Diseases are sent by Providence for the punishment of sin, and the proposed attempt to prevent them is a diabolical operation."

Then, as now, unfortunately, rhetoric was swallowing the debate. Both sides focused more on the traditional positions and arguments about abortion and cloning than on the more difficult and unique scientific and philosophical issues at the very heart of the new research. In Congress, the issue first came to a head in 2001 over the question of whether President Bush would permit federal funds to be used to fund research on stem cells derived from surplus in vitro fertilization embryos. Both sides weighed in heavily, and the lobbying was intense.

I struggled with what to do. As a pro-life senator, I had played a leading role in numerous fights over abortion, and many of the arguments being made by some of my colleagues, such as Senator Brownback and Representative Chris Smith, resonated with me both personally and professionally. Given my voting record and position on abortion, the obvious political course was to follow the lead of the Right-to-Life community and support a complete ban on this kind of research. It would be far easier—and better for my future electability—to support a ban than to endorse this most promising branch of regenerative medicine. What this position would not do, however, was help Cody Anderson and millions of others suffering from serious chronic diseases.

Moreover, the passionate defense of life should not stop at birth. We have as profound an obligation to a child outside the womb as we do to one inside. To me, an advocate for life has to consider not only our obligations to a group of cells with the potential for life but also our obligation to our fellow citizens—men, women, and children—who will face untold suffering and lose many years of life unless there is a medical breakthrough.

Using the information I had gained from all my meetings, I tried to work through the problem in a logical manner. First, was an unimplanted egg fertilized through in vitro fertilization in fact a person? Put another way, was an artificially fertilized egg, frozen and stored in a refrigerator, the equivalent of an embryo or fetus developing in a mother's womb?

Several churches argue that life is sacred from the moment of conception, regardless of how that conception occurs. A fertilized egg contains the entire human genetic code and has the potential to grow into a person. Therefore, to them, it is spiritually and ethically a human being.

Other religions, however, base their support of embryonic stem cell research on their obligation to assist not just the unborn but the whole spectrum of life, especially when assistance cannot be provided by any other means. To them, ignoring this opportunity would be immoral and unethical.

There is a third perspective, the so-called "developmental" view of life, that an early embryo, before the formation of the primitive streak that will eventually become the spinal cord and brain, does not enjoy the same legal protections as a person. This is based in part on the assessment by some scientists that for the first fourteen days, a fertilized egg is little more than a jumble of cells.

All three positions have thoughtful and sincere supporters. For many, the right interpretation is based on both religious faith and understanding, made all the more difficult as science has forced religions to review their positions on life and creation.

For me, human life begins in a mother's nurturing womb and is impossible without it. The blasotcysts used for embryonic stem cell research, whether they are developed through the somatic cell nuclear transfer process or are unused embryos from an in vitro fertilization clinic, are not the same as a person or a fetus. A frozen embryo in a laboratory refrigerator is more akin to a frozen egg or sperm. While each has the potential to contribute to human life, no frozen egg, sperm or embryonic cell can reach personhood absent a mother's womb. There is little debate over the ethical or moral consequences when these are discarded, just as there are few objections when an in vitro clinic discards unused blastocysts.

Oddly, the controversy seems to arise only when blastocysts already scheduled for destruction are used instead for scientific research. As Dr. Louis Guenin has pointed out, stopping embryonic stem cell research does not guarantee that one more baby will be born.[2]

Similarly, there are significant legal problems with the assertion that a blastocyst is the same as a person and thus that the destruction of one is the equivalent of murder. Certainly, no member of the United States Supreme Court has ever taken the position that embryos are constitutionally protected persons, and there is little likelihood that any court would order every "spare" embryo in a clinic to be taken through a full-term pregnancy. This position also conflicts with state law. Under Utah law, for example, an abortion can occur only when a fertilized egg has been implanted in a womb.

If an embryo were the legal equivalent of a person, the use of a variety of contraceptive devices, such as those that impede fertilized eggs from attaching onto the uterine wall, could potentially be considered a criminal act. For in vitro clinics, the routine act of discarding "spare" frozen embryos could become an act of murder and would, at a minimum, be inseparable from an abortion.

Regardless of one's position on abortion, there is little support for this legal result. To successfully create life through in vitro fertilization, extraordinary third-party human involvement and scientific procedures are required. Conversely, while it requires an intentional human act, the purpose of abortion is to end life. The two procedures are polar opposites and should not be considered legally, morally or philosophically equivalent.

There was a second issue to consider. What are the consequences of banning this research?

Some, particularly those in the Right-to-Life community, argue that research on adult stem cells actually holds greater promise than the study of embryonic cells. Although adult stem cell research would clearly offer a preferable political solution, most leading scientific authorities dispute this proposition and assert that embryonic stem cell research is by far the more promising course to follow at this time. For now, a ban on the use of embryonic cells could materially impede progress, and the hope that this new field represents would be diminished and, perhaps, lost.

In addition, federal involvement in stem cell research will ensure that there are controls and limits on what is being studied and what materials will be used. Experience over the last several decades has proven that federal funds are needed to underwrite most major medical research programs. The private sector simply cannot generate sufficient funding on its own. And with federal dollars come federal controls. Having the research financed by government will help ensure that appropriate limits are honored. To that end, in 2000, the National Institutes of Health published guidelines controlling the direction of the research and what could be studied. The regulations built upon the work of the National Bioethics Advisory Committee, the Advisory Committee to the Director of the National Institutes of Health, and the Human Embryo Research Panel, which was established by President Clinton. More than 50,000 comments were submitted about the guidelines when they were initially published in draft form, ensuring that when finalized they not only would be comprehensive but would pass the inevitable legal challenge. These guidelines require that only stem cells derived from embryos produced for procreation, but not used for that purpose, could be a possible source. No financial or other benefit could be offered to encourage donation, and there must be comprehensive informed consent. Most important, no funds could be used for human cloning.

After reviewing all these factors, I decided we should support the use of federal funds to underwrite controlled research into regenerative medicine, regardless of whether the stem cells are derived from unused blastocysts obtained through in vitro clinics or through somatic cell nuclear transfer applied to unfertilized eggs. This research is fundamentally different scientifically, legally and morally from abortion. Supporting it is both pro-life and pro-family.

If the potential of this field is actually realized, one day a wide range of diseases and degenerative and debilitating conditions can be cured. Lives will be saved and unfathomable pain, suffering and torment will be avoided. The purpose of the research is to save life, not terminate it.

Families of those currently afflicted also deserve consideration. When one of our loved ones is stricken by illness, more than one person is affected. The whole family shares the pain and suffering. To cope with the disease, family members have to make changes in lifestyle, in the home, even in normal daily activities. If successful, stem cell research could liberate not only the sick but their families as well.

I could not, however, find any legal, moral or religious justification for the human cloning of babies. It is morally repugnant and represents a completely unjustified intrusion into the creation of life. Bringing a new human being into the world should be the sacred responsibility of a husband and a wife.

Early in 2001, President Bush halted all federal funding of stem cell research, creating an opportunity for his administration to review the NIH guidelines and existing controls over spending. Advocates and opponents alike immediately weighed in, lobbying both the White House and Congress. Over the next several months, lobbying campaigns were inaugurated, articles began appearing in the press, and interested organizations began issuing pronouncements and analyses.

On June 13, 2001, I sent a letter to President Bush and a more detailed version to Tommy Thompson, the Secretary of Health and Human Services, outlining why I believed the administration should allow research on embryonic stem cells derived from unused blastocysts to continue. I stressed that it was consistent with our mutual pro-life and pro-family values.

I already knew that Secretary Thompson had similar views. When a person is nominated to a cabinet position by the president and thus subject to Senate confirmation, he or she will pay what is called a "courtesy call" to key senators, especially those who serve on committees with jurisdiction over the particular department or agency in question. During Tommy's courtesy call to me earlier in the year, we talked for the better part of an hour, devoting much of the conversation to regenerative medicine. As governor of Wisconsin, he had worked through many of the issues we were now confronting in Congress. I learned he was both pro-life and a proponent of the research.

Reaction to my letters was, to say the least, mixed. The opponents of regenerative medicine chastised me for abandoning my principles and called my reasoning both vacuous and scientifically inaccurate.

The pro-life community expressed its outrage both in Washington and back in Utah, and my state office was swamped with angry calls. On the other side, research proponents praised my judgment, applauded my understanding of the state of the science and commended my courage.

It's taken awhile, but I have learned not to get too excited about either assessment.

The pressure on the White House continued to build as spring turned into summer. On July 16, Representative David Weldon, a Republican from Florida, introduced legislation criminalizing the cloning of embryos for whatever purpose. If enacted, it would bar not only the use of somatic cell nuclear transfer to create stem cells but also the use of therapies based on such cells that are developed overseas. Sam Brownback had already introduced a comparable bill in the Senate.

The Weldon bill was put on a fast track. It moved through a judiciary subcommittee and the full committee in a little over a week, and was brought to the House floor on July 31. There, Representative Jim Greenwood, a Republican from Pennsylvania, offered an amendment to limit the ban to the use of somatic cell nuclear transfer to initiate pregnancy. His proposal was defeated, and the bill was passed by the House on a vote of 265 to 175, only sixteen days after it was introduced.

On August 9, President Bush weighed in. He announced he would permit federally funded research to continue on the estimated sixty existing stem cell lines already developed, but he would bar the spending of funds on any new lines. (The number of cell lines has since grown to approximately eighty, as more qualified cell lines were identified.) The President also announced the formation of a Presidential Council on Bioethics to consider the scientific and ethical ramifications of the research, to be headed by Leon Kass.

It was an ingenious political resolution. While not completely blocking scientific progress, President Bush avoided the considerable risks associated with addressing the more difficult problems involved, such as the legal status of the blastocysts. He did not have to take a position on when life begins with respect to those embryos. Several pro-life organizations, such as James Dobson's Focus on the Family, expressed limited acceptance, as did the National Right to Life Committee. Even Senators Ted Kennedy and Tom Daschle praised the decision, but noted that it did not go far enough. The number of times this quartet has agreed can be counted on one finger.

Unfortunately, the President's compromise does mean that stem cells derived from the eighty existing stem cell lines will be the only ones studied with federal funding. This group is heavily weighted toward Caucasians and Filipinos. Unless the pool is expanded, there may be insufficient materials to study diseases common to a particular race or ethnicity, such as sickle cell anemia.

This year, the debate has continued in the Senate. Senator Brownback has tried on several occasions to force a vote on his companion legislation to the Weldon bill. He has thirty cosponsors, including one Democrat, Senator Mary Landrieu of Louisiana.

More important, his bill has been endorsed wholeheartedly by President Bush. In a televised announcement, the President acknowledged that while many in the scientific community would disagree with his position, he had moral authority on his side. It was time to stop human cloning before it starts.

Several of the prohibitions in the Brownback bill are troubling, especially the provision making it illegal to use drugs and treatments developed overseas. I thought of Cody Anderson and his parents. I may appear to be personalizing the issue too much by focusing on just one person, but I have found it's often the best way to grasp the moral complexity of a debate.

How could anyone look Cody in the eye and tell him that he could not take a drug that would free him from the disease and pain that otherwise would play such a prominent role in his future? If he traveled overseas, took the drug in another country and was cured, would he be arrested if he returned? If he were my child, would I be willing to let him suffer horribly, knowing there was a cure available? I'm certain I would not, and I would rage against any law that compelled me to do so.

Concerned about what I might do, the White House asked me to come to a meeting. Karl Rove, President Bush's top political advisor, was there along with several other administration officials. Although I initially wondered whether this was the proverbial call to the woodshed, we instead had an interesting and forthright discussion about why I had decided to support stem cell research. While it was clear that the President and I had reached different conclusions, it was also clear that his staff had been struggling with many of the same issues as I had.

Shortly thereafter, I joined Senators Ted Kennedy, Dianne Feinstein of California, and Arlen Specter of Pennsylvania on a bill that would ban cloning aimed at producing a child but would permit the use of somatic cell nuclear transfer for research under limited and controlled circumstances. It has been endorsed by forty Nobel laureates, including some of the world's leading geneticists and cancer specialists.

As expected, the bill came under attack the minute it was introduced. Senator Brownback suggested that it would lead "to the creation of human embryo farms where embryos will be grown to specification." Others claimed it would lead to genetic manipulation and the creation of designer babies.

Of course, our legislation would specifically prohibit this kind of cloning, but the debate will continue through the election and over the coming years. Both sides are working on their respective bills, waiting for the Senate to vote. The bill I cosponsored will probably be amended to make it clear that it would apply only to unfertilized eggs; that both the eggs and the stem cells would have to be voluntarily provided with no financial profiteering as a result of the donation; that in the case of somatic cell nuclear transfer, the artificially created cells could be used in their first fourteen days only; and research centers must be physically separate from an in vitro clinic where the eggs are donated. It would ensure that the study of regenerative medicine will be conducted largely in conjunction with American moral and ethical standards, instead of allowing another country, perhaps one having fundamentally different priorities and proprieties, to dictate the direction of the research. And it will ensure that many of our most brilliant scientists will not be pressured to move overseas to find cures to the most painful and debilitating diseases in the world.

No matter who wins this time, the issue will be back next year and for many years after that. When Congress reconvenes in January 2003, we will start all over again. There will be new debates over old problems. We again will talk about Social Security reform, taxes, prescription drug benefits and the budget. New issues will be discovered and new solutions revealed. We will be diverted by unforeseen events and sidetracked by incidents that are impossible to predict. Still, there will be time to revisit the more vexing problems from the previous year. Regenerative medicine will undoubtedly be on this list. It is far too complicated and controversial to be resolved by only one Congress.

I have little doubt about the outcome, however. It may be caused by a remarkable scientific discovery or breakthrough. It may be determined by a handful of dedicated, compelling individuals who have the courage and persistence to step forward and convince the country that the potential benefits far outweigh the potential dangers. Maybe it will be in reaction to a terrible mistake or revelations that researchers are engaging in the very kind of human cloning feared by most Americans. Or, we may learn that, despite earlier predictions, adult stem cells can be studied just as effectively as embryonic ones.

In the end, however, we will reach a final decision because it reflects a consensus of what the American people believe and want.

The rhetoric will diminish, as it always does. Over time, as our collective knowledge grows, even the most vehement criticisms will be tempered, and we will learn that, despite our respective fears, many of our core principles were in fact not in jeopardy. This is the beauty and the frustration of our political system.

Epilogue

*I knew a very wise man who believed
that if a man were permitted to make
all the ballads, he need not care who
should make the laws of the nation.*

—Andrew Fletcher
of Saltoun, in a letter to the
Marquis of Montrose, 1704

July, 2002

I took up boxing because of music. When I was in junior high, my mother insisted I take violin lessons. Things haven't changed much: Take a skinny young man with thick glasses, make him carry a violin to school, and he is going to get picked on. I'll never know for sure whether Mom wanted me to learn how to play an instrument or how to defend myself—or maybe both—but the one quickly led to the other. I learned to read and write music and to play the piano as well, and I got to be a pretty good boxer. I certainly had enough opportunities to practice.

Thankfully, my family's survival has not hinged on my skill as a violinist. My real love was basketball. Since all teenage sons know more than their mothers, I failed to concentrate on music as much as I might. Still, I played the piano well enough to be named as the organist at the small church we attended while I was growing up, and every

Sunday I would pound out hymns on the old pump organ they had scrimped and saved to obtain.

In addition, every year in junior high and high school, my parents scraped together the $18.75 needed to buy me a season ticket to the Pittsburgh Symphony. Wearing my Sunday meeting clothes, I would walk two miles to a trolley and then ride into the city to sit by myself in what we called Peanut Heaven, the cheapest and highest seats in the auditorium. For a kid from the wrong side of tracks, a boy who thought that fighting was the answer to most problems, the ticket was a pass to a world far removed from my own surroundings, a world that valued artistry over brute strength. I got to listen to performances by some of the great classical musicians of the time—violinists, pianists and opera singers not to mention a symphony orchestra that was simply beyond my imagination. I realized that there was far more to life than the sum of my own experiences. This was an important lesson: It helped me be tolerant of other points of view and taught me that there was something in the human spirit to be cherished and celebrated.

Unfortunately, after high school, I no longer had the same amount of time to spend on music. Lately, however, that's changed.

Like many of us in Congress, I spend a lot of time on airplanes. A majority of weekends, I fly between Washington, D.C., and my home in Salt Lake City. Most of the four-hour flights home are in the evening, a perfect time to wind down from the week's events. It's a quiet time, free of interruptions, an opportunity for introspection and reflection. For me, it has also become a welcome opportunity to write music. Songwriting, be it on airplanes or in the evenings, has become a solace beyond any I could imagine. It has allowed me to look at people and problems in a different light and to discuss themes that are considered inappropriate subjects for political discourse. It has given me the chance to work through ideas and feelings, free of the restraints that often limit honest reflection for those in public office. And it has enabled me to distance myself momentarily from the demands of my profession and restore a sense of balance and joy.

I got started in 1996, when one of Utah's finest and most prolific composers of inspirational music, Janice Kapp Perry, asked whether I would be interested in writing some hymns with her after I showed her some of the poetry I had written. I readily agreed. I wrote lyrics to ten of her songs, which ultimately became a CD titled *My God Is Love*. Since then, we have written more than seven CDs together.

Working with Janice led to collaborations with Madeline Stone, a wonderful award-winning songwriter and master of love songs and ballads. I also have had a chance to work with Billy Hinsche, the guitarist and keyboard player for the Beach Boys, and Peter McCann, who wrote such hits as "It's the Right Time of the Night." Dan Truman, the exceptional keyboardist with the country group Diamond Rio, is another collaborator, as is Lowell Alexander, one of Nashville's great inspirational composers.

As is the case with most songwriters, most of my work has been ignored, but lately things are starting to pick up. Songs I have written have been recorded by Gladys Knight, Donny Osmond, John Schneider, Natalie Grant, and Brooks and Dunn. My music has also been included on the soundtracks of three movies. If you listen very carefully, about five seconds of one of my songs can be heard in the movie *Rat Race*.

Recently, I had a chance to meet several times with Paul Hewson when he was in Washington building support for his campaign against hunger in Africa and resolution of the continent's money problems. A compelling and captivating spokesman for African debt cancellation, AIDS and hunger relief, he has worked with members of Congress without regard to their ideological affiliation.

He's also a phenomenal musician, better known under his stage name, Bono. His group U2 is one of the most successful recording groups in the history of rock music, and the lists of hits they have produced is legendary.

At the end of one meeting in my office in the Senate, to the absolute horror of my staff, I asked Bono whether he would like to hear some of the music I was writing. Graciously, he responded that he would, and I played him several songs while he sat in one of the chairs in front of my desk.

"They're beautiful," he said when I turned off the CD player. "They're actually beautiful, but the brothers will never play or sing them."

"Why's that?" I asked.

"Because of who you are, man," Bono answered emphatically.

"Well, what can I do about that?" I asked.

"You'll have to change your name."

"Any suggestions?" I asked, laughing nervously.

To my surprise, Bono sat back in the chair and clearly thought for a moment, his head tilted to one side. Then, as if struck by lightning, he jerked forward.

"Johnny Trapdoor," he said, a smile crossing his face. "Johnny Trapdoor."

Such moments are rare. Whether I'm writing as Johnny Trapdoor or Orrin Hatch, I'm about as low in the songwriting pecking order as you can get, a refreshing and sobering reminder for someone in elective office. When you're a senator, doors are opened as much for the position you hold as for the person you are. People want to know what you think; they want to make sure you have access to as much information and as many people as possible. You can literally pick up the phone and call almost anyone and have the call returned. If you aren't careful, it's easy to get trapped into believing such treatment is normal.

My struggles to write songs and get artists and recording companies to pay even the slightest attention are a constant reminder that most of us don't live this way. It's often hard simply to find the right doors, let alone have them opened for us. We work hard every day to make ends meet, to provide for our families, and to fulfill our responsibilities and obligations. No one is there to say thanks or to record our efforts. And at some point in our lives, most of us need help.

The bedrock of all politics is constituent service, helping the people you represent with the myriad problems they have with federal and state government, with their careers and professions, and with their families and communities. There is no less visible activity in politics, but none is more enjoyable.

In all honesty, it's a job that can't be done without a good, hardworking staff, a team of professionals skilled in breaking through the countless walls and obstacles of every modern bureaucracy. Mine are some of the best. More often than not, they are the ones who walk constituents through the process. They can spend the time to make sure the system works fairly and that people are not left behind or ignored. I can make calls and visit government officials, but my staff members are the ones who will stay on the case until it is resolved.

Because of their dedication, we have helped people recover their missing Social Security checks. Health insurance benefits have been restored and passports have been issued. Children gone missing overseas have been found. In instances when the IRS was making legal threats over a $5 miscalculation, my staff in Utah and Washington made sure the agency made good on its promise to restore a little sanity to the process. They enabled me to provide an elderly man with his dying wish—to become an American citizen. And they have helped me expedite literally hundreds of adoptions.

On a recent Friday, I took the evening flight back to Salt Lake City after another round in the Senate. By any standard it had been a bad week. As we seem to do far too often, we had spent more time criticizing one another than working on legislation. The Senate Democrats attacked the president. The House Republicans were picking holes in Democratic proposals. The Senate Republicans were fighting with each other. We were still talking, as we have for years, about prescription drug benefits, Social Security and Medicare reform, homeland security and tax relief. Several nominations were held hostage to a continually shifting set of demands. We were way behind schedule on a growing list of must-do legislation, and it now looked certain that we would be returning after the November elections for a "lame-duck" session. By the time we adjourned for the weekend, it seemed everyone was upset about something.

I spent most of the flight home working on the lyrics of a song. It had nothing, absolutely nothing, to do with politics.

After we landed, I walked into the nearly empty concourse and saw Ron Madsen waiting for me. Ron, who's been with me for more than two decades, is as good and loyal a friend as anyone could have. He's now in his seventies, but he still puts in a full day. If he has time, he swings by the airport on his way home to give me a ride.

As we started to walk to his car, he mentioned that he had gotten a few calls while at the airport. "Guess what?" he said. "I just got a call from the P_____ family. The adoption went through. They're thrilled and said to say thanks for all you did."

"Fantastic," I said. "When will they get the baby?"

"Tomorrow," he answered. "The dad will be able to bring her home in the afternoon."

"That's wonderful. You guys did a great job."

"So, Orrin," Ron asked, "was it a good day?"

I glanced at him for a moment. When I took off from Washington I might have said no. But Ron's news, and the new lyrics, and perhaps even the distance itself had changed my perspective.

"Are you kidding?" I said. "It was a very good day."

Notes

Chapter 1

1. Adam Clymer, "Barry Goldwater, Conservative and Individualist, Dies at 89," *New York Times,* 29 May 1998.

2. Earl Warren, speech in Madison, Wisconsin, June 1955.

3. *Talmud,* rabbinical writings, first to sixth centuries A.D.

4. 370 U.S. 421 (1962).

5. 410 U.S. 113 (1973).

6. Barry M. Goldwater, a speech given in West Chester, Pennsylvania, 21 October 1964.

7. Dwight D. Eisenhower, a broadcast speech, 28 January 1954.

Chapter 3

1. For the record, this debate preceded the election of Ronald Reagan. Some Democrats have argued that deficits only became a problem after Reagan forced his tax cuts through in 1981. In fact, deficit spending was already an issue. What led to the jump in deficit levels was a combination of tax cuts and mostly increased spending, for which Congress was largely responsible.

2. James F. Jeffords, *My Declaration of Independence* (Simon and Shuster, 2001).

Chapter 4

1. I am referring here to bills that create new laws or amend existing statutes. So-called money bills, appropriations legislation, are in a world of their own. There, the key factor is whether a member of either the House or the Senate Appropriations Committee will champion a specific request for funding.

2. The compromise created new incentives for the development of innovative drugs and provided the brand companies with a patent extension for some of the time lost during the FDA approval process. The legislation also permitted generic companies to use the safety and efficacy data of the innovator companies in order to bring a generic equivalent on line once the patent expired. Bioequivalence became the critical test.

3. The day after the signing ceremony, the trade association representing the brand companies fired its president for letting the bill become law. Given how well these companies have done as a result of the bill, it was a singularly misguided and inappropriate act, unfortunately not the first or the last misstep by the organization.

4. A. F. Crocetti and H. A. Guthrie, *The Nationwide Food Consumption Survey, 1977–1978* (Anarem Systems Research Corporation, 1982).

5. Ironically, David had worked for me in the past, and I played a significant role in President Bush's decision to appoint him commissioner. He was a very public commissioner who was successful in some areas but did not implement many of the institutional changes the FDA desperately needs.

6. Both the Senate and the House have a Legislative Counsel, a group of nonpartisan, independent lawyers who work for all the members. They are responsible for turning ideas into legislation and checking the work of others to ensure that the actual language says what it is intended to mean. It can be an extremely difficult job.

7. The agency's stubbornness continues to cause problems. During the Summer Olympics in Australia, the press carried reports that the husband of the American gold medal winner, Marion Jones, had flunked a drug test. He claimed he had been victimized by a bad batch of supplements, even though experts noted that the amount of the illegal substance in his body could not be reached by consuming a bad batch of supplements.

Nonetheless, some in the press ran wild. One report breathlessly suggested that this individual would not have flunked the test if my legislation had not been enacted and that my bill might cause every American winner to be stripped of his or her medals.

The International Olympic Committee (IOC) picked up on this theme. In 2001, it held a press conference and attacked the American supplement industry, the federal law and me. Naturally, we were told that these attacks had nothing to do with the fact that the IOC itself was involved in a bribery scandal or that most Olympic doping involves the use of prohibited substances and not "tainted" supplements.

Chapter 5

1. It is often forgotten that one of the reasons the Bush Administration had the military resources and personnel to fight and win the Gulf War was the priority the Reagan Administration gave to the rebuilding the military.

2. At the time, there was as much confusion as there was fear about AIDS. People were terrified, unsure how the virus spread. Many thought AIDS could be contracted simply by touching or being around someone with the disease, and those known to have the disease were often shunned. So little was known about the disease that people were shocked when I hugged an AIDS victim during a hearing on the disease, in part to convince people that it was safe to engage in the most ordinary acts of compassion and that passive contact with an AIDS victim was not a risk.

3. After hearing my remarks, several delegates came up and said they now understood my position. They apologized for their vote. They felt they had been misled by my opponents and urged me to spend more time explaining my position to other conservatives.

Chapter 6

1. 133 Cong. Rec. S. 9188 (daily ed. 1 July 1987) (Statement of Ted Kennedy).

2. 741 F.2d 444 (D.C. Cir. 1984).

3. Congress subsequently banned the release of video rental records. I have always wondered whether this legislation gained favor because of a feeling of shame about what happened with Judge Bork, or if some of my colleagues were concerned that this tactic might be applied to them.

4. As Senator Metzenbaum liked to tell nominees after a particularly rough grilling, don't worry, it wasn't personal. It's just politics. But it sure seemed personal to the nominees.

Chapter 7

1. Nomination of Clarence Thomas to Associate Justice of the United States Supreme Court, 11, 12, and 13 October 1991, Part 4 of 4 Parts, p. 9.

2. Ibid., p. 84.

3. Ibid., pp. 157–158.

4. Interestingly, Ted would subsequently undergo his own confirmation battle when George W. Bush nominated him to be solicitor general of the United States in 2001. Many of the same people who had opposed Clarence Thomas and Judge Bork tried to block Ted, relying upon the same tactics used in the earlier fights. Again, their efforts would be unsuccessful, accomplishing nothing more than momentarily tarnishing in the media a man with an exceptional record and a proven history of legal excellence.

Chapter 8

1. Speech by Robert F. Kennedy in South Africa, 1966.

Chapter 9

1. Quoted in the *American Spectator,* 28 October 1992.

2. Congressional Record, 7 January 1999, p. S41.

3. I had previously worked with Judge Breyer. In the late 1970s, he served as the chief counsel on the Senate Judiciary Committee when the committee was chaired by Ted Kennedy. During this period, he was also a professor at Harvard Law School. Stephen was intelligent, honest and fair, always more than gracious to the Republican members and staff, not a universal sobriquet for a Kennedy staffer.

He was nominated to the appellate court by President Carter in 1980, but his nomination got bogged down as the Senate prepared for the coming presidential election. After Ronald Reagan was elected, but before he was sworn in, Kennedy asked if I could intervene on behalf of Breyer. He told me that Strom Thurmond, who was scheduled to become Chairman of the Judiciary Committee when the Senate reconvened in 1981, was blocking a vote.

I went to Strom and reminded him that Breyer had been a good chief counsel of the committee. He had been honest and decent. "Strom," I continued, "we shouldn't treat him like this." Strom looked at me and asked if I really thought that was the case. I said I did. Strom relented and said he would let Breyer's nomination move. Judge Breyer went on to have an excellent career as an appellate judge, becoming the chief judge of the First Circuit in 1990.

4. My familiarity with Judge Ginsberg was far more limited. In 1980, she,

too, was nominated by President Carter, but to the District of Columbia Court of Appeals. Concerned with the lack of progress on her nomination, a mutual friend, Ira Milstein of the distinguished New York law firm, Weil-Gottshal, called on her behalf. Ira is a well-known Democrat and an excellent attorney. We have always gotten along well and keep our political differences on a professional level. He asked if I would be able to see her. "She's deathly afraid of you, Orrin," he confided.

I readily agreed. I didn't know her personally, but I was familiar with her career and thought her to be an exceptional lawyer. She was the first tenured female faculty member at Columbia Law School and had a litigation record that would be the envy of any attorney. Six of her cases involving gender discrimination went to the Supreme Court, and she won five.

When we met, we chatted for nearly half an hour, discussing the role of judges and the Court. At the end of the meeting, I assured her I would support her nomination to the Court of Appeals. Not many people realize this, but her voting record at the appellate court was very similar to that of another subsequent Supreme Court Justice, Antonin Scalia.

5. Ken was appointed after his predecessor, Robert B. Fiske Jr., who had been selected by Attorney General Janet Reno, was asked to step down by three federal judges. They had concluded that having the President's Attorney General pick the individual responsible for his investigation created an appearance of a conflict of interest. The problem was with the appearance, not the actual performance of Mr. Fiske, who has gone on to serve the country in a variety of different and commendable capacities.

Chapter 10

1. Questioned about his amount of experience during the debate between candidates for vice president, Senator Quayle said, "I have as much experience in the Congress as Jack Kennedy did when he sought the presidency." "Senator, I served with Jack Kennedy," his opponent, Lloyd Bentsen, shot back in response. "I knew Jack Kennedy. Jack Kennedy was a friend of mine. Senator, you're no Jack Kennedy." (Omaha, Nebraska, 5 October 1988)

2. Morris K. Udall, *Too Funny to Be President* (Henry Holt and Company, 1988), p. xiv.

Chapter 11

1. Editorial, *Washington Post*, 4 May 2001.

2. Louis M. Guenin, M.D., "Mortals and Immortals," *Science* (1 June 2001).

Index